Group Work
Honoring our Roots, Nurturing our Growth

Proceedings of the XXXI Annual International Symposium of the Association for the Advancement of Social Work with Groups

---

Group Work
Honoring our Roots, Nurturing our Growth

Edited by

Ann M. Bergart, Shirley R. Simon, and Mark Doel

w&b

MMXII

Published by Whiting & Birch Ltd,
Forest Hill, London SE23 3HZ

ISBN 9781861771254

Printed in England and the United States by Lightning Source

Contents

Acknowledgements

**Association for the Advancement of Social Work with Groups
XXXI Annual International Symposium
Chicago, Illinois, 24 to 28 June, 2009**

We would like to acknowledge the many people and institutions who contributed to the success of the 31st Annual International Symposium on Social Work with Groups. Some worked on organizing the event; others took responsibility for the mountain of details which accompany each symposium; others provided financial sponsorship of various kinds; and still others provided the support which enabled those who were working directly on the event to persevere over many months.

We are very grateful for the financial support we received in the form of numerous co-sponsorships. Aurora University, also home of the George Williams College site of the Pre-Symposium Institute, co-sponsored the Symposium at the highest level of partnership. The School of Social Work, Loyola University Chicago, a faithful supporter of the Illinois Chapter of AASWG for many years, was a very generous co-sponsor. Whiting & Birch, who publish these Proceedings, also co-sponsored generously. Our additional co-sponsors were the University of Chicago School of Social Service Administration, Illinois State University School of Social Work, and Judy & Jim Klutznick. In addition to these sponsorships, we received a grant from the McGowan Gin Rosica Family Foundation which allowed us to provide scholarships for the Pre-Symposium Institute to a large number of students. Thank you, one and all, for your generous support!

The persistent efforts of our wonderful planning committees gave us a Symposium which we will all remember with pride.

Members of the 2009 Symposium Planning Committee

Symposium Co-Chairs
Ann Bergart & Joyce Webster

Symposium Coordinating Committee

Ann Bergart
Alexandra Fliess
Carlean Gilbert
Zena Goldenberg
Alyssa Keel
Kay Goler Levin
Kristina Lind
Sally Mason
Kathleen Westropp Stauber
Joyce Webster

Pre-Symposium Institute Planning Committee

Sandy Alcorn
Ann Bergart
Jon Habegger
Munira Merchant
Sue Ross
Caron Wedeking

Special thanks go to the following, for their contribution to planning:

Kimberly Berta
Amanda Blucher
Anne Kopp Hyman
Kate Jadin
Colleen Muchowski
Marcia Pantell
LaShon Parks
Jan Selander
Shirley Simon
Barney Straus
Shin Yee Tan
Charles Zastrow

The Co-Chairs are especially grateful to their partners, Mal and Bryan, for enduring the many months of their preoccupation with planning the Symposium.

Thanks also to the army of volunteers who helped out during the Symposium itself.

We are grateful to the Executive Committee of AASWG for their assistance and their faith in us.

Executive Committee of AASWG.

Nancy Sullivan	President
Andrew Cicchetti	Vice President
Dominique Moyse Steinberg	Treasurer
Michael Wagner	Secretary
Greg Tully	Membership Committee Co-Chair
Carol F. Kuechler	Interim Symposium Committee Chair
Linda McArdle	Chapter Development Committee Chair
Ellen Sue Mesbur	Commission on Group Work in Social Work Education Co-Chair; Nominations Committee and Elections Co-Chair
John Ramey	Honorary Adjunct Member

Thanks also to the AASWG Board and the Chapter Chairs who supported the Symposium in so many ways, including taking out ads, contributing to the scholarship fund, and fostering attendance.

Special thanks go to Sue Henry and Carol Kuechler, each of whom served as Symposium Committee Chair during the planning period for this event. Their mentorship and guidance was invaluable.

Ellen Sue Mesbur and David Whiting were of tremendous support to the Editors of these Proceedings. Thank you for your generous assistance with this final Symposium project!

In closing, we would like to thank all those who contributed as presenters and workshop leaders. You brought life to our dreams for the 2009 AASWG Symposium!

About the Editors

Ann M. Bergart, Ph.D., LCSW was formerly Associate Professor at the Aurora University School of Social Work. She is now an adjunct faculty member at The University of Chicago School of Social Service Administration and the Loyola University Chicago School of Social Work, and has taught both graduate and continuing education courses at both schools. Ann has published numerous articles about group work and presents regularly at AASWG symposia. In addition to her private practice, she has conducted staff training and consultation in group work at numerous social agencies. Ann is active in the Illinois Chapter of AASWG, and has served on the Board of Directors of the international organization. She coordinated the first Group Work Camp, a new AASWG initiative offering experiential training in social work with groups. Ann can be contacted at annbergart@gmail.com .

Shirley R. Simon, ACSW, LCSW is Associate Professor, School of Social Work, Loyola University Chicago, where she chairs the Group Work Practice Committee. She has been a social work educator for over thirty years, has published on group work education and history, and has facilitated over one hundred student and recent alumni presentations at professional association conferences. She has provided group work training for social work agency staff and field instructors, and is currently conducting research on the status of group work education in masters-level social work programs, the effectiveness of hybrid-online teaching of group work content, and curricular strategies for connecting students and professional associations. Shirley is active in AASWG at both local and international levels, and regularly presents at its symposia. Shirley Simon can be contacted at ssimon@luc.edu.

Professor Mark Doel, PhD, MA (Oxon), CQSW is Emeritus Professor of Social Work in the Centre for Health and Social Care Research at Sheffield Hallam University, England. He is a registered social worker and was in practice for almost twenty years, including two separate years living and working in the US. His research focuses on social work practice methods, especially groupwork, and practice education. He has an international reputation in these fields. Mark is an active

member of AASWG and has presented keynotes at three Symposia. His groupwork books, *The Essential Groupworker* (with Catherine Sawdon) and *Using Groupwork,* are widely read and based on a nine-year action research project to develop a groupwork service in a large public social work agency in northern England. Mark can be contacted at doel@ waitrose.com, with more information at:
http://www.shu.ac.uk/research/hsc/sp-mark-doel.html

The contributors

Sharima R. Abbas, MSW, is a faculty member of the Social Work Department in Universiti Utara Malaysia, Kedah, Malaysia. She is one of the collaborating partners in the Global Group Work Project and was involved in a planning committee for the 2011 Group Work Camp under AASWG. She is actively involved in humanitarian services in Indonesia, Pakistan and Chile where she uses art and play in groups with child survivors from tsunamis, earthquakes and floods. She can be reached at sharima@uum.edu.my or kaklilohawaii@gmail.com

Samuel R. Benbow, D.Ed., M.S. is an Assistant Professor, Shippensburg University Department of Social Work & Gerontology. He is a member of the Association of the Advancement of Social Work with Groups. He enjoys facilitating psychodynamically-based groups with teens and young adults. He can be reached at srbenb@ship.edu.

Susan Ciardiello, PhD, LCSW is a licensed clinical social worker with her Ph.D. in social work. Her areas of expertise are social group work with children and adolescents and AD/HD coaching. She is a member of the Board of Directors for AASWG. She is currently Supervisor of Group Programs at the Larchmont-Mamaroneck Community Counseling Center and has a private practice in Mamaroneck, NY. She can be reached by e-mail at Sue23@optonline.net.

Jennifer A. Clements, PhD, LCSW, is Associate Professor, Shippensburg University Department of Social Work and Gerontology. She currently serves on the Executive Committee and is a Board member of AASWG. She enjoys teaching group work at the BSW and MSW levels, and can be contacted at jaclem@ship.edu.

Carol S. Cohen, DSW, is Associate Professor, Adelphi University School of Social Work in Garden City, New York. She is a founding partner of the Global Group Work Project, Co-Chair of the 2002 International Symposium on Social Work with Groups, and Co-Chair of the AASWG Commission on Group Work in Social Work Education. She can be reached at: cohen5@adelphi.edu.

Alex Gitterman, EdD, is Professor, University of Connecticut School of Social Work, Hartford. He is past president of the Association for the Advancement of Social Work with Groups and has written extensively about life-model practice, vulnerable and resilient populations, and mutual aid groups. He can be reached by e-mail at Alex.Gitterman@ uconn.edu.

Alison Hahn Johnson, MSSW, is a practitioner in private practice in Louisville, KY , where, for over 30 years, she has worked with families, individuals, couples and groups. She is known regionally and internationally for her interest in the use of program and skill in group work with children and adolescents. She has taught social work practice courses in bachelor and graduate programs in KY and presented workshops statewide and internationally, and can be reached at ajcounseling@gmail.com.

Louise C. Johnson, ACSW, is Professor Emeritus, Social Work, University of South Dakota. She received her MSW in Group Work from the University of Connecticut in 1962. Professor Johnson is co-author, with Steven Yanca, of *Social Work: A Generalist Approach*, and *Generalist Social Work with Groups*. She can be reached at LCJohnson12@gmail.com.

Gerald Kellman, who holds an MA in journalism and an M.Div., recruited, trained, and mentored President Obama as a community organizer in the 1980s. Trained by Saul Alinsky, he has served as a community organizer throughout the Midwest in White, Latino, and African American neighborhoods. Having worked with the Gamaliel Foundation, Mr. Kellman is currently working with churches and community organizations around multiple issues, and is coordinating a pilot project to organize older African American and Latino Americans. He can be reached at JerryKellman@yahoo.com.

Teresa Kilbane, Ph.D. is an Associate Professor, Loyola University Chicago, School of Social Work. She is a Research Methodologist who has been working in collaboration with her colleague, Shirley Simon, on the status of group work in graduate social work programs. She can be reached by e-mail at tkilban@luc.edu.

Cheryl D. Lee, Ph.D., MSW, is Professor, School of Social Work, California State University, Long Beach. She teaches Social Group Work and HBSE. Research subjects include: Mentoring, Group Work, and Child Welfare. She is Chair of AASWG's Southern California Chapter and a member of its board, and was Chair of the Long Beach AASWG Symposium. Her e-mail is cheryllee18@gmail.com

Andrew Malekoff, LCSW, is executive director and CEO for North Shore Child and Family Guidance Center in Roslyn Heights, New York. He is editor-in-chief of the journal Social Work with Groups and author of numerous publications including the textbook *Group Work with Adolescents: Principles and practice* (Guilford Press), now in its second edition. His e-mail address is Anjru@aol.com

Eliette del Carmen Montiel, MSW, is a Psychiatric Social Worker, Los Angeles County Dept. of Mental Health. Her e-mail address is eliettemontial@gmail.com.

Hélène Filion Onserud, LCSW, is a practitioner who has written a number of papers and presented to diverse audiences, with a particular focus on the affinity between social group work and youth development. She advocates for the profession of social work to look to the growing youth development field as an arena in which to revitalize and implement social group work as a practice method. She can be reached by e-mail at helene.onserud@gmail.com

Catherine (Katy) Papell, MA, MSW, DSW, Professor Emerita, Adelphi University, SSW, Garden City, New York, was Co- editor-with Beulah Rothman of *Social Work with Groups*, and is a Founding Board Member of AASWG. She has written extensively about group work as a method of social work, and about "Experiencing Aging". She is now 95 years old, and can be reached at katy111216@aol.com.

Reineth (CE) Prinsloo,DPhil, is a senior lecturer at the Department of Social Work and Criminology, University of Pretoria, South Africa. Her fields of specialisation are social work with groups and family development and guidance. She works from a strength perspective and focuses on prevention and enrichment. She can be reached by e-mail at reineth.prinsloo@up.ac.za.

Deirdre Quirke, BSS, MA, DASS, CQSW, is a Principal Social Worker and Student-Unit Co-Ordinator within Brothers of Charity Disability Services in Cork Ireland. She is Director of a Practice Unit and has been actively engaged in practice for over three decades in both Statutory and Voluntary Sectors. Her current practice context is within Disability and she delivers a module on the subject on both B.S.W and M.S.W. and Practice Teachers programmes in the School of Applied Social Studies, University College Cork. She provides Supervision on an Individual and Group basis. Her practice approach has been in developing collaborative ways of working in Agency and Academia. She can be reached by e-mail at D.Quirke@ucc.ie.

Karen A. Ring, LCSW, is a lecturer in social work at The University of the West Indies, Cave Hill Campus, Barbados. She is past president of the Barbados Association of Professional Social Workers and has practiced clinical social work for 30 years. Besides group work, she has conducted research in disaster management in the Caribbean. She can be reached by e-mail at karen.ring@cavehill.uwi.edu.

Lorraine Ruggieri, LMSW, ASW-G is a specialist in dementia care with advanced certifications in gerontology as well as adults and families. She is a support group leader for the New York City Chapter of the Alzheimer's Association and an advocate for victims of this disease and their caregivers. She can be reached by e-mail at lmruggieri@ verizon.net.

Robert Salmon, MSW, is Professor Emeritus. He joined Hunter College School of Social Work in 1971, serving as Associate or Interim Dean for sixteen years. Among his awards was one for Excellence in Teaching. Published works include many articles and books and, with A. Gitterman, *The Encyclopedia of Social Work with Groups* (2009). He can be reached by e-mail at rssalmon@rcn.com.

Kathleen Westropp Stauber, Ph.D., has been a social work practitioner, educator, and higher education administrator, and more recently a higher education consultant with The Solutions Team. As a group worker, she provides relationship expertise, academic excellence, and financial/organizational ability to both non-profit and for-profit universities and colleges. Dr. Stauber teaches group work at Loyola University Chicago, and can be reached at kws@the-solutions-team.org.

Dominique Moyse Steinberg, DSW, has been a member of the faculty of the Hunter College School of Social Work in New York City. She writes extensively and is particularly interested in mutual aid, in the effective management of conflict in small groups, and in the translation of mutual-aid potential to varied group types and formats. Steinberg reviews for *Social Work with Groups, Journal of Teaching in Social Work,* and *Journal of Interdisciplinary Studies.* A member of AASWG since 1983 and on the Board's Executive Committee since 2006, she can be reached at dmsvt@earthlink.net.

Dr. Mary Wilson, B.S.S., M.S.W., Ph.D., CQSW is Director of the Bachelor in Social Work programme at the National University of Ireland, Cork. Her research interests and writings are reflective of her teaching and practice interests, notably the use of groupwork in the professional training of social workers. She also engages in groupwork with service users to create more empowering forms of service delivery. Her e-mail address is: m.wilson@ucc.ie.

Stephen J. Yanca, PhD, DIPLO, ACSW, LMSW, LMFT, is Professor of Social Work at Saginaw Valley State University. He has an MSW from Wayne State University and a Ph.D. from Michigan State University, and has experience in counseling, group work, child welfare, juvenile corrections, community mental health, supervision, and administration. He is the coauthor of three social work texts, and can be reached at sjy@svsu.edu.

Editors' overview

The theme of the 31st Annual International Symposium on Social Work with Groups, "Honoring our Roots – Nurturing our Growth", was inspired by social group work's rich history in and around Chicago, Illinois. This theme was also intended to highlight exciting new initiatives undertaken by the Association for the Advancement of Social Work with Groups, Inc. (AASWG, Inc.) to identify and mentor a new generation of group workers and to encourage them to become part of our organization.

The Planning Committee envisioned the Symposium as a weaving together of group work's past, present, and future. It began with a trip to the past. Prior to the meeting in Chicago, a two-day pre-symposium institute was held at Aurora University's George Williams College campus, an historic gathering place and group work training site established during the early YMCA/YWCA movement. Steeped in this history, over seventy group workers and students of diverse ages and from several nations made strong connections as they participated in experiential training which affirmed group work's roots in the use of activity to promote growth and change.

Following this institute the Symposium opened with a focus on the present. Gerald Kellman, the man who hired and trained Barack Obama in community organization in the 1980s, delivered the keynote plenary. His address illustrated the use of personal narrative, group work, and community organization in Obama's 2008 presidential campaign, clearly demonstrating the powerful and necessary interplay among all three social work modalities. The first day of presentations concluded with a pilgrimage to Hull House, where we honored Catherine (Katy) Papell, one of our founding mothers. Katy set the tone for the Symposium by reading her touching letter to Jane Addams in front of the very fireplace where Miss Addams conducted so many of her groups.

On the second day, the plenary address re-focused us on the present, as recent advances in global group work connections were described by an international group of AASWG members chaired by Carol Cohen. Next came a poster session, primarily showcasing students' work. More papers and workshops on practice, research, and educational initiatives followed. On the last morning, the plenary by Shirley Simon and Kathy Stauber urged us to embrace the future, as they shared their innovative use of technology in social work education.

This volume is organized into four parts. The first three parts address the past, present, and future of social work with groups – paralleling the theme of the Symposium. Part One ("Our Past") begins with Papell's touching letter to Jane Addams. It is followed by three articles which call us back to early group work theory and to our roots in youth development and the use of activity.

Part Two ("Our Present") begins with Kellman's keynote plenary address. This powerful presentation, along with the article which follows, highlights several contemporary issues – the resurgence of interest in community organization in the wake of Barack Obama's election; the need for organized action to protect social programs in the face of recent fiscal downturn and budget cuts; and the potential for wedding group work with community organization. The third article in this section reports on the status of group work offerings in MSW programs in the United States. Part Two continues with the plenary presentation by Cohen et al., addressing the processes and outcomes of global group work. A description of diversity education in a South African group work course, and an account of an innovative program for people with Alzheimer's disease and their caregivers, conclude this section.

Part Three ("Our Future") opens with Simon and Stauber's call to embrace technology as a means of ensuring group work's future. This plenary address is followed by two articles which highlight additional strategies for building the foundation of this future. The first of these articles focuses on advocating for group work within organizations, and the second demonstrates a model for involving students in AASWG. Part Three concludes with a thoughtful integration of the past, present, and future of generalist group work practice.

In Part Four of this volume, we present two new offerings for a *Proceedings* publication. This year, the Chicago Symposium reintroduced a poster session aimed at facilitating greater participation by students and emerging professionals. Our aim was to provide a less intimidating first experience in making a conference presentation. Part Four opens with the abstracts of the poster presentations which were presented in Chicago. Their number and diversity are clear indications of the success of this endeavor. The second new offering is based on our decision to invite additional presenters to briefly summarize their papers or workshops. These authors address the turning points in group life and the education of social work students in the use activities in groups. Part Four is meant to give the reader a wider exposure to the variety of topics and ideas which were addressed at the Symposium.

The 2009 Symposium was a stimulating and joyful gathering of our group work community. We hope that this volume conveys the essence of this memorable event.

Ann Bergart, Shirley Simon, and Mark Doel
Editors

Dedication

This volume is dedicated to Catherine (Katy) Papell, one of the "founding mothers" of AASWG. It was our incredible good fortune that Katy was able to attend the 2009 Symposium, and that we could honor her at a reception at Hull House. There, in the very dining room where meals were served at Hull House, Katy read us a letter addressed to Ms. Addams. Her letter appears in these pages.

Katy is our inspiration, as Jane Addams has been hers. In fact she *is* *our* Jane Addams! This brilliant, gentle, passionate, and compassionate woman has never let us forget where we come from. Her love of the human group and its possibilities, as well as her devotion to social justice, inform everything about her. We listen to her speak and take note – reminded that the history of social group work is rich with values that lead us to work with groups in ways which make us unique among the helping professions. We read what she writes – marveling at her ability to see patterns over time, communicate complex ideas clearly and humanely, and let us know who we are.

Thank you, Katy, for being part of the tremendous trio who saw the need for action to advocate for social work with groups itself, thereby creating our organization. Thank you again for being part of the dynamic duo who established a journal in which we could build our own theory and practice knowledge – and rebuild lost pride in our method of social work practice.

Most of all, thank you for being the very special person that you are – our beloved advocate, mentor, colleague, and friend ...

1
AASWG at Hull House for tea

Catherine P. Papell

This chapter contains the address given by Catherine P. Papell, Professor Emerita, Adelphi University, at the Hull House Reception, at the 31st International Symposium on Social Work with Groups Chicago, Illinois, June 26, 2009

Good afternoon, Miss Addams

Here we are. Your group workers – social workers who work with groups. You are our mentor. We have come today to honor you and to remind ourselves what we owe to you, what we have sought with such commitment to keep alive in the profession that you participated in building.

We know that you were not a Licensed Professional Social Worker as most of us are. That was because you lived and worked years before such technical societal matters, 1860-1935. We know too that you identified yourself with the early social settlement movement and, along with Mary Richmond (1861-1921), the charities movement, wherein lay the roots of today's Social Work Profession. We know too that, before you opened Hull House, you graduated valedictorian from the Seminary that became Rockland College, and that despite ill health which thwarted your plans to go to medical school, you traveled in Europe for two years, as was appropriate at that time for a well-educated young woman. We know that you took a second trip to Europe with Ellen G. Starr and visited Toynbee Hall in London, that you were searching for a meaningful plan for your life (as many of us have done). We know that you and Miss Starr returned to Chicago and decided to live with the impoverished immigrant community on Halsted and Polk Streets and open a Social Settlement there (September 18, 1889). We know that, like the social settlement movement, your purpose was "to provide a center for a higher civic and social life, to institute and maintain educational and philanthropic enterprises and to investigate and improve the industrial districts of Chicago" – helping people to survive and enrich their lives, to create community, and to participate in national and international problem solving.

(As an side, Miss Addams, let us tell you that amongst us gathered here are many who found our way into social work in the early half of the 20th century through the settlement movement.)

We know too that your deep and genuine humanity and love for all people and your extraordinary creativity and the breadth of your personal, intellectual, and spiritual ideology produced a program of world renown.. This description of what was happening here where we are today is found in the Nobel Foundation's Peace Prize statement (1931) about you, Jane Addams:

> "Miss Addams and Miss Starr made speeches about the needs of the neighborhood, raised money, convinced young women of well-to-do families to help, took care of children, nursed the sick, listened to outpourings from troubled people."

The Nobel Peace Prize continues,

> "By the second year of existence, Hull House was host to two thousand people every week. There were kindergarten classes in the morning, club meetings for older children in the afternoon, and for adults in the evening more clubs or courses in what became virtually a night school. The first facility added to Hull House was an art gallery, the second a public kitchen; then came a coffee house, a gymnasium, a swimming pool, a cooperative boarding club for girls, a book bindery, an art studio, a music school, a drama group, a circulating library, an employment bureau, a labor museum."

We know too that, never working alone, much of this was accomplished by you, with the on-going help of the people, educated and oftentimes privileged, who came to live with you at Hull House, and to whom you offered leadership. You shared passionately your growing insight into the vast complexity of individual and societal forces that brought pain and anguish to your neighbors. You gave your heart and mind to helping wherever it was humanly possible and to engage neighbors in working together. It was said that you, Jane Addams, had "an incredible sense of humanity that found ... [you] always explaining human tragedy as related to human longing and human search for life."

We know too that your writing and lecturing and your civic and political leadership and activities produced outcomes of national and international benefit, and your advocating against World War I led to your being awarded the Nobel Peace Price in 1931.

Let me tell you, Miss Addams, something about us who have come to have tea with you today. May I speak for us. . .

We are social workers who have spent the many decades, a century since you were the President (1909) of our first professional organization, The National Conference of Charities and Corrections (NCCC), seeking to capture and maintain for the growing Social Work Profession, the essence of your work: "helping people by helping them to help each other and themselves". We social group workers have been responsible, during the early half of the last century, for the progression of organizations of the group work movement, each of which early on was inspired by your work. We joined in 1955 with all social work organizations to become the National Association of Social Workers (NASW).

May I tell you Miss Addams, that early on some of us group workers who were social work educators entered genuinely in the search for a generic, holistic, foundation notion of social work methodology, and discovered the unintended consequences that individual and family work with primarily clinical treatment objectives seemed to be more educationally powerful for Social Work education than group and community approaches. Our organization, the Association for the Advancement of Social Work with Groups (AASWG), organized in 1979, and the journal, Social Work with Groups, emerged to restore and strengthen the place of the group and of interactional relationship in the societal purpose of the Social Work Profession.

As professional social workers with individuals, families, groups, and communities, we have sought to recapture the heart of the Settlement movement, enabling people to organize and work together in groups in order to problem-solve and create community. We have continued to believe with you, Jane Addams, that successfully and actively dealing with reality in group life is health and strength producing as well as community enriching

As did you, we have participated in the building of Social Work's academic curriculum, BSW, MSW, DSW, and PhD. We note the work of your committee that became the Chicago School of Civics and Philanthropy and then the University of Chicago School of Social Service Administration. Yes, you have been our mentor!!!

We would like you to know, Miss Addams, about how we group

workers have developed the way of engaging with suffering people that you demonstrated early on in Hull House, in order that it can be taught in education for the Social Work Profession.. Throughout the past century and today, through writing and exchanging experiences in leading groups of infinite kinds of human issues, problems, and settings, through drawing on the growing social sciences, sociology, social psychology, psychology, anthropology and, of course, education, there have been beautiful skills and concepts identified, and theories created by our group work colleagues about the professional social work role in helping humans to succeed in their group life.. We think that you would be very much interested in the *Encyclopedia of Social Group Work* (2008), edited by Gitterman and Salmon.

Certainly the new *Handbook of Social Work with Groups* (2004), edited by Garvin, Gutierrez, and Galinsky, would be helpful to you in sorting out the vast historical and spectacular group work and theory building by social workers who work with groups in the 20th century and into the 21st .

In particular, Chapter 6 of the Handbook, "The Mutual Aid Model'" (Gitterman), would have been important to you in teaching the Hull House residents, which we understand was a very important aspect of your work. Perhaps the "mainstream model" (Papell and Rothman) would have captured your imagination historically. And the Standards for Social Work with Groups (AASWG) might have been helpful to you and your residents in your work with your neighbors, the community, the city, and the wider and wider circles to which you devoted your life and to which we devote ours. We believe that what has come to be called the "mutual aid model" is the one that most closely represents the essence of your work with your neighbors.

This, Miss Addams, is what we have been doing, inspired by you and the work that has emanated from Hull House.

Those of us gathered here in 2009 and representing our organization (AASWG), would wish for me to tell you, Miss Addams, what we are certain you knew, that the struggle for depth and breadth in our helping profession is never over. It is not difficult to think systemically, holistically about the needs of humankind, but it is difficult indeed to act, to "use the self", in the social work societal role needed for the complexity of human misery in an oftentimes evil world.

The world is still at war, Jane Addams, and the essential humanity of group and community work is even more desperately needed. You would be greatly saddened and horrified, as we are, by the newfound savagery and the unspeakable human misery war has wrought. We rejoiced with the election of Barack Obama, (a community organizer!) and are certain you would have rejoiced with us. And we social group workers wept in joyful support a few weeks ago to hear our U. S. President say, when speaking in Egypt and to the world, this time about faith differences:

> So long as our relationship is defined by our differences, we will empower those who sow hatred rather than peace, those who promote conflict rather than the cooperation that can help all our people achieve justice and prosperity. And this cycle of suspicion and discord must end.

We social workers who meet here today at Hull House are amongst those who have identified themselves within the profession as social workers who believe passionately in offering our helping services through experience in group and community life. We have struggled and are still doing so to keep alive within the profession the ideals and insight and deep humanity that you exemplified in your life and work here more than a hundred years ago.

We thank you, Jane Addams, for inviting us to tea, and for giving us this opportunity, as social workers who work with groups, to be reconnected with our indebtedness to you.

You Transform The World

Written by Rev. Dr. Judy Lee
For Dr. Catherine T. Papell
On the Occasion of Your AASWG Honoring
at Hull House, Chicago, June 2009
(Revised from the original poem written in 1997 and amended in 1998)

Katy,
You are our Jane Addams
blending cause and function,
democracy and full participation,
settlement and justice,
beauty, music and art,
learning and a fair start,
bread and peace in time of war,
our ambassador abroad

and inspiring activist
for Afghan women and inclusion,
always inclusion for all people
so that the over accumulation
at one end may be shared.
You model still passion and
compassion for people and
for process equal to outcomes-
servant, savant, sage,
and yet, you know no age.

You are our Bertha C. Reynolds,
blending method and action
never bending to the popular
or the easy, your heart is
with the working people always.
Your work with those addicted
and their families, and with
the homeless and outcast
continuing into time when
others would have simply
rested.
Complex thinker, questioning,
challenging-creating higher ground
for our thinking – but your doing
is the harder and better part.
Tireless ever giving caretaker
of family and friends.

You are our loving woman,
our ever curious intellectual
with a conscience and a
heart of pure-spun gold.
You are our synthesizer and integrator
so that the theories fit like puzzle pieces
and group work is one.
You are our bright star,
our ethicist, keeping our
moral compass pointed north
anchoring us to our groupwork values.

You call us to love beyond
our powers,
to give, to think,
to challenge the way things are
and by our actions usher in
the way things are supposed to be.

Gentle and beautiful
and never letting us settle
for less than we can be,
you model the caring practitioner,
the consummate group worker,
the whole human being
who will not let anyone fall by the wayside.
Your gait is slower now, and
you are bent, but you run the distance even still
and call us to your side.

We cannot keep your pace,
but you are ever before us,
your lovely face smiling
as we come alongside.
Thank you for the example
of lifelong dedication to the work
with energy, love and caring.
Thank you for keeping on,
for teaching us, and reaching us
with who you are
and who we can be –
as social workers –
as those who serve one another –
dedicated to groups that form
and connect us to the end.
And most of all,
it is the greatest pleasure
to call you friend,
and ask you to accept the
gratitude we here extend
and our unending love.

2

Testing the applicability of the Boston Model: Worker perceptions

Susan Ciardiello

Abstract: This article discusses a dissertation study that examines the applicability of the Boston Model for the stages of group development from the social worker's perspective. The Boston Model is a prominent model of group development in social work. This quantitative study used an internet survey to question members from the Association for the Advancement of Social Work with Groups (AASWG) about group development. Factors that influence the development of closed-ended groups, such as gender and oppression status of group members, were investigated. Findings suggest that groups considered to be predominantly oppressed, of low income, non-white, and of mixed ethnicity were more likely to develop along the lines of the Boston Model.

Keywords: Boston Model, group work, group development, Relational Model, oppression status, stages of group development

Intoduction

Over the last sixty years group researchers from a variety of professional disciplines have studied group development. Since 1948, social work scholars started to develop group development models (Trecker, 1948; Sarri & Galinsky, 1974; Garland et al., 1965; Northen, 1969; Richmond, 1971; Schwartz, 1971; Vinter, 1974; Tropp, 1976; Glasser & Garvin, 1976; Schiller, 1995; 2003). Group development theorists from the fields of sociology and psychology also began their investigations around the same time (Bales, 1956; Bennis & Sheppard, 1956; Bion, 1959; Tuckman, 1965; Lacourcière, 1980; Wheelan, 1994). Regardless of discipline, group research supports the theoretical notion that groups move through a series of distinct stages. There are well over 100 theories of group development, most of which report a sequential developmental process (Johnson & Johnson, 2000). Some models describe a developmental process that is more cyclic in nature in that specific issues or problems recur over time and resolution of problems is only temporary (Wheelan & Hochberger, 1996; Johnson & Johnson, 2000). This article will focus on the Boston Model which is considered a sequential stage model.

Garland, Jones and Kolodny developed the Boston Model for the stages of group development in 1965. The Boston Model categorizes a group's life into the five sequential stages of pre-affiliation, power and control, intimacy, differentiation, and separation (Garland, Jones & Kolodny, 1965). The Boston Model has been widely accepted and used in the group work literature since its inception. The social group work literature is saturated with books and articles that reference the Boston Model or directly apply the model (Berman-Rossi, 1992; 1993; 2002; Ciardiello, 2003; Cohen, 1994; Glassman & Kates, 1990; Malekoff, 1997, 2004; Sullivan, 1995; Toseland & Rivas, 2001; Toseland et al, 2004; Travers, 1995). The Boston Model has also been used as an organizing framework for the discussion of group work in a number of social work texts and reference books (Anderson, 1997; Hepworth & Larsen, 1993; Barker, 1999). In addition, group work educators teach and examine group life through this developmental lens (Kurland & Salmon, 1998). Despite its widespread use, there is little empirical support for the model. A recent review of the literature references only one empirical study that demonstrates the applicability of the Boston Model (Kelly & Berman-Rossi, 1999).

The origins of the Boston Model

The model was developed from observations of youth groups by staff of the Department of Neighborhood Clubs of Boston Children's Service in conjunction with research studies from the fields of social psychology and social work (Garland et al., 1965). The study used a sample of convenience composed of therapeutic youth groups with disturbed and handicapped children. The group members were of both sexes and ranged in ages from 9 to 16, with various levels of social competency and socioeconomic status (SES). Informal clinical research was conducted over the course of three years. Specifically, group workers noted behaviors exhibited by different groups during staff seminars. Also, group records were analyzed. Results showed similar relational issues that changed over time. These issues were organized into a group development model. Study limitations entail findings that were subject to clinical interpretation or 'researcher bias' (Garland et al., 1965).

There were several factors presumed to influence the applicability of the model. These include the self-fulfilling prophecy (worker biases, predictions, and expectations), alterations of group composition during group life (such as members joining and leaving), age, developmental level, and socio-economic status of the members. Therefore these factors were controlled for in the study conducted by this researcher.

The developers of the Boston Model encourage workers to test the model by applying it in various settings to determine if and how it is useful as a guide for practice. They add that where the model does not apply, it may serve as a base for developing other models (Garland et al., 1965). The current inquiry is a step in that direction.

The Boston Model stages

The Boston Model describes group and worker behavior according to the five stage developmental sequence of pre-affiliation, power and control, intimacy, differentiation, and separation. During the first stage of pre-affiliation, members become acquainted with the group and each other. The major early struggle is approach-avoidance in relation to closeness. In stage two (power and control), members attempt to define and formalize relationships via status, scapegoating, conflicts, subgroups, cliques, and alliances. Power and control issues are the groups attempt to defend against intimacy. Also, the absence of punishment and the worker's permissive stance creates a 'normative crisis' causing fight or flight behaviors to occur. It seems without the external control of punishment many members will lack internal self control and fight or flee. This calls for a re-discussion of rules regarding emotional and physical safety. When this issue is addressed the members are better able to trust one another and become more intimate. In stage three (intimacy), a more intense level of personal involvement, self-disclosure, and interdependence characterizes group interactions. This allows the group to plan and carry out collective tasks more effectively. In the fourth stage of differentiation members begin to accept each other as separate individuals, the worker as a unique individual, and the group as a special experience where members are free to individualize and differentiate from one another. Now, more organization for work and play is possible. Leadership tends to be more shared and functional. The last stage of the Boston Model is separation. During this final phase of group life, members experience some anxiety over separation and loss. Approach and avoidance behaviors, similar to those displayed during stage one, can occur (Garland et al., 1965).

Highlighting two factors that influence group development: Gender and oppression status

Gender

Gender is an important variable to consider in group development. Schiller (1995; 1997) began the critical analysis of the notion that group development is not gender specific. She claims the Boston Model developers did not take into account that women's normative growth within their life cycle in general, and in groups in particular, is dramatically different from that of men. Drawing from feminist theory and self in relation theory she suggests that concepts of relationships, intimacy, and conflict have different meanings developmentally for women than for men (Gilligan, 1993; Sands & Nuccio, 1992; Schiller, 1995; 1997; Miller & Stiver, 1993). Specifically, Schiller (1997) asserts that a main difference between male and female groups includes the way they deal with conflict. Women tend to challenge and confront others after they have established a sense of safety and connectedness and mutual understanding. Women may avoid conflict because they feel it is not appropriate. A high degree of trust and safety is needed before conflict surfaces in women's groups and before members challenge each other and the worker. Considering some of these principles, Schiller (1995; 1997; 2003) altered the sequence of the stages in the Boston Model to develop a Relational Model of group development for women's groups. In similar fashion to the Boston Model, Schiller's model is often referenced in the field of social group work; however, it has only been investigated once in open-ended groups with the institutionalized elderly (Kelly & Berman-Rossi, 1999).

Oppression status

Schiller (1997; 2003; 2007) has also asserted that the Relational Model is applicable to groups with vulnerable members such as those that have been oppressed or traumatized. Group work scholars have applied the Relational Model to group work with oppressed populations such as developmentally disabled women (Berwald & Houstra, 2002), gay, lesbian, bisexual, transgender, and questioning (GLBT & Q) populations, (Gray & Healy, 2003), queer youth (Peters, 1997; Delois & Cohen, 2000; Delois, 2003), and other oppressed groups concerning race (Brown & Mistry, 2005). Many of these assertions have not been empirically tested.

The Relational Model stages

Schiller's model identifies a developmental sequence for women's groups that is similar to the Boston Model's five stages of group development. However, Schiller alters the middle three stages of the Boston Model to create the following developmental scheme: pre-affiliation, establishing a relational base, mutuality and interpersonal empathy, challenge and change, and separation. Stage one, pre-affiliation and stage five, separation, are the same in both models (Schiller, 1997).

During Stage one, pre-affiliation, the group character is one of exploration and approach-avoidance behaviors. Stage two, establishing a relational base, involves creating a sense of connection with the group via sharing of personal stories and common problems. This creates a sense of safety and is a prerequisite for greater intimacy and self-disclosure. This sense of safety in the group allows the members to be better prepared to deal with conflict when it arises. Thus, rather than jumping into the area of greatest difficulty for women, that is dealing with conflict, authority, and power as in the Boston Model, women first set the stage with what they do well – give support, bond around common issues, and generally do not challenge each other or the worker early on.

During the third stage, mutuality and interpersonal empathy, members are not yet engaged in overt conflict or challenges. Rather, this is a time during which there is a deeper level of intimacy that allows for both empathic connection and appreciation of difference. The Boston Model separates the stages of intimacy and differentiation which is in line with developmental psychology that notes differentiation precedes intimacy. However, feminist researchers have asserted that these processes are different for women. Specifically, for women, these tasks are merged. The Boston Model does not consider this developmental difference. However, the Relational Model does acknowledge this difference by integrating these processes into the same developmental stage.

During the fourth stage, challenge and change, authority issues emerge; challenging the authority of the worker and each other develops later in this model. The women know they are liked which frees them up to allow conflict to emerge. The main challenge during this stage is often at the heart of growth for a woman, which is how to engage in conflict without sacrificing the bonds of connection and empathy. Therefore the task during this stage is to hold connection within conflict.

The final stage of separation is the same as the stage noted in the Boston Model. Specifically, the members may regress to earlier stage behaviors in the face of loss. The group reviews and evaluates the group experience and works through the process of letting go (Garland et al., 1965; Schiller, 1995).

The Boston Model vs. The Relational Model

When comparing the Boston Model to the Relational Model the following difference is noteworthy. The placement of conflict is different in each model; in the Boston Model conflict precedes intimacy or the development of close bonds and in the Relational Model intimacy precedes conflict.

As mentioned earlier there is limited empirical evidence that supports the Boston Model and the Relational Model. However, this researcher found one empirical study that demonstrates the applicability of both models. Kelly and Berman-Rossi (1999) conducted a qualitative study on group development in open-ended groups of the institutionalized elderly. The groups observed in the study were compared to the Boston Model and Relational Model. The researchers studied the process recordings of two groups: a new resident group composed primarily of women from 14 different floors and the floor group comprised of 31 men living together on the same floor that were served over time. Findings suggest the two groups developed differently. The new resident group (consisting of mostly women) had greater member turnover and fewer persons returning. As a result, fewer members remained to carry on group norms, themes, and culture and the group did not progress to a consistent place of intimacy however beginning stages of the Boston Model were observed. The floor group was composed of all men with the addition of one woman later in the group. This group's developmental sequence was more reflective of Schiller's Relational Model. The fact that the members were known to each other proved to significantly influence how the group developed overtime. The researchers encourage further investigation to identify with more accuracy group development patterns for different populations served by social group work (Kelly & Berman-Rossi, 1999). The open-ended structure of one of the groups seemed to influence group development.According to Galinsky & Schopler (1989) groups that are open-ended or have members entering and leaving consistently interferes with group development. Therefore only closed groups were used in the current inquiry.

Study design

This study uses a quantitative design to investigate group workers' perceptions of group development with an emphasis on the factors that influence a group's developmental pathway. IRB approval was sought and received to conduct the current inquiry.

Study questions and variables

The main research question is: Are there different factors that influence the development of closed-ended groups as perceived by group workers? Study questions and their related hypotheses used to guide this research were:

SQ1: Is there a significant relationship between worker perception of group development sequence and the gender of group members?

H1: Women's groups will be described as displaying conflict later (Model B: Relational Model)) than men's or mixed groups (Model A: Boston Model).

SQ2: Is there a significant relationship between worker perception of group development and mandated membership?

H2: Mandated/Involuntary groups will display conflict earlier than non-mandated voluntary groups despite gender.

SQ3: Is there a significant relationship between worker perception of group development sequence and worker perception that members are predominantly from an oppressed group?

H3: There will be a significant relationship between worker perception that members are predominantly from an oppressed group and worker perception of group development sequence in that members that are perceived as oppressed will be more likely to be perceived as following the development sequence of Model B: Relational Model.

Research was conducted and data was generated to answer these questions.

Regarding study variables, there were two dependent variables used to measure group development: 1) DV1 (Dependent Variable 1): group developmental sequence observed and DV2 (Dependent Variable 2):

conflict variable. DV1 was measured via participants choosing from three descriptions: Model A (Boston Model), Model B (Relational Model), and other (they write it in). DV2 was measured via asking the participants about the placement of conflict in the group development sequence (conflict before close bonds are developed represents the Boston Model and conflict after close bonds developed represents the Relational Model). Independent variables in the study include gender of group members and oppression status of group members. Mandated membership was also investigated because it has been noted to influence group development. Specifically, because mandated members have not chosen freely to participate but were rather coerced or forced to do so, they have a resistance to group involvement that often causes behaviors such as anger and frustration at the worker and each other during the beginning stages before close bonds are developed (Rooney & Chovanec, 2004). Demographic variables include worker gender, worker education, worker primary employment setting and main employment function, location of primary employment setting, therapeutic approach used in the group, worker group experience. The confounding variables in the study are income level, ethnicity, and age of group members, group duration, group size, session length, session frequency, worker group developmental theory ascribed, and presenting problems of members.

Study sample

650 American members of the Association for the Advancement of Social Work with Groups (AASWG) were selected from a sampling frame of 879 international and national members from the 2005 membership list. Permission was granted by the Executive Committee of AASWG to use the membership list for this inquiry. Participation for the study was conducted via internet survey completion and members were contacted to participate via e-mail. This researcher sent e-mails to all members who have known e-mail addresses, which were 530 of the 650 American members. This is roughly two-thirds of the total membership. Therefore, a sample of convenience of 530 AASWG members was used in the study. International members were excluded due to limited temporal and financial resources (Patten, 2000; Rubin & Babbie, 2001; Cone & Foster, 2001).

Instrumentation: The group development survey

Eight experts in the field of social group work research and practice reviewed the group development survey. Changes were made based on recommendations provided. To assess construct and criterion validity, Linda Schiller, the developer of the Relational Model, reviewed the survey to ascertain if the description of her model was a valid and accurate representation (Schiller, 1995; 1997). Some changes were made to the Relational Model in response to her recommendations. The group development survey was pilot tested with a sample of five group workers who did not participate in the main study and no serious adjustments were needed based on their feedback (Patten, 2000; Rubin & Babie, 2001; Cone & Foster, 2001).

Procedures

530 AASWG members with known e-mails were entered into a study group distribution list so that electronic mail could be sent anonymously to all participants at one time (Sills & Song, 2002). The survey was sent in three waves, each two weeks apart. The survey was accessible via a web-based link making it easy to get to, complete, and return. Participates were informed that their involvement was voluntary and confidential and that no harm would come to them. With the rapid growth of the Internet over the last decade, web-based surveys have become a method for conducting scientific research. For particular populations that use the Internet on a regular basis, e-mail and web-based surveys have been found to be a sensible way to secure meaningful data (Sills & Song, 2002). Of the 508 e-mails that were sent, 405 (79.7%) were successfully delivered over a six week period. Participant completion of the survey constituted consent (Patten, 2000; Rubin & Babbie, 2001). A total of 144 returned surveys provided a 35% response rate.

Data analysis

The data were analyzed using the computer program, SPSS for windows, 15.0.

Frequencies and descriptive statistics were run for all demographic variables and to answer the exploratory study questions. Also, chi-square tests were conducted to test the relationships between variables. To ascertain the extent to which the independent variables are predictors of the Boston Model and the Relational Model, a logistical regression with a hierarchy of two levels was used. To check for subjective analysis problems and to control for experimenter expectancy or researcher bias, an expert in the field of social work research reviewed the data gathered (Rubin & Babbie, 2001).

Demographics

A major question in this study was, 'Have you facilitated a closed-ended group in the past two years?' This reduced the 130 respondents to 49 respondents therefore reducing the amount of salient data for the study. In other words, only 37.7% of the sample (49 of the 130 respondents) ran a closed-ended group in the last two years making the N equal to 49 (N=49) for the current inquiry.

Main study sample (N=49)

Of the 49 members who ran a closed-ended group within the last two years, there was an average of 10.6 members in the groups (with a minimum of 2 members and a maximum of 80 members). The median number of members was 8 and the mode was 8. As shown in Table 2, most groups were of mixed gender or all female and for the mixed gender groups, most had more females than males. Most group members were adults/elderly followed by adolescents and then children. Of the 49 groups, most groups were voluntary or non-mandated (See Table 1).

Table 1
Gender of group members and membership type

	%
Gender	
All female	40.8
All male	8.2
Mixed	51.0
Gender mix	
More females	60.0
More males	20.0
About even gender mix	20.0
Member age	
Children	4.1
Adolescents	28.6
Adults/Elderly	67.3
Member type	
Voluntary	89.8
Involuntary	10.2

In regards to how often the groups met, most groups met once a week for 1-2 hours (see Table 2). The groups continued for an average of 7.40 months (median = 5 months, mode= 3 months).

Table 2
Group frequency and session length

	%
Group frequency	
Once a week	73.5
Twice a week	12.2
Every other week	8.2
monthly	6.1
Session Length	
Less than an hour	18.4
1-2 hours	69.4
2 + hours	12.2

Psycho-education was the predominant therapeutic approach used in the groups (see Table 3).

Table 3
The predominant therapeutic approach

Therapeutic Approach	%
psycho-therapeutic	6.1
feminist-relational	10.2
support group	12.2
psycho-educational	26.5
socialization group	16.3
cognitive-behavioral	8.2
task group	6.1
other	14.3
Total	100.0

As Table 4 indicates, the proportion of members who were of low income exceeded the proportion of members of mid-upper income. More group members were considered oppressed by the group workers than not oppressed and most had a multiple oppression status indicating they were oppressed in more than one way. Regarding the predominant ethnicity of group members, there were more whites than non-whites (see Table 4).

Table 4
Income, oppression status, oppression type, and ethnicity

		%
Predominant income level	low	53.1
	mid-upper	46.9
Oppression status	yes	59.2
	no	40.8
Oppression type	income	3.4
	presenting problem	13.8
	multiple oppression status	82.8
Predominant ethnicity	white	51.0
	non-white	24.5
	mixed	24.5

In regards to the predominant presenting problem of group members, the most common presenting problem was interpersonal problems followed by socialization issues and academic work. Table 5 shows a full list of the predominant presenting problem of group members. This data was condensed for advanced statistical testing to social problems (65.3%) consisting of the following categories: interpersonal, child welfare issues, socialization issues, family functioning and other issues, and individual problems (34.7%) consisting of substance abuse, psychiatric disorders, trauma, academic/work, and behavioral problems.

Table 5
Predominant presenting problem of group members

Problem	Members presenting (%)
Substance abuse	4.1
Interpersonal	24.5
Child welfare issues	6.1
Psychiatric disorders	4.1
Trauma	8.2
Academic/work	14.3
Behavioral	4.1
Socialization issues	20.4
Family functioning issues	4.1
Other	10.2
Total	100.0

Worker characteristics for the main sample (N=49)

There were more female than male workers with most holding an MSW/MSSW degree (see Table 6). As Table 6 shows, the group experience of the workers was about even across categories with the higher proportion of workers having 11-20 years of experience.

A large percentage of the workers reported the main employment functions of direct service/clinical and education/training/research and the most common practice area comprised children and youth followed by education, mental health, and school social work (see Table 7). These variables were condensed for advanced statistical testing in the following way. Two categories were created for workers main

Table 6
Worker gender, academic degree, and group experience (%)

Gender	
Male	26.5
Female	73.5
Academic degree	
BA/BSW	4.1
MSW/MSSW	61.2
PhD/EdD/DSW	34.7
Group experience	
0-10 years	32.7
11-20 years	34.7
21+ years	32.7

Table 7
Worker's main employment function and practice area (%)

Main employment function	
Direct service/casework	2.0
Direct service/clinical	38.8
Consultation	6.1
Education/training/research	32.7
Management/Administration	14.3
Retired	2.0
Other	4.1
Practice area in primary employment setting	
Children and Youth	24.5
Family Services	8.2
Medical/Healthcare	6.1
Public Assistance/Welfare	2.0
Services to the Aged	2.0
Occupational	4.1
Community Organizing/Planning	2.0
Mental Health	10.2
Substance Abuse	7.7
School Social Work	10.2
Education	18.4
Other	4.1

Table 8
Primary employment setting and group theory guiding practice (%)

Primary employment setting	
Social service organization	22.4
Hospital	6.1
Nursing home	4.1
Elementary/secondary school	8.2
Outpatient facility	8.2
Private practice	14.3
College/university	30.6
Other	6.1
Location of primary employment	
Southeast	6.1
Northeast	65.3
Midwest	18.4
Southwest	8.2
Northwest	2.0
Group development theory	
Boston model	12.2
Relational model	28.6
The relational model and the boston model	12.2
Mutual aid model	4.1
No particular model	26.5
Other	14.3

employment function: direct service/clinical (38.8%) consisting of only that one category and other (61.2%) consisting of all other categories (see Table 7). Three categories were created for workers' practice area: children/youth/family (32.7%) involving the categories of children and youth and family services; school/education (28.6%) involving the categories of school social work, and education; and other (32.7%) involving the categories of medical/healthcare, public assistance, services to the aged, occupational, community organizing/planning, mental health, substance abuse, and other.

In order of frequency, workers primary employment settings were predominantly the following: college/university, social service organization, and private practice/self-employed and most workers lived in the northeast (See Table 8). For advanced statistical testing, the data for primary employment setting was condensed to outpatient (44.9%) consisting of social service organization, outpatient facility, and private practice; inpatient (10.2%) consisting of hospital and nursing home; and school social work/education (38.8%) consisting of elementary/secondary education and college/university. Finally, for the main study sample, it seems the Relational Model guides the practice of more workers than the Boston Model and 12/49 or 26.5% of the group workers said that no particular group development model guides their practice (Table 8). When considering number of years of group experience, of those 12 workers, 33% have been practising group work for 11-20 years and 25% have been practicing for 0-5 years.

No group sample (*N*=81)

The no group sample consists of the 81 AASWG members who had not run a group in the previous two years. Most of the workers in this sample were female, MSW/MSSW educated with 21+ years of experience working with groups. The largest percentage of the workers had the main employment function of education/training/ research, worked in the practice area of education, in the primary employment setting of college/university in the northeast. From this data it can be inferred that many respondents in this study were academics that did not run a group in the last two years who seem to be affiliated with AASWG for reasons other than collegial support for the groups they are currently running. This was an unexpected result that unfortunately lowered the amount of usable data to answer the study questions.

Group development data: Two dependent variables (DV1 & DV2)

To check the validity of the dependent measure, group developmental theory observed, another measure was created on the survey that asked if conflict emerged before the development of close bonds (the main premise of the Boston Model). In particular, this is called criterion validity and it is when an outside measure is selected because it is believed to be an appraisal of the same variable that the question intends to measure (Rubin & Babie, 2001). The conflict variable was included in the survey for that purpose. When comparing the final results, for the group development sequence observed, 42.9 % observed the Boston Model and 57.1% observed the Relational Model. The conflict variable generated different information. In regards to the placement of conflict in the developmental sequence, 69.4% reported YES, conflict did emerge before close bonds were developed (Boston Model) and 30.6% reported NO, conflict did not emerge before close bonds were developed (Relational Model) (See Table 9). Results show that the group developmental theory observed responses were inconsistent with the conflict question responses. Thus, a clear discrepancy is present and the measure did not produce information it was intended to generate. Also, a correlation coefficient test was run to assess the correlation between these two measures. The variables were found to have a correlation coefficient of .36 (p=.01), which is significant but low, adding support that the measures were not correlated. The discrepancy may be due to the lengthy description in the group development sequence question versus the concise question presented in the conflict question. As a result of this discrepancy, it was decided that there will be two dependent variables for the study to test the conception of group developmental theory observed by the worker: DV1: the dependent variable of group developmental theory observed and DV2: the conflict variable (did conflict emerge before close bonds developed) to see if any significant differences are present. There was no significant associations identified for DV1. However for DV2, when participants were asked if conflict developed before close bonds were developed, significant associations were found. Therefore only data for DV2 will be presented in this article.

Table 9

Group development data by frequency of model

Dependent Variable	DV 1		DV 2	
	n	%	n	%
Boston Model	21	49.2	34	69.4
Relational Model	28	57.1	15	30.6

Data analysis

Chi-square analysis

In the chi-square test, if the difference is statistically significant ($p \leq .05$), the null hypothesis is rejected (Green & Salkind, 2003). Using the chi-square test, no significant associations were found between gender and the placement of conflict in the group development sequence observed. Therefore the hypothesis that women's groups would be described as displaying conflict later than men's groups or mixed groups was not supported by the data generated. In addition, no significant associations were found between the placement of conflict in the group development sequence and membership type (mandated/non-mandated). Thus, the hypothesis that mandated involuntary groups would display conflict earlier than non-mandated groups despite gender was also not supported.

There were however, three statistically significant associations found (see Table 10) using the chi-square test. Oppression status and the placement of conflict in group development were found to be significantly associated, Pearson x^2 (2, N=49) =3.29, p=.035. This allows the researcher to reject the null hypothesis that there is no difference between oppression status and the placement of conflict in group development. This suggests that there is a difference in developmental sequence observed by group workers according to the oppression status of the members. However the difference was not one that was hypothesized by the researcher. The researcher predicted that in groups in which members were considered predominantly oppressed conflict would emerge after bonds were formed (Relational Model). However, according to this finding, conflict emerged before close bonds developed (Boston Model). Specifically, in oppressed groups, workers observed the Boston Model (79%) of group development more often than the Relational Model (21%).

The second statistically significant association involved the variables of predominant ethnicity (whites, non-whites, mixed ethnicity). People can be considered oppressed based on their ethnicity. Therefore predominant ethnicity was used as an indicator of the independent variable oppression status. Predominant ethnicity and the placement of conflict in group development were found to be significantly associated, Pearson x^2 (2, N=49) =7.46, p=.024. This indicates the workers' perceptions that groups that are predominantly nonwhite and of mixed ethnicity are more likely to demonstrate the Boston Model of group development than the Relational Model. In particular, in non-white groups, workers observed the Boston Model more often (83.3%) than the Relational Model (16.7%). In mixed ethnicity groups, workers observed the Boston Model more often (91.7%) than the Relational Model (8.3%). However, the data must be interpreted with caution because two cells had an expected frequency of less than 5 (Weinbach & Grinnell, 2001).

The third statistically significant association involved the variable of predominant income level. People can be considered oppressed based on income. Therefore income was used as an indicator of the independent variable oppression status. Predominant income level and the placement of conflict in group development were found to be significantly associated, Pearson x^2 (1, N=49) =6.04, p=.014 (Weinbach & Grinnell, 2001). In other words, groups with members that were perceived by the worker to be predominantly of low income were more likely to be observed as following the Boston Model than the Relational Model. Namely, in low income groups, workers observed the Boston Model (84.6%) more often than the Relational Model (15.4%).

Table 10
Summary of statistically significant chi-square (DV2)

Variable	*F* value /χ^2	Degrees of Freedom (*df*)	Probability (p)
Oppression status	3.29	2	p=.035
Predominant ethnicity	7.46	2	p=.024
Predominant income	6.04	1	p=.014

The rest of the study variables were not significantly related to the placement of conflict in the group developmental sequence (see Table 11).

Regarding answering the exploratory question involving an association between the age range of the members and the group developmental sequence observed, no significant associations were observed. Namely, of the two children's groups surveyed, both were observed to develop like the Boston Model. Of the 14 adolescent groups surveyed, ten were observed to develop like the Boston Model and 4 the Relational Model. Of the 33 adults groups surveyed, the Boston Model was observed in 22 of the groups and the Relational Model was observed in 11 of the groups. However, these findings were not statistically significant.

Table 11
Non-significant chi-square statistics for DV2 (N=49)

Variable	F value /χ^2	Degrees of Freedom (df)	Probability (p)
Group membership type	.231	1	p= .631
Gender mix	1.76	3	p= .759
Oppression type	4.35	2	p= .113
Member age	1.02	2	p= .599
Worker theory that guides practice	3.59	2	p= .165
Worker academic degree	.998	2	p= .607
Worker group work experience	.018	2	p= .991
Group length	2.61	3	p= .455
Group frequency	1.27	3	p= .737
Session length	4.92	2	p= .085
Presenting problems of members	.018	1	p= .894
Worker primary employment setting	.783	3	p= .853
Worker practice area	.812	2	p= .812
Worker employment function	.452	2	p= .798

Multivariate analyses

The type of multivariate analysis used in this study was binary logistical regression. Logistical regression identifies independent variables that best predict membership into one of two groups (Boston Model and Relational Model) (Mertler & Vanatta, 2002). All independent variables and dependent variables were used in the analysis. Results of this study indicate no statistically significant predictions.

Discussion of the findings

The main research question for the study was: Are there different factors that influence the development of closed-ended groups as perceived by group workers? It was hypothesized based on the Relational Model that women's groups will be described as displaying conflict later than men's or mixed groups. However results found no significant relationship between gender and the placement of conflict in group development.

It was also hypothesized that mandated/involuntary groups would display conflict earlier then non-mandated groups despite gender. Results showed no significant relationship between mandated membership and the placement of conflict in group development.

In addition, it was hypothesized that there would be a significant relationship between worker perception that members are predominantly from an oppressed group and worker perception of the placement of conflict in group development in that members that are perceived as oppressed will be more likely to follow the developmental path where conflict occurs after close bonds are developed (Relational Model). A significant association was found between worker's perception that members are predominantly from an oppressed group and the placement of conflict. However the relationship was not one predicted by the researcher. Members that were perceived as oppressed by the worker did not follow the developmental sequence of the Relational Model, but rather, the Boston Model. In other words, conflict will emerge before close bonds are developed in groups considered by the worker to be predominantly oppressed.

The literature notes case studies of oppressed groups that follow the Boston Model of group development as well (Cohen, 1994; Travers, 1995; Groves & Schondel, 1996). When considering the reason why groups that were considered to be predominantly oppressed were more likely to develop along the lines of the Boston Model, oppression psychology may supply a worthy explanation. Specifically, according to oppression psychology, oppressed people may have internalized the dominant message of oppression and then treat each other in oppressive ways (Gitterman & Shulman, 1994). The conflict observed by the workers during the beginning stages of group life could be testing behavior or a way the members test to see how safe the group is going to be. In other words, the conflict may be the way in which the members find out if the worker and the group will create a safe environment for them and treat them with respect. Also, oppressed people may have had a disruption in their experience of safety. Therefore it may take them a longer time to develop the experience of safety.

Another finding of this study was that predominant ethnicity was significantly associated to the placement of conflict in group development. For example, groups with members who are perceived by the worker to be predominantly non-white and of mixed ethnicity are likely to follow the group developmental sequence in which conflict occurs before the development of close bonds, i.e., the Boston Model. According to Brown & Mistry (1994; 2005), mixed racial groups can influence group development and when mixing groups there is potential for conflict between them. These researchers also add that the race of the members have a significant effect on group behavior and group process. They assert that patterns of social oppression will be repeated in social work groups because groups are a social microcosm of the wider society. Indeed, in our society, racial and ethnic segregation persists. Neighborhoods and schools are still often segregated (Rodenborg & Huynh, 2006). Each group member evaluates the group based on their socially determined frame of reference. For instance, part of the frame of reference for black/African American group members may be the experience of living each day in a racist society controlled by white persons. Often, the frame of reference for white group members takes for granted their superior status and power in relation to black/African American people and other minorities. These differences in frames of reference may cause conflict during the beginning stages of group development. Brown and Mistry (2005) add: 'There is extensive evidence that the structurally determined oppressions of racism are replicated as a powerful dynamic in small groups of mixed membership' (p.140). Thus, born out of a lifetime of oppressive experiences, mixed groups often import distrustful attitudes. According to Rittner et al. (1999), in groups with mixed races, problems or conflicts usually emerge during the beginning stages, when obstacles to engagement are most likely to occur. Unaddressed tensions generated by diversity can cause damaging prejudices which often result in dissatisfied group members.

Another possible explanation is that conflict occurs during beginning sessions in mixed groups because oppressed people might bring to the group feelings of anger and rage generated by their oppressive experiences. Challenging behaviors by non-oppressed members in beginning groups might trigger reactions in the oppressed members because that anger from being victimized is activated, causing anger to surface and be expressed during group interactions. Continuing work to analyze group development through the lens of power and privilege can help generate a more complete understanding of the interactions in mixed ethnicity groups (Delois, 2003).

Also, in this study, predominant income (lower income and mid-upper income) was found to be significantly related to the placement of conflict in group development. For example, groups with members who are perceived to be of low income by the worker are likely to follow the group developmental sequence in which conflict occurs before the development of close bonds, i.e. Boston Model. It is interesting to note here that the Boston Model was developed with a population that conforms to this finding. In particular, the model was developed from observations of therapeutic social youth groups with children of varying socioeconomic status (SES). According to the developers of the model, the SES of the members influenced the applicability of the model (Garland et al., 1965).

Furthermore, others have asserted that income level influences group development (Garland et al., 1965; Northen, 1969). In Northen (1969) socioeconomic status (SES) was listed as a factor that influences group development. According to research conducted by Stern, Smith, and Jang (1999), poverty significantly affects mood, disrupts relationships, and causes the externalization of problems. Carlson (2006) adds that higher levels of poverty are significantly related to higher levels of direct exposure to school violence, dissociation, property damage, and violence proneness. Therefore, it may be possible to infer that people of low income may deal with conflict during group interactions differently than people of other income levels because of the inherent stress and problems that enduring poverty can create.

Finally, the developers of the Boston Model, Garland et al., (1965) recommended that workers test their theory with various types of groups, populations, agency settings, ages, developmental levels, and class of the members to see where it does or does not apply. This study responded to the developers of the Boston Model's call to test their model on current group work practice and found their theory applicable to the oppression status involving ethnicity and, as they suspected, the income level of group members.

An exploratory inquiry: The age of group members

There was also information generated in an exploratory manner, or in a manner that did not include any predictions or hypotheses. One of these inquiries sought to ascertain which group developmental sequences were most common to which age ranges of group members. Results show the two children's groups that were facilitated in the study both followed the Boston Model. Also, twice as many adult groups followed the Boston Model than the Relational Model. Further, adolescent groups followed the Boston Model (11/14), two thirds more than the Relational Model (3/14).

What the findings suggest about current group work practice

Based on the demographic findings of this study, it seems that in current group work practice there are more mixed groups than same gender groups. Psycho-educational groups and socialization groups are the most common type of therapeutic approach used by group workers. Also, the average length of a group is approximately 7.5 months. The average size of a group is 8 members. Most groups are voluntary and occur once a week for 1-2 hours. Few groups are facilitated with people of high income, most are low to middle income. More AASWG members run adult groups than adolescent and children's groups. As to be expected, groups are most often used for clients struggling with interpersonal and socialization issues than other presenting problems. When groups are predominantly oppressed, most are oppressed in multiple ways rather than in one particular way.

The findings of this study imply that many group workers questioned do not have any particular group development theory in mind when they run their groups. This is a concern for social work education. Specifically, 12/49 or 26.5% of the group workers said that no particular group development model guides their practice. When considering the number of years of group experience of those 12 workers, 33% have been practicing group work for 11-20 years and 25% have been practicing for 0-5 years. Thus many new social workers, as well as experienced ones, do not seem to be adequately informed about this important group work principle. Without knowledge of group development theory one will have difficulty knowing where the group or individual members should be or strive to move towards (Lacourciere, 1980). Also, an understanding of group development is needed to guide workers on the appropriate timing of interventions and activities. Indeed some knowledge about group development is needed to run groups in a purposeful way. Therefore, group work educators should strongly consider integrating the teaching of group development to social work students to better prepare them for real life practice situations.

Limitations of the study

All findings need to be interpreted with prudence because of the limitations of the study. One of the major limitations of the study was that the sample size was small. Surprisingly, only 37.7% of the respondents conducted a group in the last two years limiting the number of cases to use in the analysis. Future research should consider expanding the study population to include other groups of social workers. Also, the sample was one of convenience, which limits its empirical power. Future studies should yield data from a larger sample size that is random in nature. Also, the ethnicity of the worker was not generated in this study. Future studies should add this variable to ascertain if the presence of conflict might be explained by differences in ethnicity between members and the group worker. Finally, the results of the ethnicity variable need to be accepted with caution because chi-square rules were violated. Also, logistical regression analyses yielded no significant findings, further limiting the study.

Future research based on the limitations of the study

Of the 49 groups that were investigated in this study, only 12 were non-white. Considering that one of the main findings of the study involved the ethnicity variable, future research should seek to study the developmental path of more non-white groups including the variable of worker ethnicity to ascertain if it has an influence on group development. Also, in this study there were only 4 all male groups. Thus more attention should be paid in future research to obtain a more balanced pool of same sex groups. In addition, only the perceptions of AASWG members were investigated. Therefore future studies should consider including other groups of social workers. These findings are exploratory in nature, therefore they must be considered preliminary at best. This study was just a first scientific look considering there were practically no previous studies examining this topic in an empirical way. Indeed, given the limitations, it is clear that more studies are needed to clarify the impact that oppression status has on group development and to continue to test whether or not the variable of gender alters the developmental pathway of groups.

References

Anderson, J. (1997). *Social work with groups: A process model.* NY: Longman.

Bales, R.F. (1956). A theoretical framework for interactional process analysis. In D. Cartwright & A Zander (Eds.), *Group dynamics: Research and theory.* NY: Row, Peterson and Co, 30-38.

Barker, R.L. (1999). *Social work dictionary.* Washington, D.C.: NASW Press.

Bennis, W. & Shepard, H. (1956). A theory of group development, In W. Bennis (Ed.), *Planning of change: Readings in theory of group development.* Plenum Publishing.

Berman-Rossi, T. (1992). Empowering groups through understanding the stages of group development. In J.A. Garland (Ed.), *Group work reaching out: People, places, and power.* NY: Haworth.

Berman-Rossi, T. (1993). The tasks and skills of the social worker across stages of group development, In S. Wenocur, P.H. Ephross, T. V. Vassil & R.K.

Varghese (Eds.), *Social work with groups: Expanding Horizons.* New York: Haworth, 69-81.

Berman-Rossi, T. (2002). My love affair with stages of group development. *Social Work with Groups, 25*(1/2), 151-158.

Berwald, C. & Houstra, T. (2002). Joining feminism and social group work practice: A women's disability group. *Social Work with Groups, 25*(4), 71-83.

Bion, W.B. (1959). *Experiences in groups.* NY: Basic Books.

Brown, A. & Mistry, T. (1994). Group work with mixed membership groups. Issues of race and gender. *Social work with Groups, 17*(3), 5-21.

Brown, A. & Mistry, T. (2005). Group work with mixed membership groups. Issues of race and gender. *Social Work with Groups, 28*(3/4), 133-148.

Carlson, K.T. (2006, April). Poverty and youth violence exposure: Experiences in rural communities. *Children and Schools, 28*(2), 87-96.

Ciardiello, S. (2003). *ACTivities for group work with school age children.* Warminster, PA: Marco Products.

Cohen, M.B. (1994). Who wants to chair the meeting? Group development of homeless people. *Social Work with Groups, 17*(1/2), 71-87.

Cone, J.D. & Foster, S.L. (1993). Dissertations and theses from start to finish: Psychology and related fields. Washington, D.C.: American Psychological Association.

Delois, K. & Cohen, M. (2000). A queer idea: Using group work principles to strengthen learning in a sexual minorities seminar. *Social Work with Groups, 23*(3), 53-67.

Delois, K. (2003). Gender bending: Reflections on group work with queer youth. In M.B. Cohen & A. Mullender (Eds.), *Gender and Group work.* London: Routledge, 107-115.

Galinsky, M.J. & Schopler, J.H. (1989). Developmental Patterns in Open-Ended Groups. *Social Work with Groups, 12*(2), 99-114.

Garland, J. Jones, H. & Kolodny, R. (1965). A model for stages of development in social work with groups. In S. Bernstein (Ed.) *Explorations in group work: Essays in theory and practice.* Boston, MA: Boston University School of Social Work, 17-77.

Gilligan, C. (1993). *In a different voice: Psychological theory and women's development* (2nd ed.). Cambridge Mass: Harvard University Press.

Gitterman, A. & Shulman, L. (1994). *Mutual aid groups, vulnerable populations, and the life cycle* (2nd ed.). New York: Columbia University Press.

Glassman, U. & Kates, L. (1990). *Group work: A humanistic approach.* California: SAGE.

Gray, B. & Healy, T.C. (2003). From support to empowerment: Caregiver

Connections. In M.B. Cohen & A. Mullender (Eds.), *Gender and group work*. London: Routledge.

Green, S.B., Salkind, N.J. (2003). *Using SPSS* (3rd ed.). Upper Saddle River, N.J.: Prentice Hall.

Groves, P. & Schondel, C. (1996). Lesbian couples who are survivors of incest. Group work utilizing a feminist approach. *Social Work with Groups, 19*(3/4), 93-103.

Hepworth, D.H. & Larsen, J. (1993). *Direct social work practice: Theory and skills* (4th ed.). Pacific Grive, CA: Brooks/Cole.

Johnson, D.W. & Johnson, F.P. (2000). *Joining together: Group theory and group skills,* (7th ed.). Boston: Allyn & Bacon.

Kelly, T. B. & Berman-Rossi, T. (1999). Advancing stages of group development theory: The case of institutionalized older persons. *Social Work With Groups, 22*(2/3), 119-138.

Kurland, R. & Salmon, R. (1998*). Teaching a methods course in social work with groups.* Alexandria, VA: Council on Social Work Education.

Lacourcière, R. (1980). *The life cycle of groups: Group developmental stage theory.* NY: Human Sciences Press.

Malekoff, A. (1997). *Group work with adolescents: Principles and practice.* New York: The Guildford Press.

Malekoff, A. (2004). Strength based group work with children and adolescents. In C. Garvin, L.M. Gutierez, & M. Galinsky (Eds.), *Handbook of social work with groups,* NY: Guildford, 227-244.

Mertler, C.A. & Vannata, R.A. (2002). *Advanced and multivariate statistical methods: Practical application and interpretation* (2nd ed.). Los Angeles, CA: Pyrczak Publishing.

Miller, J.B. & Stiver, I.P. (1993, August). A relational approach to understanding women's lives and problems. *Psychiatric Annals, 23*(8), 424-425.

Northen, H. (1969). *Social work with groups.* New York; Columbia University Press.

Patten, M.L. (2000). *Proposing empirical research: A guide to fundamentals.* Los Angeles, CA: Pyrczak publishing.

Peters, A.J. (1997). Themes in group work with lesbian and gay adolescents. *Social Work with Groups, 20(*2), 51-69.

Richmond, M. (1971). *Social diagnosis.* NY: The Free Press.

Rittner, B., Nakanishi, M., Nackerud, L. & Hammons, K. (Fall, 1999). How MSW graduates apply what they learned about diversity to their work with small groups. *Journal of Social Work Education, 35*(3), 421-431.

Rodenborg, N. & Huynh, N. (2006). On overcoming segregation: Social work and intergroup dialogue. *Social Work with Groups, 29(*1), 27-44.

Rooney, R. & Chovanec, M. (2004). Involuntary groups. In C. Garvin, L.M.

Gutierez & M. Galinsky (Eds.), *Handbook of social work with groups*. NY: Guildford, 561-577.

Rubin, A. & Babbie, E. (2001). *Research methods for social work* (4th ed.). Belmont, CA: Wadsworth Publishing.

Sands, R.G. & Nuccio, K. (1992). Postmodern feminist theory and social work. *Social Work, 37*(6), 489-94.

Sarri, R.C. & Galinsky, M.J. (1974). A conceptual framework for group development, In P. Glasser, R. Sarri & R. Vinter (Eds.), *Individual change through small groups*. NY: Free Press, 71-88.

Schiller, L. (1995). Stages of group development in women's groups: A relational model. In R. Kurland & B. Salmon (Eds.), *Group work in a troubled society*. NY: Haworth, 117-138.

Schiller, L.Y. (1997). Rethinking stages of development in women's groups: Implications for practice. *Social Work with Groups, 20*(3), 3-19.

Schiller, L.Y. (2003). Women's group development from a relational model and a new look at facilitator influence on group development. In M.B. Cohen and A. Mullender (Eds.), *Gender and group work*. London: Routledge, 16-31.

Schwartz, W. (1971). On the use of groups in social work practice. In W. Schwartz & S. Zalba (Eds.), *The practice of group work*. New York: Columbia University Press, 3-24.

Sills, S.J. & Song, C. (Spring, 2002). Innovations in survey research: An application of web-based surveys. *Social Science Computer Review, 20*(1), 22-30.

Stern, S.B., Smith, C.A. & Jang, S.J. (1999, March). Urban families and adolescent mental health. *Social Work Research, 23*(1), 15-27.

Sullivan, N. (1995). Who owns the group? The role of worker control in the development of the group: A qualitative research study of practice. *Social Work with Groups, 18*(2/3), 15-32.

Toseland, R.W. & Rivas, T. (2001). *An introduction to group work practice* (4th ed.). Massachusetts: Allyn & Bacon.

Toseland, R.W., Jones, L.V. & Gellis, Z.D. (2004). Group dynamics. In C. Garvin, L.M. Gutierez & M. Galinsky (Eds.), *Handbook of social work with groups*. NY: Guildford, 13-31.

Travers, A. (1995). Adversity, diversity, and empowerment: Feminist group work with women in poverty. In R. Kurland & B. Salmon (Eds.), *Group work in a troubled society*. NY: Haworth, 139-156.

Trecker, H. (1948). *Social group work: Principles and practices*. NY: American Book Stratford Press.

Tropp, E. (1976) Developmental group work. In R.W. Roberts & H. Northen (Eds.), *Theories of social work with groups*. NY: Columbia University

Press, 198-237.

Tuckman, B.W. (1965). Developmental sequence in small groups. *Psychological bulletin, 63*(6), 384-399, 9-33.

Vinter, R. (1974). The essential components of social group work practice. In P. Glasser, R. Sarri & R. Vinter (Eds.), *Individual change through small groups.* NY: Free press.

Weinbach, R.W. & Grinnell, R.M. (2001). *Statistics for social workers* (5th ed.). Needham Heights, MA: Allyn & Bacon.

Wheelan, S.A. (1994). *Group processes: A developmental perspective.* Boston: Allyn & Bacon.

Wheelan, S.A. & Hotchberger, J.M. (1996). Validation studies of the group development questionnaire. *Small Group Research, 27*(1), 143-170.

3
Going back to our roots:
Social group work, the ideal method for youth development

Hélène Filion Onserud

Abstract: The purpose of this paper is to raise awareness about the desirability of using social group work methodology in youth development programs, and the value of employing social group workers in those programs. To demonstrate the similarities between youth development and social group work, this paper draws parallels between their histories. It describes a community-based agency that uses the social group work method in its youth development programs.

Keywords: youth development; community building; social group work; Beacon program; leadership training

Introduction

As programs for youth have grown exponentially over the last twenty years, the field of Youth Development has shifted its focus from early deficit-based assumptions about adolescence to a strengths-based appreciation of young people. These advances have not, however, produced a methodology upon which to base standards of practice, program models, and staff training for the numerous youth programs in urban centers throughout the country. This paper provides a brief overview of the Youth Development movement, and of social group work as it relates to this field. It describes how one agency, based in an urban community, has used social group work to organize its school-based programs and, more recently, the agency itself. The paper discusses how the values inherent in social group work produce a culture in which the positive development of youth, family, and community takes place within this agency's school-based sites.

Youth development

History

Youth Development is a field of practice whose existence spans the last three decades. During the 1950s, and even more during the 1960s, major demographic shifts resulted in a rise of the national poverty level, divorce rates, and single parenthood (Calatano, Berglund, Ryan, Lonczak, & Hawkins, 1999, p.2). These factors resulted in a crisis which began in the 1960s and continues to this day, as inner city neighborhoods have been "strained and torn by the ravages of increasingly concentrated poverty and isolation; and by the arrival of cheaper and more addictive drugs along with the rivalries, violence and fear that those drugs introduce" (Hyman, 1999, p. IX). Before the 1960s, adolescent development was defined mainly in relation to deficits. There was no positive developmental model in the social science literature (Quinn, 2004). Consequently, agencies serving youth and families initially responded to these societal changes in a reactive fashion, which was insufficient to deal with the scope of the needs. Hyman (1999) points out that a deficit-based approach to services does not do justice to the complexity of the issues underlying the presenting problems of "at risk youth". Moreover, he argues that this approach assumes that youth who are *not* deficient on a set of arbitrary criteria are neither at risk nor in need of critical attention and supports (p.9).

Emergence of a strengths-based approach

As it became clearer that the deficit reduction, remedial, and even prevention models were not yielding sorely needed solutions or results, Youth Development emerged as a new strengths-based approach toward the complex challenges facing young people, especially those living in inner city neighborhoods. This approach does not attempt to replicate the organic individual maturation from childhood to adulthood, but instead strategizes to promote the development of those aspects of personality that will lead to successful adulthood. "Youth development is the strategic, systematic process of guiding the acquisition of societally determined skills and competencies..." (Peak, 2001, p.4).

This new field assumes that young people are an important segment of society, and that the passages from childhood to adulthood (particularly to middle school and then to high school) require attention that is not available through the traditional channels of family and school. As Strobel *et al.* (2008) point out, at these key points in their development young people need "supportive relationships, opportunities for autonomy and choice, and a sense of competence in their dealing with the world" (2008, p. 1679). They suggest that the after school context is ideal for meeting these needs, since it is a " 'developmental niche' -- a core context rather than [a] supplemental context of development" (p. 1680).

Beacons

In 1991 New York City developed programs known as Beacons, a publicly funded initiative that used schools as community centers during non-school hours. In this initiative, the city funded community based organizations to operate and run programs for youth, families, and communities every night and on weekends. The Youth Development Institute, under the auspices of the Fund for the City of New York, provided technical assistance to Beacons in a public/private partnership with the city. This initiative expanded from ten Beacons to eighty between 1991 and 2001 and still stands today, even as its mission and direction have shifted away from the multigenerational community-building aspect that was once its hallmark. This paper will later describe how the Center for Family Life has used Beacon funding and has adapted the model to fit some of its school-based sites.

Family strengthening youth development model

One of several trends that emerged within the field of Youth Development was the family strengthening youth development model, promoted first in 1998 by the Annie E. Casey Foundation. As stated in a 2001 report, "the Foundation's longstanding interest in promoting the well-being of children and youth has expanded to recognize the reality that young people are inextricably tied to families as well as to their community (Gutierrez *et al.*, p. 1)." This model endeavors to purposefully integrate families into the mission and practices of youth-serving agencies and organizations (Peak, 2003). It brings together three overlapping areas: youth development, family development, and community development.

Community Youth Development movement

The Community Youth Development movement, conceptualized in 1993, is another trend in Youth Development. It seeks to integrate youth in community development and mobilize communities "to embrace their role in the development of youth" (Hughes & Curnan, 2000, p. 7). Echoing the concerns of the Annie E. Casey Foundation and the Community Youth Development movement, Hyman (1999; 2000) suggests that community must be an indispensable ingredient if successful youth development outcomes are to be achieved. He is aware, however, that when one realizes the importance of community in the process of youth development, actualizing this integration poses an enormous challenge.

> Simply put, if "it takes a village to raise a child," you first have to have the village -- a community that is, in many senses, "communal"-- a place where adults share a set of common interests, beliefs and/or goals for themselves, for their young people, and/or for their community, and are willing to organize and maintain themselves, as a group, to pursue and preserve them; a place where residents feel, and act upon, the connectedness and obligation they share toward one another for their mutual benefit (2000, p.3).

Challenges for youth workers

Since the emergence of Youth Development programs, youth workers have faced numerous challenges beyond those having to do with the lack of family or community context mentioned above. Engaging youth to become involved in programs on an ongoing basis can be difficult. A number of studies report that while there is evidence that young people benefit from attending youth programs, the benefits are only clear when there is consistent attendance (Harvard Family Research Project, 2004). Yet as programs have become more widespread, it has become evident that the young people who most need services are often those who participate and attend least often.

Building caring relationships with youth is a complex process, especially when youth workers – though often highly invested in their work – are without credentials, adequate supervision, or professional training (Wilson-Ahlstrom, 2008). They also frequently lack a theoretical foundation for their practice. Based on his comparative study of youth programs in five different countries, Sherraden (1992) suggests that Youth Development in the U. S. is in need of a body of knowledge:

> Ideally, like many other western nations, the United States would develop a national perspective on youth professionals and establish educational standards defining a youth work training curriculum. However, in looking at other countries, the content of this curriculum remains largely undefined and there are many opinions about what it should be (pp. IX-X).

Where is social group work?

KixMiller & Onserud (1993) comment that "it seems surprising that the profession of social work (and particularly social group work, with its rich tradition of working with youth) is not making a larger contribution to the theories and practices of youth development in the cities of the United States today" (p. 204). As Grace Coyle, an early group work theorist, notes,

> With our American traditions we have always put our faith in the school and the church as the major instrumentalities outside the home for these purposes. Within the past century, however, we have invented an additional institution. This new organ is our familiar set of organizations of, for, and by youth. (1948, p. 10)

Coyle (1948) further suggests that programs for youth should involve young people in community building. A report from the Carnegie Council on Adolescent Development echoes Coyle, referring to a "third leg to the triangle of human development. If family and school constitute two of these legs . . . the third leg is surely those experiences that young people have in their neighborhoods and the larger community" (Carnegie Council, 1992, p. 18). This report suggests that in a postindustrial economy young people experience growing demands for education and training, just as community and family supports are eroding. It further points out that community, "this sense of place, of belonging, is a crucial building block for the healthy development of children and adolescents. And it is especially crucial for young people who are growing up in disadvantaged circumstances" (p. 19).

When social group work became a profession, it had a dual commitment – to individual growth and to democracy. Newstetter (1935) states that "[t]he underlying social-philosophical assumption [of social group work] is that individualized growth and social ends are interwoven and interdependent; that individuals and their social environment are equally important" (p. 297). As KixMiller & Onserud (1993) point out, however,

> [S]ince Grace Coyle elaborated her ideas on the nature of an institution for the development of youth, very little prestige, status, financial rewards, or theoretical interest have been attached to this endeavor in the social sciences in this country, even within the profession of social work. As a result, the promising strides group workers made early on in this direction eventually were superseded by more rewarding ventures into clinical group work (p. 206).

It would be outside the scope of this paper to give a full account of the causes underlying this change of orientation within social group work methodology, which Janice Andrews-Schenk (2001) discusses in considerable detail. Nevertheless, it is clear that there has until 1993 been no mention within the field of Youth Development of adopting social group work as a desirable professional methodology (KixMiller & Onserud, 1993). However, more recently, this situation appears to be changing.

In the face of increasing national dialogue about the potential connection between Youth Development and social group work methodology, leaders in the field of Youth Development have begun to express enthusiasm for, and interest in employing this methodology. They recognize that they know *what* needs to be accomplished with young people, but are missing knowledge about *how* to reach these goals.

Center for Family Life: A case example

The Center for Family Life was founded in 1978 by two sisters of the Good Shepherd, who were also social workers. They understood the individual in the context of a relationship to something or someone else – the family, the group, and the community. Like early settlement workers before them, they saw a direct relationship between the strengths (or lack thereof) of the family and its members, and those of the surrounding community.

Even though the sisters had no formal training in group work, their orientation was close to that of early group workers. They viewed the Center as something akin to a settlement house, and they thought that its services should be based on the community's need, rather than on whatever source of funding happened to be available at the time. Thus the sisters implemented programs which were based on their understanding of what the community needed. These included:

- after-school programs serving single parent families and working parents needing family support and/or child-care during after-school hours;
- evening programs providing alternative group experiences for teens at risk of joining gangs;
- year-round employment programs for adults, and summer programs for youth;
- a community service center/thrift shop, providing advocacy

services for entitlement programs and basic necessities such as clothing and food;
- family counseling, helping families with concrete as well as counseling needs; and
- a community foster care program, helping children and families to work on reunification within the neighborhood.

Attracted by the sisters' vision for the Center, many of the staff who came to create programming or work at the school-based sites were group workers. Naturally they organized programs and groups employing this methodology. Since 2000, when a group worker became co-director of the Center, much of the organization of staff within the Center has reflected this methodology as well.

An example of the Center's programming efforts in one of its Beacons demonstrates the integration of a social group work orientation within its services. The Center for Family Life Beacon at Public School 1 includes a few different programs:

- School-Age Child Care (SACC), including after school and summer day camp for over 500 children a year (ages five through thirteen), is comprised of a Lower Camp (ages five through eight) and Upper Camp (ages nine through thirteen). SACC is very structured, with programs for most of the groups divided into units along age and gender lines. These units provide a "home base" for participants, who go from one activity to another with their unit, following the weekly schedule. Activities include visual arts, performing arts, sports, club meetings, homework help, and games.
    - A weekly period called Options, mixes individuals in the older upper camp into two large groups (according to age), and participants get to choose between different offerings for an eight week cycle.
    - There is also a Leaders-in-Training component for the graduating participants in Teen Camp (unit 12), the oldest group. This program operates from 3 to 6 PM during the school year, and from 9 AM to 3 PM during the summer.
    - A Counselor-in-Training program for more than 50 teenagers a year is a natural next step for young people graduating from Teen Camp. This program offers an internship for those young people who want to volunteer and take on leadership training and work experience. The Counselor-in-Training group forms the pool from which most of the part-time assistant group

leaders are hired.

    - In the Community School Project, the Counselor-in-Training program for School-Age Child Care creates a bridge between the upper camp and lower camp programs. Specialists and other senior staff members, including directors, are used in both of the School-Age Child Care components and in the Neighborhood Center, and have overlap among programs.

- Neighborhood Center, an arts and recreation program that includes over 1000 youth and 200 adults a year, operates four evenings a week and Saturdays. It offers a wide range of activities including sports, dance, art, and sewing. There is also an open games, homework, and reading space for participants to socialize and build relationships with staff and each other. It includes adult education classes every evening. In contrast to School-Age Child Care, Neighborhood Center offers participants the opportunity to choose activities based on their interests, and to decide about the frequency of their participation in program. During the summer, the Neighborhood Center moves outside to the schoolyard. It offers drop-in programming in arts and games, in addition to more structured activities such as baseball and soccer teams. This is in contrast to the very structured summer day camp. Neighborhood Center has its own Counselor-in-Training program.

As stated earlier, one of the major challenges for youth workers is to facilitate and maintain the participation of young people in ongoing services. The Center's group work orientation has resulted in the development of programs which encourage youth to remain engaged and involved throughout their maturation, even into adulthood. This outcome appears to be related to the following aspects of program design:

- Participants have choices. They can be part of the more structured School-Age Child Care program, or they can join the Neighborhood Center and have a variety of options in terms of the activities and the frequency of their participation.
- The setting is familiar to many of the young adolescents who have participated since childhood. As they are making big adjustments while going through puberty and starting middle or high school, it can be comforting to have a stable setting where they know most

of the people and feel cared about.

- Groups and programs are meaningful places for young participants. The people they have known in the program since childhood are not just acquaintances. They symbolize important relationships built over time – through activities, special events, and projects enjoyed together, as well as through conflicts and struggles they have experienced with each other.
- There is a path participants can follow, with models of leadership to emulate when they get ready to leave a familiar group or program. The counselors-in-training and staff are close enough in age to make the reality of following in their footsteps within reach.
- Young people quickly become natural leaders as they internalize the social group work culture. They are generally open and eager to begin civic engagement. As participants in the Leader-In-Training program, they can play a leadership role with younger participants. Through community service projects in teen camp, they can become leaders in the larger program or the neighborhood.
- As youth age-out of the school-age child care program, they still have opportunities for civic engagement through volunteering as coaches in Neighborhood Center or helping with program in other ways. They can also choose one of the more popular Counselor-In-Training programs.

While other youth programs and Beacons include many of the elements mentioned above, the pervasive use of social group work methodology makes a difference in the quality and intensity of experiences young people have in the Center's programs. The level of participant and staff retention is high, largely because the programs foster a strong sense of community.

Community building via social group work

Social group work creates a culture in which people are given space to be themselves while being thoughtful and responsible about others – individually, within a group, and within a program. The values which create this culture include: (1) having room to experiment and make mistakes, while also being accountable for them; (2) being open to conflict and dealing with authority issues directly; and (3) problem solving and cooperative decision making about activities, projects, events, and group issues.

These values permeate the program environment, so that participants and staff from all programs recognize it as something they have in common. Because of the attention social group work brings to both personal growth and social change, there is a reciprocal nature to the environment of the Beacon – a built-in civic engagement that is integrated slowly over time. Young people are given support to work on themselves within the group, while developing a sense of responsibility toward others. Many look forward to being in a position to become leaders with the younger participants and/or with the community as a whole.

Another aspect of the community building process is the common vision which encompasses all programs of the Beacon, while still maintaining the integrity of each separate part. Just as individual groups become increasingly cohesive as they go through the stages of group development, the community can become more cohesive when there is a concerted effort to plan a calendar of events and activities that will encourage this process. First, individual groups must have a sense of cohesion and ownership within themselves. In one of the Beacons run by the Center for Family Life events such as Halloween, Potluck Thanksgiving dinner, Winter Wonderland, and the CIT Holiday event offer a progression throughout the fall. Each individual program has a chance to have its own event, with help from staff from other programs. It is as if each program is showcased and appreciated by the others for what is uniquely theirs to contribute. Once this is achieved, further integration can take place; program or Beacon-wide events and activities are planned to progressively allow groups and individuals to become part of a wider community circle. Within this particular Beacon, the process culminates in a spring show, in which participants or groups from all programs, including parents, come together. They work on props, backdrops, or costumes, or they act or dance in an event that truly brings the community together – as performers, stage hands, or audience. This multigenerational process contributes to the development of a cohesive community.

Retention and leadership development

Most of the group leaders and assistant group leaders in the School-Age Child Care program have either grown up in the program or climbed some rungs on the ladder of leadership.

> When they transition to the Counselor-in-Training program, [...] young people begin to practice as leaders the group work skills they have absorbed over the years. They continue to learn and integrate knowledge and information through experience, supervision and formal training. [...] This ladder of leadership results in retention of youth from elementary age through college as they progress into paid staff positions. [It is a concrete manifestation of the social group work culture]. There is a continuity of service, a deepening sense of community, and the ongoing cultivation of new leadership as youth who began as program participants become counselors-in-training, group leaders, coordinators and directors. (Onserud *et al.*, 2009, p. 10)

In an example of this type of retention, of the twenty-four staff members in one Beacon – ranging in age from sixteen to twenty six (with an average age of nineteen and a half) – thirteen have been employed for two to five years, and eleven from seven to fifteen. The site director, as well as two of the coordinators who grew up as participants since age five, have been at the community school project for twenty-five years.

In order to achieve a common vision, a concerted effort is made at Center for Family Life to ensure that there is integration among different groups and programs. This process of integration takes place at all levels of the Beacon and the agency. Leaders of the different groups and programs are brought together in several levels of staff groups.

> For example, the CFL Beacon at PS 1 holds a weekly leadership team meeting that brings together staff leaders of the Lower Camp, Upper Camp, Neighborhood Center and Counselor-in-Training programs in different representations depending on the purpose at hand. That group must develop the common vision of the Beacon community that will bring together their separate programs and staff. In another important function of the leadership team, the directors, coordinators and more seasoned specialists guide the rest of the staff in a parallel group work process that mirrors the experience of participants. This allows everyone to keep learning experientially and establishes integrity of practice. We do not ask participants to open themselves up to a process we are not

> willing to embrace ourselves. Within the leadership team and within each individual program, staff go through the same stages of group development and experience the excitement, struggles, and rewards of being group members. (Onserud *et al.*, 2009, p. 10)

As a result of this process, staff continue to deepen their involvement with the participants, with each other, and with the community.

Conclusion

The social group work methodology, utilized in programs such as those described in this paper, offers a valuable professional framework for the field of Youth Development. It helps staff think about, understand, and work with program participants. This framework offers ideas about how to organize individuals within groups, groups within programs, and each of these units within a community. Social group work offers an ideal tool for a holistic, intergenerational, community-building model such as the one created by the Center for Family Life. There needs to be a bridge between the fields of Youth Development and social work – to expand the opportunities for linking Youth Development with social group work education and training.

References

Andrews-Schenk, J. (2001). Group work's place in social work: A historical analysis, *Journal of Sociology & Social Welfare,* 28 (4), 45-65.

Carnegie Council on Adolescent Development. (1992). *A matter of time: Risk and opportunity in the nonschool hours.* Report of the Task Force on Youth Development and Community programs. New York: Carnegie Corporation.

Catalano, R., Berglund, M., Ryan, J.; Lonczak, H., & Hawkins, J. (1999). *Positive Youth Development In the United States: Research Findings on Evaluations of Positive Youth Development Programs.* Unpublished paper submitted to the U.S. Department of Health and Human Services, Office of the Assistant Secretary for Planning and Evaluation, National Institute for Child Health and Human Development.

Coyle, G. (1948). *Group work with American youth.* New York: Harper & Brothers.

Gutierrez, M., Berkey, M. and Bergson-Shilcock A. (2001). Strengthening families to promote youth development. Report of the *Annie E. Casey Foundation's roundtable discussions.* Philadelphia, PA: OMG Center for Collaborative Learning.

Harvard Family Research Project (2004) Moving beyond the barriers. *Issues and Opportunities in Out-of-School Time Evaluation.* 6 (July).

Hughes, D. M. & Curnan, S. P. (2000). Community Youth Development a framework for action., *CDY Journal,* 1 (1), 7 – 13.

Hyman, J. B. (1999). *Spheres of influence: A strategic synthesis and framework for community and youth development.* Baltimore, MD: The Annie E. Casey Foundation.

Hyman, J. B. (2000). *Building the village: Exploring social capital as the vehicle for strengthening resiliency in youth.* Washington, DC: The Urban Institute.

KixMiller, J. and Onserud, H. F. (1993). A community center model for current urban needs. In R. Kurland & R. Salmon (Eds.), *Group work practice in a troubled society: Problems and opportunities.* Binghamton, NY: Haworth Press, 203-216.

Newstetter, W. (1935). What is social group work? In *Proceedings of the National Conference of Social Work,* 291-299.

Onserud, H, Stein Brockway, J. and Mancell, K. (2009). Practices to keep in after-school and youth programs: The social group work approach promoting individual growth and community building. New York: Youth Development Institute.

Peak, G. L. (2001). *Family-Strengthening Youth Development:* A Position Paper. Unpublished paper submitted to the Annie E. Casy Foundation, Baltimore, MD.

Quinn, J. (2004). Professional development in the youth development field: Issues, trends, opportunities, and challenges. *New Directions for Youth Development,*.104 (Winter) 13-24.

Sherraden, M. (1992). Community-based youth services in international perspective. Washington: Carnegie Council on Adolescent Development and William T. Grant Foundation Commission on work, family and citizenship.

Strobel, K., Kirshner, B.,O'Donoghue, J. and McLaughlin, M. (2008). Qualities that attract urban youth to after-school settings and promote continued participation. *Teachers College Record,*110, (8).

Wilson-Ahlstrom, A., Yohalem, N., Pittman, K. (2008). Unpacking youth work practice. *The Forum for Youth Investment.* (June).

4
The use of program and activities: Purpose, planning and structure

Alison H. Johnson

Abstract: This article is based on the premise that many group practitioners are unfamiliar with the concept of 'program' and its appropriate use. They employ curricula without modifications, create topic centered groups, and often use activities only to fill the time they have with clients. Frequently, this manner of group work lacks a clear and shared understanding of the group's purpose and the role of the activity toward that purpose. The skilled practitioner's use of program seeks to fit activities to the purpose and stage of development of the group as well as to take into consideration the individual needs of members. The use of program is a group work approach demanding the worker's simultaneous attention to the whole group, the individual members, the stated purpose, the relevance of content, and the value of process and experiential learning. This invitational workshop sought to define program and illuminate its use as an integral part of successful group work.

Keywords: group work; use of activities in groups; use of program in groups; group development

What is 'program'and how do activities fit into the program?

Social work with groups offers a rich history of the use of program to achieve the purpose of the group and to select activities to further the work of the group. Program embodies the content, the process, and the purpose of a group that helps members to communicate feelings, use present reality, and address group relationships. It is the medium through which members express interests and needs of which they are unaware or which they are incapable of expressing in words (Wilson & Ryland, 1981). Program is the expressive dimension of group life where the 'what and how' of group are meshed organically (Middleman 1981, 1988). Steinberg (2004)) expands 'what and how' to include the 'why' of group when she makes purpose explicit as an element of program: 'What members do together to achieve a certain end (such as talk or activity) reflects content. The end to which they do what they do (why they are talking or engaging in a certain activity) reflects purpose' (p. 74). The 'what and how' flows from the 'why' (purpose) of a group.

> Program assists the work of groups in members' experiencing each other in real time and affords the worker an indirect means of influencing groups and their members and is deliberately used to achieve desired objectives. (Glasser, Sarri, & Vinter, 1974, p. 233)

Activities are a primary socializing mechanism, helping human beings to learn how to get along with others in life, to innovate, create and develop a style of interacting with others. Aligning programmed content (talk or activities) with group purpose and the stage of group development moves the group and members toward cohesion and work. Regardless of the purpose of a group, a frequent objective is the pursuit of improved self-regulation of members. Self regulation is the way individuals learn to modulate their behavior when stimulated by their emotions to match the circumstance, setting and social expectations for behavior. Toward this end, activities simulate or create opportunities in which members can practice expression or suppression of emotion and behavior, adjustment, and tolerance of the self in relation to others. Groups designed to incorporate experience via activities allow participants to behave less self consciously, as they would in real life. When engaged experientially, members lose themselves in the action, showing strengths and flaws in character in the here-and-now. Members get the chance to act as they are rather than how they wish to be (seen), adding a richness to the group experience.

Many activities in groups are designed as prompts to move the group on to deeper work (Doel, 2006, p. 78). Groups experiencing conflict and intimacy develop greater awareness of self and self in relationship. This, in turn, generates reflection, discussion and possibilities for change. When members recognize their impact on each other, it can be both subtle and profound ('Hey, I matter and so do you! We're more alike than different.'). Once sharing begins, members learn how to give and receive feedback more gracefully. Members develop empathy and offer kindnesses, challenges, and acknowledgements. They recognize and commiserate with pain and develop mutuality and camaraderie.

Program as process and 'thinking group'

Middleman and Wood (1990) advised workers to 'think group,' considering the group as a whole first and individual members second when initiating or responding to others (pp. 96-97). Individuals remain a critical concern of the practitioner, but they develop and achieve their goals through attention to the group itself.

Group offers members an experience where 'we-ness' can develop. We-ness is that sense of the group as an entity in itself, and is as important as the individual in the group. We-ness provides support and allows for change to occur. When skillfully used by the worker, 'thinking group' recognizes that we have choices in our lives, promotes individual experimentation and empowers group decision making. This we-ness and individual change can happen in a group when a worker recognizes the importance of the use of program in concert with a purpose that meets the group members needs.

The value of program and the role of activities

Program, including talk as well as separate and cumulative activities, is the means to achieve individual and group goals. (Brandler & Roman, 1991, pp, 128 -131; Ciardiello 2003; Clements & Benbow, 2009; Doel, 2006; Glasser, Sarri, & Vinter, 1974; Glasser, Sarri, & Vinter, 1985; Middleman, 1980; Middleman, 1988; Stuecker & Rutherford, 2001; Sweeney & Homeyer, 1993; Vinter, 1985; Wilson & Ryland, 1981). These authors suggest the following considerations for using activities in a group to foster individual growth and development:

- To include clients who are uncomfortable or unable to express themselves verbally.

- To encourage socialization and/or social responsibility.
- To teach and practice specific social and coping skills.
- To help members to feel competent, worthwhile, and validated -- spiritually, emotionally, and intellectually
- To surface differences and challenge members to try new behavior and attitudes.
- To sufficiently distance threatening subject matter in order to address it and to problem solve around it.
- To promote members individual strengths.
- To prize similarities and to learn to negotiate, collaborate, and cooperate toward common goals.
- To have fun.
- To help members to express socially unacceptable or conflictual feelings.
- To help develop higher levels of frustration tolerance and self regulation.
- To aid in diagnosis, interpretation and treatment.

Vinter, Glasser, & Sarri (1985) recommend that the worker attend to the evolving nature of the group and its developmental needs as an entity in itself. They advise attention to the following attributes of a successful group that includes the use of program:

- Deciding the degree and range of rules for conduct.
- Making clear who enforces the rules or ensures safety, e.g. umpire, captain, etc.
- Determining the extent to which participants are required or permitted to move about in the activity setting.
- Considering the minimum level of skill required to participate in the activity – skills may be physical, cognitive, emotional, and/or social.
- Providing for participant interaction to accomplish the work – verbal/nonverbal, cooperative/competitive, and degree of intimacy or personal disclosure/emotional distance.
- Using a reward structure – offered by leader and by other members.

In developing the effective use of program in this era of curriculum, manual, topic, and diagnosis driven group, workers must ask themselves two questions: 1) does the activity make sense, given the group's stage of development? and 2) to what end(s) does the activity address the purpose and goals of the group? Planning and program go hand in hand, evolving with the group, and program is especially effective when the worker recognizes program as process and content that flow from the purpose (Kurland, 1978). Stuecker and Rutherford (2001) add that the greatest success lies in a worker's ability to provide a program that addresses the group members' heritage and culture, while attending to the assets and needs of individuals within the context of the group's identity and purpose (Stuecker & Rutherford, 2001). To summarize, program is more than a set of activities. It embodies the use of content and process to accomplish the purpose of the group.

Manuals and curricula are very helpful in identifying usable content that fits a group's needs (de Anda, 2002; Haasl and Marnocha, 1992; Leban, 1994; McGinnis and Goldstein, 2003). They run the risk of becoming cumbersome, functionally repetitive, and mind-numbing when used from A – Z as written, or when used as a one-size-fits-all approach to responding to the so-called 'purpose' of a group.

Workshop overview

This workshop defined the concept of 'program' and illustrated its use according to the stages and purpose of the group by including examples of activities that could be used at beginning, middle, and ending stages of the group. The author envisioned the workshop as a single session group, replete with all group stages as well as the unique challenges presented by a single-session group.

The use of program in a group includes the content (what they do) and process (how they do it) that reflects the purpose (why they do it). Basic concepts regarding the 'what' and 'why' of the programmed use of content (in this case, activities) were offered by the author, followed by an activity. The purpose of the beginning stage activity, *Get Up and Move,* was to have fun, so as to facilitate comfort and integration of the material and facilitate sharing as the workshop proceeded. At the conclusion of the first activity, more didactic information was shared. The second activity, *Plan a Trip,* was intended to move the group into deeper connection. Didactic material was then shared in a more informal way prior to ending the workshop. In closing the workshop, the author engaged the group in an ending activity, *Share a Gift Received.* The intended purpose was to anchor the workshop experience and the mutuality which developed among participants, to highlight a shared understanding of the use of program, and to bring closure to the group.

Reflection on the program activities used in the workshop

By design, the author planned to include herself in the beginning and ending activities, so as to reduce the emotional distance and power differential between the members and herself and to establish trust and safety. Because of the nature of the middle activity chosen and the one-session format of this group, the author decided not to participate. This change was made in order to help the members to bond with each other as a group and to support their connectivity without interference.

The Beginning Activity was introduced to workshop participants after the author shared how she came to know and understand the use of program through her teacher and mentor, Ruth Middleman, and after a didactic introduction of the use of program. The objective was to offer participants an experience relevant to the cognitive material. The activity chosen was *Get up and Move.* Members were asked to form a circle with their chairs minus one chair to allow room for a person in the center of the circle. The author, as worker, started off in the center with a challenge, 'Get up and move if you _______________', filling in the blank with common experiences such as 'want to do this activity, like to eat pizza, ever cheated on a test, won an award, lied to your parents, visited a foreign country, are a newcomer to the Symposium', etc. The instruction to the group was that anyone to whom the sentence applied must move to a new chair. The person unable to find a seat became the new person in the center and was asked to issue the next challenge.

This activity is particularly good for helping members to get to know each other, to expose the group to physical and emotional regulation, and to transition to deeper content. This enjoyable activity can be used with groups of all ages, although it does require mobility. It invites risk-taking in sharing and identifying interests, attributes, mistakes and feelings. In addition, it challenges members to name 'parts' of themselves in a way that encourages recognition of similarities and appreciation of differences. Many personal attributes reveal themselves in addition to what is verbally stated, such as cooperation, competition, lying, getting physical, provoking others, trying to 'stump' everyone, avoiding the center, teasing others, moving slowly so as to get more turns in the center of the circle, and not moving to avoid taking a turn in the center.

Usually this activity begins with a low personal risk sentence completion. As the activity proceeds, the worker can alter the sentence object when he or she finds herself in the center again, to fit the circumstance or go deeper and encourage the members to do the same. The length of the activity depends on the stage of the group and the objective, so in this case it was planned to be relatively short (about seven minutes plus about ten minutes to process). The purpose of this activity was to help members of the workshop loosen up and share information about themselves so as to facilitate deeper learning and sharing as the workshop proceeded.

In the case of this workshop, the author's sentence stems were intentionally lower risk and humorous to suit the circumstances of a one-time session and Symposium setting. As the workshop group processed the experience, the author shifted the discussion to applications of the activity, allowing members to draw from their own experiences in the group. Aspects of the process and content were explored. In particular, the participants, were asked, 'How could the same activity, altered, serve the purpose and process of another group and at other stages in a group's life?' Feedback from the members indicated success as measured by participants' enthusiasm, admission of greater comfort with each other, adjustments made to accommodate a member who could not move quickly, and members' offerings of challenges that evoked laughter and a desire to get all to come to the center of the circle. A concern relevant to our experience was the fact that one member could not physically move quickly, so we discussed how the activity could be adapted to accommodate varying levels of physical capability. The author acknowledged that she had failed to consider this in planning the workshop. The extent to which the members wanted to continue to converse rather than get back to the workshop content was unanticipated, yet relevant, so more time elapsed than was planned.

After briefly sharing further information regarding the uses and value of activities as related to program and purpose, a Middle Activity was introduced. The intention for the activity was twofold -- to get the group active again (shift the energy) and to move the group into conflict/intimacy. The activity, *Plan a Trip*, is a team challenge to plan an all expense paid trip for the 'company's work team' to which they all belonged, for two weeks. However, they all must agree on the destination, travel together and participate in the decided agenda. Conflicting roles were distributed, such as 'A is afraid of flying, B likes human density; C is all about relaxation, likes the night life and good restaurants, and prefers to sleep in late; D detests tour vacations, and cruises are out of the question; etc'. Roles can be tailored to fit a particular group's goals and member idiosyncrancies (either to exaggerate them or offer an alternate experience).

This activity was intentionally aborted by the group due to their desire to interact verbally around the workshop content. The author assessed that the group had quickly developed a sense of ownership and so adjusted the program to fit their need to engage more informally, moving between content and discussion. This change also suited her needs as the teacher and worker due to time considerations and her desire to spend more time on the content. Given the fact that all were attendees at a Group Work Symposium where many were presenters as well as participants, it appears in hindsight that the need for intimacy trumped the need for conflict. These members did not need to experience the traditional group stages to become a group! In fact, the group's development most closely resembled the relational model of group work (Schiller, 1995). This group experience reinforced a valuable skill -- the ability of the worker to move with a group's need and abandon his or her plan.

Although it was not the case in this workshop, there are occasions when it is important for the worker to press on with content. This is particularly important when the leader senses that the group is avoiding the work or is derailing the process of pursuing sensitive or taboo material. Usually this avoidance shows up in a group as subject changes, digressions, side conversations, clowning, moving about and other evasive actions.

After the exchange of information, reactions, and reflections regarding the material in the changed format of the workshop, the author introduced an Ending Activity, *Share a Gift Received,* in which she participated. The intention was to complete the process established in this workshop and to demonstrate the importance of endings, in particular this group's termination. Colored index cards and pens were distributed to each member. Participants were asked to write and/or draw a picture of something that was gained from the person to their left and to sign it. They shared and handed their cards to that person – a gift to take away. The workshop objective was to demonstrate the use of program offering content (what we did) and process (how we did it) that reflected the purpose (why we did it). An associated workshop objective was to develop mutuality, which the author believes is integral to any Social Work with Groups endeavor. The group members hugged each other and lingered to chat. This was interpreted as some indication of the success of the workshop's program.

Conclusion

So why are program content and process important to successful group work? 'Activities are the way people learn to socialize with others throughout human development. They are serious and real in themselves, paralleling life in their demands for ingenuity, choices, and attention to others.' (Middleman, 1980, p. 58).

Beyond the fact that activities are basic to human interaction, activity within the framework of program provides group workers opportunities for interventions that arise from spontaneous interactions occurring in the group in real time. It allows opportunities for the worker to teach social skills and corrective behaviors and for members to experience new behavior. Experiencing oneself in the here-and-now (conflict, mistakes, apology, helpfulness, humor, harmful or playful teasing, taking a stand for self or another, expressing feelings, etc.) allows individual members to integrate thinking, feeling, and action. It offers options for life outside of the group. Our attributes show up more quickly in a group, especially when program activities are well designed and managed. These include competiveness, sarcasm, grace, crankiness, irritability, empathy, gloating, sullenness, withdrawal, invasions of physical and emotional space, resignation, seductiveness, provocative actions, thoughtfulness, acquiescence, frustration, tolerance, quitting, and more. Once our attributes are out in the open, more meaningful work can be accomplished. The interpersonal and intrapersonal management of self is a major component of group work. Planfully managed, program allows the group to seize opportunities for individual and group development toward mutuality, respect, challenge, and caring.

References

Brandler, S. & Roman, C.P. (1991). *Group work: Skills and strategies for effective interventions.* Binghampton, NY: Haworth Press, 128-131.

Ciardiello, S. (2003). *ACTivities for group work with school age children.* Warminster, PA: Marco products, Inc.

Clements, J. & Benbow, S. (2009). Presentation. 31st Annual Symposium of the Association for the Advancement of Social Work with Groups, Chicago.

De Anda, D. (2002). *Stress management for adolescents: A cognitive-behavioral manual.* Champaign, IL: Research Press.

Doel, M. (2006). *Using groupwork.* New York: Routledge Press.

Glasser, P., Sarri, R. & Vinter, R. (1974). *Individual change through small groups.* NY: The Free Press, 233.

Haasl, B. & Marnocha, J. (1992). *Bereavement support group program for children.* Levittown, PA: Taylor & Francis Group.

Leben, N. (1994). *Directive group play therapy: 60 structured games for the treatment of ADHD, low self-esteem and traumatized children.* Austin, TX: Morning Glory Treatment Center for Children.

Kurland, R. (1978). Planning: The neglected component of group development. *Social Work with Groups, 1*(2), 173-180.

McGinnis, E. and Goldstein, A.P. (2003). *Skillstreaming in early childhood: New strategies and perspectives for teaching prosocial skills.* Champaign, IL: Research Press.

Middleman, R.R. 1980. *The non-verbal method in working with groups: The use of activity in teaching, counseling, and therapy.* Hebron, CT: Practitioners Press.

Middleman, R.R. (1981). The Pursuit of Competence through Involvement of Structured Groups. In A.N. Maluccio (Ed.), *Promoting competence in clients.* New York: The Free Press.

Middleman, R.R. (1988). Use of Program: Review and Update. *Social Work with Groups, 3*(3).

Middleman, R.R. & Wood, G.G. (1990). *Skills for direct practice in social work.* New York: Columbia University Press.

Schiller, L.Y. (1995). Stages of development in women's groups: A relational model. In R. Kurland, and R. Salmon, R. (Eds.), *Group work practice in a troubled society.* New York: Haworth Press.

Steinberg, D.M. (2004). *The mutual aid approach to working with groups: Helping people help one another.* (2nd ed.) New York: Haworth Press, 74.

Stuecker, R. & Rutherford, S. (2001). *Reviving the wonder: 76 activities to touch the inner spirit of youth.* Champaign, IL: Research Press.

Sweeney, D.S. & Homyer, L.E. (1999). *Group play therapy: How to do it, how it works, whom it is best for*. San Francisco: José-Bass, Inc. Publishers.

Vinter, R.D. (1985). Program activities: An analysis of their effects on participant behavior. In M. Sundel, P. Glasser, R. Sarri & R. Vinter (Eds.), *Individual change through small groups.* (2nd ed.) New York: The Free Press, 237- 250.

Wilson, G. & Ryland, G. (1949, 1981). *Social group work practice, Part II.* Boston: Houghton Mifflin.

3
The power of group work and community organizing in the 2008 U.S. Presidential race

Gerald Kellman

Abstract: This chapter reports the Beulah G. Rotham Memorial Plenary Address 31st Annual International Symposium Association for the Advancement of Social Work with Groups Chicago, Illinois June 26th, 2009. It illustrates the use of personal narrative, group work, and community organization in Barack Obama's 2008 presidential campaign. The chapter demonstrates the powerful and necessary interplay among all three social work modalities.

Keywords: community organization, personal narrative, group process, Barack Obama, African American

I'd like to say how pleased I am to be here. Social workers have touched many persons' lives and I am no exception. When I was a headstrong teenager, I was a leader on the east coast in the B'nai B'rith Youth Organization, an international Jewish organization. The group's advisor, Gus Unger, was a social worker. He challenged me to be responsible, to use my gifts, and to serve others. He was a second father to me and he died far too young. When I think of social workers, I think of Gus.

I'll begin by sharing some of President Obama's inner struggles during the time he was organizing and how his training as an organizer helped him with these struggles.

When I met Barack Obama for the first time at a coffee shop in New York City in 1985, most of the issues that he would have to grapple with in political life, *and* the gifts that he would draw on to overcome them were already present. Barack was African American on the outside. But on the inside, he was a citizen of the world. He was struggling to figure out how to respond to the varied misconceptions that people had of him. People judged him by his skin color. Some liked it; some did not. People judged him by his pattern of speech and the prestige of his education. Some liked it and some did not. Being judged by who people think you are, rather than who you know yourself to be is difficult for anyone, but it was particularly difficult for a young man who wanted to make a difference in the world.

What Barack learned in his time organizing in Chicago, was to not let others define him but to define himself. This was the single most important lesson Barack learned as an organizer. It may be the most important lesson that any of us ever learn. It is the lesson which enabled him to be elected President. The power of Barack's ability to define himself has been so great that in the process he has redefined America for Americans. And he has redefined America for the rest of the world. Of his two major opponents in the election, Hillary Clinton also did a wonderful job of defining herself. Unfortunately for Secretary Clinton, she never had the opportunity to work as an organizer on the south side of Chicago. So as good as she was at defining herself, Barack was better. This ability to define himself, rather than having others define him, was fundamental to Barack's campaign for President and will be fundamental to how we will engage in community organizing in the future.

One of the amazing things about the 2008 Presidential campaign and the beginning of Barack's Presidency is how much Barack Obama has become a symbol. He is a person, a political leader with a set of policies, but for the majority of the people in the world, he is also a symbol. This is particularly true outside of the United States and among young people. The power of the symbol that is Barack Obama is greatest among those who feel they had the least opportunity to influence the actions of the government of the United States. For them, Barack is a symbol of change. He is a symbol of how those outside the normal channels of power and decision making can bring about change. Barack is also a symbol of diversity. He is a symbol of our ability to cross walls that have been established to divide us: by race, prosperity, religion, ethnicity, nation, age, and even political ideology.

I hired Barack to reach out to those who were on the outside, folks who were poor and Black on the south side of Chicago. But Barack had never been poor or Black. Well of course, he had been Black, but largely he had been protected by his life from the problems of racism.

But what Barack had been almost his entire life was an outsider. We all know the biography. Barack told it to you in his book as he told it to me in that coffee shop almost twenty-five years ago. An American kid growing up abroad, not knowing his father, sometimes physically separated from his Mom, moving to Hawaii where he was one of a very few African Americans, he was very much an outsider. Outsiders basically have two choices. They either try to be like everyone around them or they identify with other outsiders. Barack chose to identify with other outsiders and in time become a symbol for outsiders throughout America and the world.

I want to describe how this ability to define himself, although he was an outsider, was shaped by his experience as an organizer and how in turn he used this experience to shape his campaign for President.

There was a peculiar resonance, between who Barack was when I met him and the training with which we would provide him as an organizer. When Barack and I came to know one another, he was torn between the idea of a career in public life and a career of telling stories, of writing fiction. The first thing he was assigned to do as an organizer was to listen to people's stories. The basis of organization is relationships. Relationships are built at the deepest level around personal stories and narrative. Like any organizer, Barack spent hour after hour in one-on-one interviews, in small group discussions listening to people tell their stories. It was in learning to tell his own story that Barack was able to define himself. It was in teaching others to tell their stories that Barack learned to be an organizer and later a leader.

I think it is worth noting that as gifted as Barack was, like most new organizers he struggled with this in the beginning. His connections could be superficial. Again and again, I would challenge Barack to go deeper, to connect with others at the level of their deepest grief and their strongest longings.

The Catholic spiritual writer Paula D'Arcy says that God comes to us disguised – as our own life, as our own story. Stories are powerful because they describe and name the world for us in a more profound way than any data or even photograph can convey. If you can tell your story, you know who you are. If you cannot tell your own story, others will define you. Were the lower income African Americans and Hispanics that Barack worked with, and that I continue to work with, on the south side people who were ONE – lazy and could not compete – OR TWO – victims of closed factories and bad luck – OR THREE – part of a multigenerational struggle to overcome the worst kind of adversity? Would they find a way to overcome obstacles once again? Knowing what you do of Barack, what message do you think he learned to convey to people? Well if you listened to his inauguration address, you know he learned to hear the story of how if we struggle, we can overcome adversity. The poet T.S. Elliot wrote that 'we had the experience, but missed the meaning.' We tell stories so that we won't miss the meaning.

David Axelrod, the strategic heart of the Obama campaign, believes that politics is about competing stories. So responding to his own experience as an organizer and Axelrod's advice, Barack told his story again and again. He told the story he wanted to tell about himself. He told us that he came from a family that has overcome adversity, from a grandmother who overcame barriers of discrimination against women, from a father who believed America was the promised land, from a single mother who gave him everything he needed, from a wife who grew up in the most segregated city in America but went on to live the American dream.

The campaign organizers decided to empower individuals through a deliberate use of group process. They gathered people in small groups, asking potential campaign workers to discuss three questions. The first was 'What is happening in your life that you are participating in this discussion? What life experiences brought you here?' In other words, they were asked to tell their stories.

The next question was 'How does your story connect with the others who are here and with others in the United States?' The discussion participants came to see that what unites us is always greater than what divides us if we are listening to one another's stories. Those in power pursue a strategy of divide and conquer. Organizers help people find their commonality via group interactions. The great secret of those who try to take away your dignity for the sake of their own power is that they do it by turning brother against brother and sister against sister. One understanding of the Biblical Hebrew word for Satan is that it means 'one who divides.' The Holy Spirit can only arrive when people are gathered together. For as long as I remember, the key to political power in Chicago has been keeping Whites, African Americans and Hispanics divided. Barack learned that the key to opening the doors of power to others was to connect people using group work to develop empowered groups. When we connect with one another at the level of our grief and hope, there is no power on earth that can keep us divided.

There was a third question, and that was 'How do the stories we have told and heard relate to this Barack Obama, this obvious outsider who believes that he can be elected President of the United States?' Organizers will recognize that question from countless house meetings and small theological reflection groups. Although Barack was taught to ask it like this, more or less: 'Understanding your grief and hope, and how your grief and hope connect you to one another, what is the opportunity of the present moment?' For organizers, this is the action question.

Because as much as we use stories to define ourselves and not let others define us, as much as we use stories to connect ourselves to others whom we previously thought we had nothing in common with, only to discover that they were just like us, stories without action were incomplete. They were a dream without a future.

We use stories to define ourselves and to prevent others from defining us. We also use stories to form connections. But those who are busy defining us and taking more and more for themselves, who are busy eating off the plate of a hungry brother and sister, would like nothing more than to have us tell our stories to one another all day long. If you want to define yourself, your stories must always result in action. We describe large efforts for social change as movements. The first instruction that Jesus gives to the Disciples is to keep moving. Sooner or later, we get to the point where we say to ourselves 'I don't have to live this way.'

I tried to teach Barack about action by modeling it for him. And he modeled it for the leaders he pulled together on the south side. I think we learn the most difficult things by watching. I taught Barack to do one-on-one interviews by having him watch me do them. I learned about the things that he understood and the things that he did not quite grasp by watching him. This is also the way he was taught about action.

Action, movement for organizers, is not flailing around. It is disciplined and reflective, as Barack was during the campaign. It recognizes emotion, but saves emotion for when we are among friends or when it furthers what we want to communicate, as Barack did during the campaign. In the heat of the moment, we remain as cool as we can be, careful not to react to everything that comes our way, choosing our battles, careful to communicate what we intend to communicate. This is what a good organizer and a good group worker does and we saw that in Barack during the campaign. Good organizers model this approach to action for others. Organizers project these action characteristics so that those they work with will learn to imitate them. Barack projected this and created the expectation that his campaign team was to behave the same way. From the campaign team, this attitude permeated to all levels of the campaign. The Obama campaign displayed a remarkable ability to collaborate and to remain consistent. Sarah Palin, Rudy Giuliani and other Republican leaders who ridiculed organizing at their convention could have helped their candidate if they urged him to be *more* like a community organizer.

There is another aspect to action in organizing and in the campaign that I want to highlight. Early in the campaign journalists speculated that Barack was not tough enough to triumph in the cutthroat world of a presidential campaign. His response was that he had been an organizer on the south side of Chicago and that nothing he encountered in the election was likely to demand as much toughness as that. And indeed, Barack demonstrated a steely toughness again and again. Community organizing teaches us that if something is important it is worth fighting for. Since the forces you are up against are likely to be ruthless and powerful, you need to decide what your ethical limits are and then be willing to do anything you need to do, ANYTHING within those limits. This includes fighting fire with fire, and compromise as needed.

Action changes us. It teaches us about risk, about solidarity, to get knocked down and get up again, and to discover capacities we did not think we had. It did these things for Barack when he first experienced action as an organizer and it did these things for the millions of people, particularly young people, who put themselves out there for the campaign

For those of you who are not aware of a unique aspect of the campaign, it is important to know that unlike any other modern Presidential campaign, this campaign allowed people to build their own campaign events, organizations, even strategies. Political campaigns at this level are about control. The local political powerhouses and workhorses are wooed and asked to register voters, identify who is favorable, and turn them out. In the primary, Hillary Clinton had most of the powerhouses and workhorses behind her. So the Obama campaign did the unthinkable. They opened up their website so people could use social networking to build their own team, gave them the basic tools of lists and suggestions and set them loose. How unprofessional!!! Except it was the most effective and best organized campaign in American history. But of course it was nothing new for the organizers. What we do is give people some basic tools and set them free. We then bring them back to evaluate and learn from what went wrong and what went right.

Well, I have talked at length about what Barack learned from organizing. I want to spend a few minutes talking about how organizing may need to change as the result of Barack's election.

Other than Barack himself, two men are most responsible for Barack's election. I am not talking about David Axelrod and David Plouffe, his strategist and campaign manager. Barack's election simply could never have happened without the work of two other men. Their names are George Walker Bush and Dick Cheney. During eight years, America was deconstructed and Americans had become so demoralized that they were willing to rethink the previously unthinkable, the election of an African American to the most powerful position in the world. Our ethics had been so compromised, our economic well-being so damaged, our budget so crippled, our place in the nations of the world so tarnished, our justice system so abused, that it was a kind of national death. If we use William Bridges' work on transitions as a guide, then there are always three parts to a transition. Keep in mind that a transition is not simply the external changes, but the inner experience of these changes. There is an ending, a long period of confusion, and then a new beginning. The ending was the destruction visited upon a standard of public life and prosperity that had developed over several generations. The transition was the campaign and the beginnings of this presidency so mired in crisis. The beginning has yet to come, but it will come. In fact, it is organizers who will help create it. What we now know more than ever is that redemption is always possible on a national, not just a personal basis, and perhaps worldwide. Destruction is painful, but it does create an opportunity for new life and creation. Transitions, the in-between times, are times of confusion, doubt, and frustration, but they are often the most fertile times that we will ever experience. Organizers must now figure out how endings give rise to opportunities and how to maximize the possibilities inherent in the in-between times, the times of transition.

The changes keep coming. We plant our feet, only to have the earth shift. The persons who will create and build something of value in an environment of constant change will be those who are committed to a lifetime of learning and who create what Peter Senge has called 'Learning Organizations'. Those who will make history will be those who work as teams and understand, as group workers already do, that no one person can ever be as smart as a group of persons fully collaborating. Those who survive the inevitable mistakes and setbacks will be those who are willing to admit mistakes, and those who will be strong will be those who are willing to admit and even show the vulnerability which is part of their humanity.

Barack learned what Saul Alinsky taught us about self-interest, but also learned the importance of hope and a call to be part of something larger than himself.

I took a fifteen year sabbatical from organizing because I felt we needed to change hearts as well as structures. In the future, organizing will be about changing both.

6
The use of group work to fight external threats to a community-based organization during harsh economic times

Andrew Malekoff

Abstract: In dire economic times, often there is a tendency towards fatalism and a sense of helplessness among many human services professionals. This article addresses the use of group work in a community-based outpatient children's mental health agency to respond to financial threats by County and State government during the economic downturn of 2008–2009. Three specific threats that came within months of one another are discussed: (1) the threat to close down a chemical dependency treatment service for youth, (2) severe funding cuts to an outreach program for immigrant youth and their families and (3) a State government plan to restructure / reform reimbursement for outpatient mental health services that promises to reduce access to care for underinsured families. Group work was used to organize, educate and activate staff, board, community and consumer groups, in large and small groups, to counter the threats and build a culture of advocacy. Lending a vision, empowering potential advocates, managing polarity and shaping the advocacy message were essential elements of the advocacy process.

Keywords: Group work, advocacy, organizational crisis, managing polarity, economic downturn, coalitions, mental health, chemical dependency, youth services, controlling the message, not-for-profit

Introduction

The 2008-2009 downturn in the US economy impacted not-for-profit human services agencies. This article offers a snapshot in time of three specific threats, by government agencies, to a leading children's mental health agency in suburban Long Island, New York. The author is a group worker and the agency's chief executive officer. In this paper, he discusses the use of group work to counter the threats and develop a culture of advocacy.

As the economy plummeted in 2008–2009, States and Counties across the nation reported growing budget shortfalls. This places community-based, not-for-profit human services agencies at risk. North Shore Child and Family Guidance Center (the Guidance Center), a leading children's outpatient mental health center in New York, was confronted, in a matter of a few months, in late 2008 and early 2009, with funding threats that promised to decimate essential services, at a time when families were experiencing more stress than ever. To add insult to injury, the notification process by government officials came without warning, demonstrating a total disregard for the agency's longstanding and valued place in the community.[1]

The threats included (1) closing down a chemical dependency treatment service for youth, (2) severe funding cuts to an outreach program for immigrant youth and their families and (3) a State government plan to restructure/reform reimbursement for outpatient mental health services that will reduce access to care for underinsured children and their families.

Organizing for advocacy

Groups were organized and activated quickly to ensure a rapid response. Utilizing a social work with groups planning model (Northen & Kurland, 2001) to get groups going, was a critical first step in getting people organized and motivated to take action. There was no time to waste. Lending a vision (Schwartz, 1961), empowering potential advocates (Taylor, 1987; Sunley, 1983), managing polarity (Johnson, 1992) and shaping the advocacy message (Bartlett, 2008) were essential components of the advocacy effort.

As a social work method and agency function, advocacy requires 'study, planning, action and evaluation' (Sunley, 1983, p.1). In the present case studies, this included demystifying the issues and educating group members (staff, board, community and consumer/clients), creating talking points and protest letter templates for communicating with legislators and public officials, and developing a story to tell that would make the issues interesting and important to people that needed to be reached.

Children, youth and advocacy

Although adolescent clients were included in the efforts in rallies and letter writing/email campaigns, it must be noted that advocacy for children and young people is different from advocacy for adults (Oliver & Dalrymple, 2008). In the former, most often adults take a stance of knowing 'what is best' for children and youth, raising important questions about the power dynamics in the advocacy equation and what it takes to bring young people's voices to advocacy campaigns.

Oliver and Dalrymple (2008) state that, 'if advocacy is about 'having a voice' and 'speaking up,' children and young people that need advocacy are routinely silenced and marginalized by other, more powerful, individuals and decision-making systems' (p.12). In the case studies described in this article, youth was engaged in the cause and participated directly in the efforts to save chemical dependency and youth services funding. A key principle of strengths-based group work with adolescents is maintaining a dual focus on individual change and social reform (Malekoff, 2004). The Guidance Center has a history of engaging youth in advocacy efforts ranging from fighting homophobia in high school and promoting gay-straight alliances (Peters, 2003) to fighting for humane bathroom conditions in a special education setting (Malekoff, 1999).

Legitimacy of cause in advocacy

Taylor (1987) advises that, 'to feel empowered to advocate, we must both feel ethically comfortable with the right to advocate and convinced that we can develop a power base sufficient to the task' (p.28). She adds that legitimacy of the cause; legal, moral or constitutional rights of clients; belief in the dignity and value of each human being and his or her right to the best possible life; and the ethical code of the profession give us the right to advocate.

Some important questions to consider in determining the legitimacy of an advocacy effort are: who are your potential allies? why do you believe advocacy can work in your agency? what obstacles do you expect to face? and what do you need to do to garner support for advocacy? What follows is a first look at the three threats that constitute the basis for the advocacy efforts described herein.

The threats

Counting what counts: The threat to chemical dependency treatment services

> *Not everything that can be counted counts and not everything that counts can be counted.*- Albert Einstein

In mid-December, 2008, just three weeks before the end of the contract year, the New York State Office of Alcoholism and Substance Abuse Services (OASAS) sent the Guidance Center a new contract that signaled the end of its adolescent chemical dependency treatment program. The depleted contract came with no explanation. After making several phone calls, the author (CEO of the agency) learned that the loss of funding was based on a State consultant's calculation that the 'cost of service' was twenty dollars too high. Cost of service is calculated by dividing units of service (e.g. counseling sessions) into the gross budget.

Organizing to fend off helplessness and demoralization

The consultant was a stranger to the agency. In making the advocacy case the CEO stated that this consultant 'is someone that does not know who we are, what we do and how well we do it.' He added, in meeting with various groups that:

> *The decision to cut funding was made completely devoid of context. It was a decision made by State bureaucrats without any consultation whatsoever with local government regarding community need or the agency's stellar reputation and fine track record for quality of care that had been formally evaluated and validated for decades.*

When the news of the potential loss of this service was delivered to the Guidance Center, it was met with a combination of outrage and deflated spirits. The outrage needed to be stoked to ward off feelings of resignation that can breed demoralization and a sense of helplessness during dire economic times. The potential for inertia and inaction was a major obstacle that needed to be headed off at the pass by 'rallying the troops' to fight back.

The advocacy process began by *organizing internally* and activating board committees, staff groups, consumers of services and community partners (e.g. local schools); and *organizing externally* by identifying and engaging key public officials and legislators. Although it was an option that we considered, we decided not to reach out to similarly affected agencies. Time was of the essence and there was no immediate confirmation about who was affected and how, nor was there any first hand knowledge of the quality of the services of other agencies.

Twenty-first century smoke signals

Four groups that were engaged immediately included two board committees: (1) the Executive Committee (composed of the board leadership) and (2) The Legislative Affairs and Advocacy Committee; (3) A group of staff members – roughly 25 people – that are located at the site where chemical dependency services are provided; and (4) A group of local State legislators – three assembly and one senate representative. Additional groups were engaged in the next phase, including groups of youth and parent consumers and an agency-community advisory council.

These groups were organized in three ways – face-to-face meetings, telephone conference calls and email groups. Face-to-face is ideal, but other means were necessary due to time constraints, as the contract year was about to end in a matter of weeks.

Communicating by phone and internet could have presented an obstacle for the advocacy effort. The ability to truly connect with one another and pick up nuance is limited in phone and email conversation. Advantages of electronic communication, however, include overcoming obstacles of time and distance, and extending the advocacy reach (Lohman & McNutt 2005). With only a short window to take action, all means of communication were activated.

No wrong door: The threat to outreach and prevention services

In the second scenario the Nassau County Executive, whose human services motto was 'No Wrong Door,' sent the Guidance Center a registered letter that promised to wipe out a much valued outreach and prevention service to immigrant families in the Hispanic community. In his letter, he implored us, and 42 other agencies, to lobby local State legislators for 'revenue enhancers' that included increased cigarette taxes, red light traffic cameras and larger fines for traffic violations. He said nothing in his letter about the cost effectiveness of youth services that kept high risk youths at home and out of costly institutions at great expense to taxpayers.

The advocacy approach in this case was participating with a wider coalition of 43 youth agencies that were similarly and simultaneously threatened; and, the same time, organizing our board, staff, clients and community supporters to advocate by writing letters, sending emails and making phone calls. Essential in coalition advocacy are agreeing to pursue a common goal, coordinating resources and adopting common strategies to reach the goal (Roberts-DeGennaro & Mizrahi, 2005). This is consistent with good group work that requires establishing a clear group purpose and utilizing appropriate content or program (means) to achieve group goals (Northen & Kurland, 2001).

The impact, if the threatened youth services cuts were realized, would be the near total destruction of County-funded youth development services in the County serving over 60,000 youth and family members annually. The services included suicide prevention, alternatives to gangs, after school enrichment, summer jobs for youth, counseling for returning veterans and their families, and respite services.

Youth and parents were engaged in this advocacy effort to participate in rallies, attend legislative hearings, lobby legislators, write letters and emails, and develop advocacy messages using art and video.

Clinic reform: The threat to core mental health treatment services

The third threat is more complex and, therefore, required a different kind of response. While the first two threats were delivered in the form of sudden, cut and dry, written communiqués, the third was presented as a statewide policy change in the reimbursement method for outpatient mental health services.

This new financing plan, referred to as 'clinic reform,' will discriminate against the underinsured middle class, lower middle class and working poor that represent three-quarters of the Guidance Center's clientele. This plan will make the Guidance Center's current business model unsustainable, threatening the viability of the agency itself. Our fight was not only to stay in business, but to ensure that underinsured families would not be denied mental health services. The legitimacy of cause is a powerful motivator in this case, as of course is survival of the agency.

At first, the Guidance Center found few allies in this fight. Others, whose nests were feathered with the largesse of Medicaid dollars, seemed uninterested in supporting universal mental health care as long as the movement to a residual Medicaid model of care did not threaten their survival. The author (CEO) presented the case to a local coalition of County mental health providers. Aside from one director who expressed gratitude for the Guidance Center's public stance and advocacy efforts on this issue, the presentation was met with silence, as well at least one dismissive comment regarding those with private insurance needing to fend for themselves.

The lack of support from sister agencies presented a potential obstacle in the advocacy effort. Although it was dispiriting to find such little support from colleagues, being a lone voice had its advantages and could be used to build group cohesion within a smaller circle.

In retrospect, a more successful approach in engaging the other agencies might have been to meet with agency directors individually to discuss the issues and the impact of clinic reform. Presenting complex issues to a large group within a limited time frame was, perhaps, not the ideal way to recruit and secure allies and build consensus.

Responding to the threats

Group work planning

Knowledge of and skill in group work planning (Northen & Kurland, 2001) are indispensable in thinking about how to organize groups to fight back. This includes deliberating and deciding on what groups to organize (*composition* – pre-existing and newly formed groups), how to bring them together (*pre-group planning, structure, context* – being the 'boss' helps in sanctioning and directing groups to meet), what information to provide and how to deliver it (*content* – shaping the message and creating talking points and sample letters) and what actions to encourage and initiate (*purpose and goals* – rescinding cuts, restoring funding; being the boss helped in getting the groups together, but how groups respond is more a matter of how the message is delivered regarding our purpose) around what *needs* – universal access to services, saving lives, keeping kids at home and out of costly institutions, preserving families.

Established coalitions composed of groups of agencies that are similarly affected can be instantly organized to advocate, particularly when this is their mandate. Of course, the success of these efforts depends in large part on any coalition's leadership and history of working together to advocate as a group to address needs and confront crises and threats. The coalition's willingness to agree on strategies was also critical. In the case of the threatened cuts to youth services the coalition responded swiftly and strongly.

In the case of clinic reform there was disinterest among the members of the earlier referenced local mental health coalition and, thus, there was no immediate response as a group. Many of these agencies felt that clinic reform would not have a negative effect because of the high Medicaid percentage in their 'case mix.' The ethic – 'all for one and one for all' – seemed non-existent in this group.

Accessing mass media

A director of a statewide advocacy organization sought information from the Guidance Center after she learned that it had taken a public position, including in the print and electronic media. She commended the Guidance Center leadership for 'going on record.' She stated that most of her member agencies preferred to have the statewide coalition speak for them, as they were reticent to go public out of fear of reprisal. The position of the Guidance Center leadership was to be bold and to act quickly. Too much was at stake to take a 'wait and see' approach. Nevertheless, speaking out in the media can present further threats.

From a strategic perspective, making the case in the media presents risks, including the possibility that opposing points of view might be presented in a more favorable light, solidifying the opposition (Sunley, 1983). There was also the possibility that acting alone, without the support of a broader coalition, could place the Guidance Center in a vulnerable position. These factors were considered and discussed with board and staff leadership. Nevertheless, the decision was to move ahead in an assertive manner given what was at stake.

Variable stakeholder interests

Of course, even if activated, coalitions can be tricky when there are competing interests. This was the case with the threatened cuts to youth services. In this situation there were 43 agencies of various sizes and budgets. Some agencies faced being shut down completely if the budget cuts held. Others would survive, as youth services funding constituted only a small part of their overall funding. The latter was true for the Guidance Center. Nevertheless, the Guidance Center joined the fight as full partners – all for one and one for all.

Standing groups with stable memberships (e.g. board committees, staff teams, consumer groups) can be activated and organized quickly to advocate for critical needs. In contrast, the composition of *newly formed advocacy groups* needs to be carefully considered to include individuals that are affected and or outraged by an issue and that are motivated to take action.

At the Guidance Center, first convening agency leadership groups – board and staff – in ad hoc (and even spur-of-the-moment) meetings was critical in making decisions about how to shape the message and tell the story about the impact of the threats. Controlling the message involved quite a bit of sorting facts and information to present the case clearly and powerfully. As Indian activist and essayist Arundhati Roy states, it is important to see:

> ... the schism between what we know and what we are told...between what is revealed and what is concealed, between fact and conjecture, between the real world and the virtual world. (2004, p.96)

Controlling the Message

Controlling the 'counting what counts' advocacy message

The key issues that were considered in deciding how to tell the story and shape the advocacy message about the threat to our chemical dependency treatment funding were: (1) the State's rationale and decision to cut our chemical dependency treatment funding was based on a *cost of service* calculation that was devoid of context and based on an adult services model, (2) the labor intensity necessary to work with children, youth and their families that are impacted by substance abuse and addiction requires a different *quality of care* standard than working with adults. (3) A new quality of care standard must be calculated into the cost of service that includes attention to collateral contacts, home and school visits, crisis intervention, and high risk case conferencing, for example.

Therefore, to shape the debate and control the message, a different story needed to be told than the story that the State was telling regarding what was important to count in providing chemical dependency services for children, youth and their families. It had to be one that would demystify the issues for advocates and that would reframe and broaden the focus of services for children and youth. We could not allow the *cost of service* rationale for reducing funding to stand alone without being challenged. The goal was to redefine the same circumstances by adding *labor intensity* and *quality of care* into the equation. We had to find a way to make the message memorable, to emphasize the importance of what we later referred to as 'counting what counts.'

We had to make a strong argument that the State must rescind the cuts, restore our funding and then help to establish a units-of-service expectation that corresponds with the high risk and high needs population that we have consistently welcomed into our program.

Managing polarity

An understanding of *managing polarity* (Johnson, 1992) is key. The idea being that if we took an either/or position – cost of service or quality of care – our fight would not stand up to scrutiny. However, if we took a both/and position – quality of care and cost of services – then our argument would be more difficult to disregard.

In a managing polarity perspective there is not one right answer, rather a paradoxical relationship between two poles that could be made to appear as interdependent opposites. In this case the argument needed to be made that both cost of service *and* quality of care are critical; that the cost of service for what the Guidance Center provides to the population that it serves – children and youth – is more labor intensive by definition, and therefore requires a different set of criteria for measuring cost of service.

In the advocacy group meetings, this concept was presented and examples were solicited from the group that told the story about the need for greater labor intensity in kids' services. Illustrations included responding to frequent crisis calls, meeting with relevant others in the children's and youths' lives, school visits, home visits, high risk case conferencing and more.

It should be noted that for the staff group of about 25 people that were organized to address this issue, they understood immediately that some of their jobs were at stake. This question was raised and answered at the meeting.

From dazed and confused, to motivated to fight back

Hearing the news of the threatened loss of funding that could lead to the end of the service and loss of jobs was first met with shock. At first there was a sense of disoriented silence in the room. You might say, to borrow from an old movie title, that the group was *dazed and confused*. In time, as the details were shared and the group was encouraged to fight back, the group slowly came to life. The author (CEO) shared his vision for the fight and the story that needed to be told. Talking points were reviewed and soon the group discussed, plotted and added their own ideas for tactics that included reaching out to multiple client and community groups. By meeting's end, the group took the fight to the State without hesitation or ambivalence.

The advocates needed to think about, talk through and, ultimately, own the story – the idea that more labor intensive work was indicated for this population and that any calculation of cost of service had to include this in the equation. They had to have a compelling argument and story to tell about why the service needed to be *counted* differently and what the impact of the loss of the service would mean to the community.

Counting what counts

The hook or phrase that was used to capture both the importance of cost of service and of quality of care, was *counting what counts.* What this means is that counting what counts in kids' services is different than counting what counts in adults services and, therefore, must be subject to different standards in arriving at the cost of quality care.

Talking points and sample letters to go to State officials and legislators were provided to the groups that emphasized and illustrated this stance. It should be noted that staff and board groups then carried the message to client/consumer groups and community supporters and enlisted their support as advocates – youth and parents and other adults. Advocacy became contagious.

The good news is that in a matter of days, due to the powerful response by the various advocate groups, as well as local government, the cuts were rescinded and the funding fully restored by the State. The 'icing on the cake' was a written response by the State OASAS commissioner that formally acknowledged our argument that kids' services are by definition more intensive and therefore deserve a different set of criteria for calculating cost of service.

Controlling the 'no wrong door' advocacy message

Fear is a great motivator. Such was the case when Nassau County (NY) Executive Thomas Suozzi announced that he would eliminate youth services in Nassau County, New York in 2009. He said that this was due to a 130 million-dollar (and growing) County budget deficit. He added that the only thing that might reverse the cuts was if bills for 'revenue enhancers' were passed by the State legislature. These so-called revenue enhancers included new cigarette taxes, red light traffic cameras and traffic violation reform, all of which, we were told, promised to bring millions of dollars into the local economy and *could* be used to fund youth services. *Could* is emphasized here since no guarantee was ever made that if funds were secured that they *would* be used for this purpose on an annual basis, in perpetuity.

Revenue enhancers and cost savings

Despite the County Executive's cry for revenue enhancers, what was curiously obscured from his message, and that Guidance Center leadership thought needed to be brought to light, was the real cost savings that these services represented by keeping kids at home and out of jail and psychiatric institutions. The facts are that preventing incarceration or institutional placement for even a relatively small number of youths would represent cost savings to taxpayers that would support keeping these services intact.

As indicated above, many of the 43 agencies that were threatened were small operations that depended on this funding to stay in business. The coalition that all 43 were a part of held regular meetings and communicated through email to plan rallies, testify at legislative meetings, write letters, make phone calls, and go to the County legislature and State capital to lobby.

It was soon clear that the group and their constituents quickly became the County Executive's unpaid lobbyists for the revenue enhancers that, if passed by the New York State Legislature, might be used for other purposes than youth services. The Guidance Center organized the board and staff to lobby for the revenue enhancers and also went on record publicly regarding the cost effectiveness of youth services and the long term savings to the County and taxpayer.

The author decided to take a public position on what he thought the threatened cuts revealed. He presented his position to large groups in public forums and in the newspaper. He was warned to be careful not to anger the County Executive; that he might be vindictive if crossed. Following, is an op-ed piece that appeared in a chain of local newspapers that also contains the core content of an address to a group of about 200 parents, youths, school officials, legislators, agency staff and board members at a bi-annual 'Community Unity Event' (see Appendix I for text of address).

Long Beach Herald

No Kudos for Suozzi

By Andrew Malekoff, March 26 – April 1 2009

In its March 19th editorial *The Herald* offered 'kudos' to County Executive Tom Suozzi for exploiting the County's most vulnerable citizens by enlisting them to become unpaid lobbyists to advocate for cigarette tax and traffic violation reform. His strategy was to advise 43 community-based programs serving over 60,000 youth and family members that they would be closed down or crippled unless these revenue enhancers were passed through Albany.

Let us take just a moment to recognize that sometimes when political figures speak that there is a gap between what is revealed and what is concealed, between what we know and what we are told. We are told that revenue from cigarette taxes and traffic violations is the solution for vulnerable youth. Yet, what we know is that slashing and burning youth services will not save the County money, but will increase costs to the County to the tune of tens of millions of dollars, as growing numbers of young people will not pass go, but will go directly to jail or psychiatric lock up as front end services disappear. We are told by Mr. Suozzi that his human services motto for Nassau County is 'no wrong door,' yet what we hear is the unmistakable sound of a door slamming shut.

During these harsh economic times when all of our best efforts are needed to preserve families, Mr. Suozzi's cuts will not only destroy the service system that has been carefully constructed to support them and increase the long term burden to the taxpayer, but will bear an even greater cost in lives lost, kids plucked from their homes and families splintered and destroyed. The federal government bails out powerful financial institutions and Nassau County tosses its most vulnerable children and youth overboard.

If and when the revenue enhancers are passed and Mr. Suozzi rescinds the cuts, will he permanently earmark and enhance these monies for youth services? And, will he start referring to them as essential human services versus the pejorative 'discretionary services?' Maybe then, and only then, will kudos be in order.

The author thought that the County Executive was presenting an either-or proposition that sounded something like this: 'Lobby for cigarette taxes, red light traffic cameras and traffic violation reform, or there will be no funding for these services.' The alternative argument that we promoted is that by eliminating youth services, costs to the County would increase dramatically as more young people would be 'put away.' We advocated for both/and, encouraging others to advocate for revenue enhancers and making the case for cost effectiveness, that youth services save the County money by keeping kids out of jail and psychiatric institutions.

The result of this process was that only one of the three revenue enhancers passed the New York State legislature. The County Executive would not commit those funds to youth services, even though they would have covered the cost of the proposed cuts. Another source of income was 'found' at the eleventh hour that enabled about 75% of the 43 agencies to continue their youth services through 2009, including the Guidance Center. The remaining agencies or youth services folded. The fight continues for restoration of full funding in 2010.

Controlling the clinic reform advocacy message

Addressing clinic reimbursement restructuring for outpatient mental health services was more complex and required meetings with high ranking public officials in County and State government. These included County and State Commissioners of Mental Health, the County Executive, local State Assembly and Senate representatives, the State Comptroller and a liaison from the Governor's office. The key message was that the clinic reform plan, as proposed, would discriminate against the underinsured middle class, lower middle class and working poor.

What became clear from these high level meetings was that, despite differences, there are areas of mutual interest and concern that could be addressed together – government and not-for-profit, bureaucrat and consumer. For example, an issue that both Office of Mental Health (OMH) and the Guidance Center had to address was the substandard reimbursement rates established by insurance carriers. In the author's public testimony (see below), he added this issue to the mix, beyond playing the discrimination-by-government card. It is a step towards establishing common ground between the government (OMH) and the not-for-profit agency. This and similarly stated opinion pieces that appeared in local newspapers were used as tools for organizing and educating advocacy groups.

Testimony by Andrew Malekoff, June 22, 2009, delivered at New York City, City Hall on Mental Health Clinic Reimbursement Restructuring

More low income and middle-class families than ever are in need of low cost, high quality community-based mental health care. Yet, the New York State Office of Mental Health (OMH) in conjunction with the New York State Department of Health is aggressively pursuing a 'reform' plan (clinic reform) for these critical services that will result in a system of community care where only those children and families with Medicaid 'fee for service' insurance coverage will be assured continued access to care. This will leave a significant number of children and adults in the lurch.

The reform plan sets up a mental health service delivery system that will no longer assure access to mental health care for children regardless of their parents' ability to pay. This policy shift represents a dramatic departure from what I see as a statutory responsibility on the part of New York State to make sure our most vulnerable citizens – our children – get care, regardless of their families' economic status.

Clinic reform signals movement away from a universal model to a residual model of care that discriminates against the underinsured middle and lower middle class and working poor children and families. Because of the lack of parity between government rates and rates paid by commercial insurers for behavioral health care, many children with what seems like adequate health insurance coverage will no longer receive behavioral healthcare services from community clinics.

Community clinics are the last bastion in addressing the needs of children and adolescents with serious emotional disturbances and their families. Private psychotherapists and counselors, with rare exception, cannot and will not afford to offer the labor intensive work necessary to properly serve families that are struggling with serious emotional disturbances.

I recommend the following: (1) The State Department of Health must demand that commercial Medicaid managed care carriers increase their rates to match Medicaid rates (2) The New York State Department of Insurance must to do the same with commercial insurers that underpay for behavioral health care. Commercial carriers that cannot demonstrate an 'adequacy of network' can, and should, have their licenses revoked.

(3) Consumers must be educated about these issues so that they can join the fight now and later, when denied community-based services, because their carriers cannot offer an adequate network of care (4) New York State Office of Mental Health, in conjunction with local governments, must restore and enhance local assistance funding – a partnership between local and State government, the local community and client-consumer – for specialty children's outpatient mental health clinics that serve a significant proportion of underinsured families.

If implemented in its current design, the Office of Mental Health's clinic reform plan will move us further away from access to mental health services regardless of ability to pay and toward a model that guarantees narrowly-defined treatment only for those with Medicaid eligibility.

Action must be taken now to reverse the course of clinic reform.

Coalition to save children's mental health services

In order to further the issues described in this testimony, multiple group meetings were held with staff and board groups, as well as groups of legislators at the County and State level. The Legislative Affairs and Advocacy Board Committee dubbed themselves the Coalition to Save Children's Mental Health Services in Nassau County[2] and used that moniker on petitions that were signed by well over a thousand citizens (and counting) and mailed to County and State officials in several installments to keep the issue in the forefront of their minds. The Nassau County Mental Health Commissioner Arlene Sanchez was invited to a meeting and she participated to clarify the impact of clinic reform from her perspective and validate her support for the Guidance Center, which served to strengthen our board members' resolve in this fight.

Convening an influential ad hoc group

Another example is an ad hoc group that was formed that consisted of board members, influential and politically-connected and savvy community supporters, and staff leadership. In all there were nine people. The author asked the more politically-connected members of the group if they would call a meeting with the County Executive, as he would be more likely to agree to a meeting called by key financial backers, versus the head of an agency who might just be perceived as 'looking to save his job' (like everyone else in the County). The group came together to plan strategy for the meeting with the County Executive.

The author began the meeting by giving a summary of the history of mental health financing and the current concern regarding the impact of clinic reform on funding going forward. It was recommended and agreed that what was needed was to ask the County Executive for something very specific in addition to his support in the fight against the proposed new State reimbursement policy for outpatient mental health services.

The Guidance Center had just sustained a significant short term financial hit (impacting on its cash flow) that was a direct result of the State's clinic reform plan.[3] After some discussion the group agreed that we would request an immediate increase to the County portion of the Guidance Center's contract, that represented the difference between decades of no 'cost of living' increases and the Agency's current contract. We understood that this request would be floated at a time when the County Executive had already gone on record publicly about a hundred-plus million dollar budget shortfall. Nevertheless, it was agreed that this had to be put on the table at the meeting and put in the context of the agency's viability.

To further make the case, several of participants said, 'We need to show that we provide services to residents from the entire County.' Their concern, they said, was that since 'North Shore' was in the Guidance Center's full name that he might construe that to mean that our services did not cover the entire County, but just a part of the County. It was recommended that a document be prepared that would demonstrate the broad 'reach' and value to the entire County versus only the 'north shore' region that include many affluent enclaves. The document would show the names of as many as 80 communities and 30 of 56 school districts across the County that used the Agency's services in the past year, many of which are perceived as deeply troubled, low income, minority communities.

The development and final approval of this document and a shorter page of 'talking points' for the ad hoc committee that would meet with the County Executive helped to establish common ground for the group. Everyone proved to be a 'fast study,' were well prepared for the meeting and contributed to telling the story. Also in attendance was the County Mental Health Commissioner Arlene Sanchez who once again presented herself as a strong advocate who validated our concerns and the story we told.

Advocacy on clinic reform is ongoing. There is some reason to be optimistic as the issue of the underinsured being carved out of the clinic reform process is starting to take hold in a way that it now 'has legs.' A key polarity in the clinic reform advocacy process is regarding the question of which children and youth get outpatient community-based mental health care. As presented thus far, Medicaid recipients benefit most from services that should benefit all consumers and taxpayers. We need to get beyond the debate between Medicaid recipients *or* the underinsured middle class and find ways to ensure universal access to mental heath care for children and youth.

Conclusion

This paper discusses the use of group work to organize a response to three significant financial threats to a specialty children's outpatient mental health agency in 2008–2009, during the downturn in the U.S. economy; a time that local and State governments are facing dramatic budget shortfalls. Consequently, in some instances, they are seeking ways to reduce government costs by cutting funding for services to the most vulnerable populations.

Organizing to fight back is a powerful way to give voice *to* and *with* vulnerable groups. Each group that can be organized and energized can contribute to a culture of advocacy that is an antidote to inertia and demoralization during dire economic times.

The advocacy efforts described herein have been carried forth in a six-month period of time and are ongoing. In the case of the threatened loss of chemical dependency funding, all cuts were rescinded by the State and funding was fully restored. The State Commissioner has validated the Guidance Center's position about the need to devise a new way to calculate the more intensive treatment approach to working with children and youth. That fight continues.

In the case of youth services cuts, a percentage of the cuts were restored through 2009. That battle still wages on.

Finally, in the case of clinic reform, by going on record, the Guidance Center has become a leading statewide voice for underinsured middle class, lower middle class and working poor. At first it felt as if we were a lone voice.

The risk to speak up appears to have paid off, at least in garnering wider support. We are not alone anymore.

Notes

1. It should be noted that, in addition to the circumstances described in this paper, the Guidance Center lost its endowment (on December 11, 2008) that was fully invested in Bernard L. Madoff securities. The author (CEO) also made half a million dollars of cost savings (budget cuts) in February, 2009.
2. The idea of naming the effort was recommended in a personal communication, during consultation with clinical professor of social work and community organizer Lee Staples from Boston University School of Social Work.
3. Although there is not enough space here to fully describe the history of outpatient mental health financing in New York State, the clinic reform plan called for an immediate 'rebasing' of one source of revenue for community-based agencies. What this meant was that in the first months of 2009 agencies had to retroactively (to July 1, 2008) return revenues in a matter of ten weeks or face interest costs if they exceeded the ten-week deadline. The 'take back' of monies, without adequate warning, impacted the cash flow of the agency. The 'rebasing' also meant that budget projections for the current year would have to be modified.

References

Bartlett, D. (2008). *Making your point: Communicating effectively with audiences of one to one million*. New York: St. Martin's Press.

Johnson, B. (1992). *Polarity management: Identifying and managing unsolvable problems*. Amherst, MA: HRD Press.

Lohman, R. & McNutt, J. (2005). 'Practice in the electronic community.' In M. Weil (Ed.), *The handbook of community practice*. Thousand Oaks, CA: Sage, 636-646.

Malekoff, A. (2004). *Group work with adolescents: Principles and practice*. New York: Guilford.

Malekoff, A. (1999). Pink soap and stall doors. *Families in Society, 80*(3), 219-220.

Northen, H. & Kurland, R. (2001). *Social work with groups*. (3rd ed.) New York: Columbia University Press.

Oliver, C. & Dalrymple, J. (Eds.), (2008). *Developing advocacy for children and young people: Current issues in research, policy and practice*. Philadelphia, PA: Jessica Kingsley Publishers.

Peters, A. (2003). Isolation or inclusion: Creating safe spaces for lesbian and gay youth. *Families in Society, 84*(3), 331-337.

Roberts-DeGennaro, M. & Misrahi, T. (2005). 'Coalitions as social change agents,' In M. Weil (Ed.), *The handbook of community practice*. Thousand Oaks, CA: Sage, 305-318.

Roy, A. (2004). *An ordinary person's guide to empire*. Cambridge, MA: South End Press.

Schwartz, W. (1961). The social worker in the group. In *New perspectives on services to groups: Theory, organization and practice*. New York: National Association of Social Workers.

Sunley, R. (1983). *Advocating today: A human service practitioners handbook (with a special chapter on how to work effectively with state and local government)*. New York: FSA.

Taylor, E. (1987). *From issue to action: An advocacy program model*. Lancaster, PA: Family Service.

Appendix I

Address by Andrew Malekoff to North Shore Child and Family Guidance Center's *Community Unity Event* at the Westbury Manor, Westbury, New York, March 5, 2009

Community unity is a beautiful thing. Community Unity is about neighbors united in good times and bad; Community Unity is about people of all ages and backgrounds standing together; Community Unity is not a fly-by-night, hit and run operation, but a sustained and determined effort; And so it is because this bi-annual event represents neighborhood at its best, I am proud to be here. I thank all of you for coming out, for being present this evening; I thank you for your solidarity and I ask for your help on behalf our sister youth serving agencies all across Nassau County.

Just a few short weeks ago youth serving agencies all across Nassau County received the horrific notice from our County Executive that will negatively impact the lives and futures of our children.

Nassau County has decided to turn its back on our young people and no longer provide the necessary funding for programs within our communities which save lives and help kids to become healthy and productive adults.

Due to these cuts, Nassau County Youth Board programs across all of Nassau County, including the communities represented here, will close immediately on March 31st.

In total, youth programs service just under 60,000 youth, families and members of the community annually.

Before the looming cuts, Nassau County had more than 40 youth service agencies. These agencies offer hundreds of programs which address issues such as: suicide prevention, homelessness, runaways, drugs addiction, gangs, employment, family crisis, eating disorders, anger management, sexual abuse, physical abuse, teen pregnancy and many more.

At North Shore Child and Family Guidance Center in coordination with our sister agencies across the County, we have been and will continue to ask County Executive Tom Suozzi to reinstate funds to these vital programs that are scheduled to close down on March 31st.

The cuts *will not* save the County money, but will dramatically increase costs to the County, State and taxpayers as increasing numbers of kids will require costly out-of-home institutional placements as front end services disappear. It is estimated that every child who drops out of school becomes a $1.5 million burden on the social services system with entitlements over their lifetime. It is clear that the funds spent on these programs today pay for themselves many times over in the years to come.

During these harsh economic times when all efforts are needed to support vulnerable children and preserve families, these cuts will not only decimate the service system that has been carefully constructed to support them, but will bear an even greater cost in lives lost, kids leaving their homes by choice or force and families splintered and destroyed.

Recently, at the Guidance Center, we were faced with the loss of our drug and alcohol treatment program, a mainstay in the County for two decades. We stood to lose all of almost $350,000 because a clerk with the New York State Office of Alcoholism and Substance Abuse Services drew a line through our budget without the benefit of knowing who we really are, who we serve and how effective we have been for decades. We responded – staff, board members, community activists, youth and parents, many of whom are here this evening – we responded swiftly and strongly. The Commissioner of that State Office that sought to close us down was flooded by phone calls, emails, faxes, and letters and guess what? – the funding was fully restored in a matter of days. Who says you can't fight City Hall?

And now we need to do it again, but this time it is not just for vital services for immigrant youth at the Guidance Center – as our Hispanic Family Life Center is at risk – but this time we need to fight for all youth services across Nassau County.

On each table is a list of people to contact and a simple message. One to Mr. Suozzi that says restore youth services; and one to State legislators that says support new revenue streams to help support youth services.

I ask each of you to commit to contacting at least one of the people on these pages by phone, fax, mail, email or phone. Let your voice be heard. If you have the time to hand write a note and mail or fax it that will be great. Hand written letters carry much weight despite the electronic age we live in. Let your voice be heard and let's demonstrate that Community Unity is more than a slogan but something real, something powerful and something that can truly make a difference.

7
Group work in graduate social work education: Where are we now?

Shirley R. Simon and Teresa Kilbane

Abstract. This paper presents the preliminary results of a national survey assessing the extent of group work offerings within masters level social work programs in the United States. The study replicates and expands upon a 1994 investigation by Birnbaum and Auerbach. Findings are compared with the earlier study to identify changes and trends in group work education.

Key words. group work, social work education; social work methods; generalist social work education; history of social work education in the United States

Introduction

Group work has a long-standing history as a core method within the profession of social work. However, for decades, social group work leaders have expressed serious concerns about group work's diminished place within social work education. Warnings about group work's demise as a distinct modality within social work date at least as far back as 1978, and have become increasingly dire in recent years (Drumm, 2006; Kurland et al., 2004; Middleman, 1990; Simon & Webster, 2009; Tropp, 1978).

The Council on Social Work Education's (CSWE) 1969 decision to merge individual methodological approaches, primarily casework, group work and community organizing, into a single generalist perspective, is often cited as the beginning of the decline of group work within social work education (Goodman & Munoz, 2004; Salmon & Steinberg, 2007). When programs altered their curricula to accommodate this generalist orientation, the number of concentrations and specialized courses in group work declined significantly (Birnbaum & Auerbach, 1994; Goodman & Munoz, 2004; Middleman, 1990; Simon, Webster, & Horn, 2007). (For the purposes of this article, a program is defined as a CSWE accredited MSW degree granting institution. Within these programs, some institutions offer tracks or areas of practice such as clinical/direct practice, administration and/or policy. These tracks may be offered as concentrations or specializations, terms that are sometimes used interchangeably. Both concentrations and specializations typically require specific courses and/or a specific range of courses to be completed. A course is defined as a class or unit of study in the curriculum of the program taken for either one quarter or one semester depending on the institution.)

Unfortunately, this decrease in educational focus has led to a critical disconnect between social group work education and the practice arena, as a resurgent demand for group work services has arisen (Goodman & Munoz, 2004; Strozier, 1997). This demand is often financially motivated based upon the concept that one can treat/service six to ten clients in a group in the same time one can see one or two clients individually. Occurring largely as a result of reimbursement requirements by HMOs, insurance companies and other managed care companies, agencies – even traditionally psychodynamic, one-on-one treatment agencies – are now mandated to offer extensive group work services. Additionally, core areas of client services are increasingly reliant on the effective use of the group work modality. Service providers in the areas of addictions, domestic violence, grief and loss, trauma, the chronically and mentally ill, veterans services, youth and adolescence, immigrants and refugees, lesbian, gay, bisexual and transgender populations, and the elderly are but some of the fields that rely upon group work in order to best help their clients (Garvin, Gutierrez & Galinsky, 2004). However, according to the most recent study of group work offerings in schools of social work, many social workers have graduated without even one course in group work, and many supervisors lack the knowledge and expertise to effectively train students and new professionals (Birnbaum & Auerbach, 1994).

In 1994, Birnbaum & Auerbach published a landmark study on the state of group work education in masters level social work programs in the United States (Birnbaum & Auerbach, 1994). Birnbaum and Auerbach's work was cited in virtually all ensuing publications on U.S. group work education. However, many years had passed, and this critical study had not been replicated. Anecdotal accounts from group work leaders and educators suggested that the situation had only gotten worse, but valid, accurate data had not been collected. Thus, planning and decision-making by social work schools, accrediting bodies, and practitioners were being made without the benefit of current, validated information. Recognizing this void, and with the encouragement of Martin Birnbaum, the lead researcher in the 1994 study, *Group work in graduate social work education: The price of neglect,* (Birnbaum & Auerbach), the authors began work on the replication and expansion of the earlier study in 2008.

Methodology

The current study used Birnbaum and Auerbach's interview guide as its foundation. However, the methodology used by the current authors differs from that used in the previous study. While Birnbaum and Auerbach collected data through phone interviews, the authors developed an online survey adding questions of current interest. Birnbaum and Auerbach's study contained data from phone interviews (N = 80) and course catalogs (N = 9) with a response rate of 92%. Interviewees were group work faculty identified through the 1990 Membership Directory of the Association for the Advancement of Social Work with Groups (AASWG). If there was no AASWG member at the school, additional steps were taken to identify a faculty member or administrator with knowledge about the group work curriculum.
The current study used online methodology to reach the much larger universe of masters level social work programs (N = 200 in 2008 vs. N = 97 in 1991). The online survey was pilot tested by group work instructors from local universities. Once the survey was refined, it was submitted to the Institutional Review Board of the authors' University for approval. The researchers then consulted with the Information Technology department to create the online survey using Opinio, a

University-sanctioned software package. An email with a consent form and a link to the online survey was sent to the deans of all masters level social work programs in the U.S. directly from the dean of the researchers' home school. Emails were distributed to the 200 accredited MSW programs, and deans were requested to forward the email to the faculty or staff members most qualified to respond to questions about group work in their curriculum. Three additional emails were sent to increase the response rate. By June 2009, 59 usable surveys were collected, representing a 30% response rate. Although this response rate falls into an acceptable range (Sheehan, 2001), the researchers plan to continue to collect data through other avenues to increase the number of responses.

Description of current study respondents

Programs in the current study sample are more likely to be found at public universities (*N* = 31, 56%) than at private universities (*N* = 24, 44%). The majority of programs are from non-religiously affiliated universities (*N* = 47, 85%). Two-thirds of the programs are in urban settings (*N* = 37, 67%) with the remainder divided between suburban (*N* = 10, 18%) and rural (*N* = 8, 15%) settings. For almost half of the programs, the primary focus of their curricula is advanced generalist (*N* = 26, 47%) while a third (*N* = 18, 33%) of the programs classify themselves as clinical or direct practice. Only one program identifies itself as having a policy/administrative track and ten programs (18%) have a single track or focus unique to their respective schools. Three quarters of the responding programs have an advanced standing option (*N* = 44, 75%). Half of the programs have their own bachelor's programs (*N* = 31, 52.5%), while only a third have Ph.D. programs (*N* = 20, 34%).

As an indicator of representativeness, the current sample was compared to the findings of the Council on Social Work Education's report, *2008 Statistics on Social Work Education in the United States*. The CSWE survey (*N* = 183, response rate = 96.3%) reported a higher percentage of public institutions (75% vs. 56% in the current study) and a higher percentage of programs offering bachelor degrees in social work (72% vs. 52.5% in the current study). National statistics on the primary locations of the schools were similar to those of the current study (urban, 63%; suburban, 20%; rural, 17% vs. 67%, 18% and 15% in the current study) (Council on Social Work Education, 2008).

The number of enrolled students varies widely because some responding universities have multiple satellite programs. Full-time students range from 24 to 500 (M = 189, Md = 170); part-time students from 0 to 700 (M = 92, Md = 50). Likewise, the number of faculty members varies widely; full-time faculty range from 6 to 80 (M = 19, Md = 17) and part-time faculty from 0 to 90 (M = 21, Md = 12).

Results

This paper presents the preliminary results of the current study as of June, 2009. One of the objectives of the study was to be able to compare current findings with those of the Birnbaum and Auerbach study. Thus, questions similar to those of the earlier study were incorporated in the online survey. Both studies included questions about program concentrations, required and elective courses, and field education in group work. The current study added questions on full-time and part-time MSW faculty expertise in group work, teaching experience, research endeavors, association membership, efforts to link students with professional associations, and use of online technology in group work education.

The Birnbaum and Auerbach study (1994) found a substantial decline in the number of schools offering group work as a concentration in their curriculum – 'from 76% in 1963 to 7% in 1991' (p.329). Nearly two decades later, the current study continues to observe a decline in schools offering a group work concentration – from six schools to four schools. Table 1 lists the schools with a group work concentration, the number of students in each concentration, and the percentage of the student body represented in each school's group work concentration. In addition to a decline in the number of schools offering group work concentrations, the schools that continue to offer a concentration report a drop in the number of students enrolled in their group work concentrations.

The current online survey asked the question: How many courses are offered in your curriculum whose primary focus is group work? Respondents were instructed to answer regardless of whether the course was part of their concentration in group work. Nine responding schools

Table 1
Social work schools with a group work concentration

School	Birnbaum & Auerbach Study Number of students	Birnbaum & Auerbach Study % of All Students	Current Study Number of Students	Current Study % of All Students
Hunter College	90	18	40	20
University of Connecticut	80	30	60	18
Yeshiva University	36	15	18	5
Boston University	30	12	15	5
Washington University	30	20		
Rutgers University	25	10		

Table 2
Required courses, elective courses and field education by program

	Birnbaum & Auerbach (*N* = 89)		Current Study (*N* = 59)	
	n	%	*n*	%
Offer Required Courses	45	50	27	46
Offer Elective Courses	41	46	22	37
One course	27		18	
Two courses	13		1	
Three or more	1		3	
School policy:				
Group experience part of field work	25	34	30	52

(15%) do not offer any such courses in their master's programs, while in the earlier Birnbaum and Auerbach (1994) study only 3 percent of the responding programs did not offer group work courses. With a range of 0 to 6 courses, social work schools offer an average of 1.48 courses (Md = 1.0, *N* = 50) that focus primarily on group work. Each program was allowed to enter up to a maximum of four group work courses in the survey. These 50 schools offer a total of 74 group work courses. Only six of these 74 courses do not contain the word 'group' in their course titles, which seems to support the premise that these courses contain group work content.

Both studies investigated whether the group work courses offered in schools of social work are required and/or elective courses. In the Birnbaum and Auerbach study (1994), half (50%) of the programs offered required courses (see Table 2). In their study, the six schools

(7%) with a concentration in group work required 2 or more group work courses; 12 schools (13%) required one group work course for non-group work concentrations; 10 schools (11%) offered a group work course as a required option within clinical sequences for non-group work concentrations; and 17 schools (19%) required group work courses for all students. In the current study, the percentage of schools requiring group work courses is slightly less, 46% (*N* = 27). The majority (*N* = 14) require a single group work course; eleven programs require two courses and two programs require three or more courses. In the current study, the number of elective courses has decreased: from 46% (*N* = 41) of the programs in the Birnbaum and Auerbach study to 37% (*N* = 22) in the current study. Programs in the earlier study also tended to offer a broader range of elective courses whereas programs in the current study almost exclusively offer only a single elective course (see Table 2). Given the overall decrease in the percentage of programs offering group work courses, it is logical that there would be a decline in the percentage of programs offering required and elective courses. Finally, both studies investigated whether schools had a policy requiring a group work experience in a student's field work placement. Current programs (*N* = 30, 52%) more often formally require group work in the student's field work experience than programs in the past study (*N* = 25, 34%). It should be noted that only schools offering required or elective group work courses were included in this question in the earlier study; programs not offering group work courses were asked not to respond.

The current study also looked at additional factors: whether schools have group work expertise on their faculty, whether their faculty is affiliated with group work professional associations and actively linking and promoting such affiliations among their students, and whether online technology is being used as a method to deliver group work content in the curriculum. Nearly three-quarters (72.0%, *N* = 42) of the programs state that there are full-time faculty members who specialize in group work at their school (see Table 3). Nearly one-half (45.0%, *N* = 26) of the programs have part-time faculty members who specialize in group work. Three-quarters (76.0%, *N* = 32) of the full-time faculty specializing in group work also teach in this area on a regular basis. A much lower percentage of full-time faculty, 31.0% (*N* = 18), conduct research in group work. AASWG is a leading professional organization for social group work educators and practitioners. Twenty-two programs (38.0%) responded that full-time faculty are members of AASWG; another eight programs (14.0%) stated that full-time faculty

Table 3
Number of programs by faculty interest in group work, teaching, research and professional memberships

	n	%	Total
Full-time faculty members who specialize in group work	42	72	58
Full-time faculty who specialize in group work and teach on regular basis	32	76	42
Full-time faculty who conduct research	18	31	58
Full-time faculty members who belong to AASWG	22	38	58
Full-time faculty members who belong to other professional groups	8	14	58
Part-time faculty who specialize in group work	26	45	58
Link students to professional associations	17	30	57

members belong to other groupwork associations. Nearly a third (30.0%, *N* =17) of the programs report supporting a curricular and/or extracurricular effort to link students with professional group work organizations.

The use of technology in teaching has made great strides since the Birnbaum and Auerbach (1994) study. Social work courses are now taught in the traditional face-to-face manner, as hybrid courses that combine face-to-face and online classes, and in a purely online format where there is no formal face-to-face classroom contact between the faculty member and students. Only nine of the 74 required and elective group work courses are taught as a hybrid course; no totally online courses are offered.

Discussion

The number of schools offering a group work concentration had drastically declined when Birnbaum and Auerbach (1994) did their study nearly two decades ago. The percentage of schools offering a group work concentration declined 'from 76% in 1963 to 7% in 1991' (p.329). This trend continues in the current study. The six schools with group work concentrations in the Birnbaum and Auerbach study have now declined to four. In addition, during this time period, the percentage of programs that do *not* offer courses with primary content in group work has increased from 3 to 15 percent. Thus, the current study also demonstrates a decline in the percentage of required and elective courses. When the final results incorporating additional respondents are available, it will be important to note whether these trends remain the same.

A positive change for group work education since the earlier study is the increase in the percentage of schools requiring students to have group work experience as part of their field work placement. This could be a critical change, since it is through field work that students have the opportunity to actually practice their group work skills. However, only half of the responding schools state that they typically enforce this requirement.

While online education was not a consideration when Birnbaum and Auerbach conducted their study, it is now an increasingly important offering within higher education. During the 2006-07 academic year, there were an estimated 12.2 million enrollments in college-level credit granting distance education courses with 77% of enrollments in online courses, 12% in hybrid/blended online courses, and 10% in other types of distance education courses (U.S. Department of Education, National Center for Education Statistics, 2008). Given this rapid growth, it is important to consider group work education's response to this trend. With only nine out of a total of 74 group work courses in the current survey taught in a hybrid online format, and none at all taught in a purely online format, one must raise the question of whether group work education is sufficiently embracing this newer modality of education. While there are legitimate questions about the effectiveness of non face-to-face group work education, it seems an important avenue for further exploration (Simon & Stauber, 2009).

The current survey requested respondents' comments regarding the trends and changes in group work education since the Birnbaum and Auerbach study (1994). The comments indicate that some schools have actually introduced group work courses or group work content within the last few years. Other schools have reduced the number of courses due to limited resources. Many schools indicate that they chose to place more emphasis on the infusion of group work content into integrated courses rather than offering separate group-focused courses. Since the current study's instruction was to list only courses whose primary focus was group work, the study's ability to capture group work content in infused courses was limited. Another influential factor in the offering of group work courses and content is the importance of having a faculty member committed to group work. Some respondents stated that the retirement of a dedicated group work faculty member led to a decline in the emphasis on group work within the school. The absence of a strong voice for group work content and the aging of a large cadre of group work's spokespersons have been cited as significant concerns for the survival of group work as a strong modality within social work (Simon, Webster & Horn, 2007).

Limitations

The preliminary findings presented here are tentative and require more in-depth analysis. At this time the current study has a somewhat low response rate and plans are underway to increase the number of completed surveys. The authors are preparing to file an amendment with their university's Institutional Review Board to allow them to directly contact non-responding schools to ascertain the name and contact information of the faculty member or administrator with group work expertise. These identified contacts will then be sent an email introducing the study with a link to the survey. Next, for schools who still do not respond, basic data will be collected from the school's website description of their master's programs.

The authors also understand that while the online survey format may be convenient, its length and detail may have inhibited some respondents from finishing the survey. Many surveys were opened using the online link but not completed. Conversely, schools with committed group work faculty or group work offerings might be more likely to complete the survey and, therefore, skew the results. Finally, the current survey does not give a complete picture of group work offerings since the content of infused courses was not addressed. Such courses contain group work content, but the relative extent and depth of its focus as compared to other areas of course content is not addressed in this survey.

Conclusion

The preliminary results of this study indicate a loss of two programs offering a concentration in group work since the 1994 study, bringing the total number of schools currently offering a group work concentration to four. In addition, the percentage of required and elective group work courses continues to decline. On the other hand, the current study does demonstrate a change toward more schools including a group work requirement in the student's field work experience. It remains to be seen whether these trends will continue when the final results are tabulated. Having a clearer picture of the educational landscape with regard to group work offerings in master's level social work programs is an essential first step in making appropriate curricular and extracurricular decisions. The authors hope that the final results of this study will provide useful knowledge for making these critical decisions and will stimulate increased professional dialogue and collaborative action among group work educators, AASWG members, and schools of social work regarding the future of group work education.

References

Birnbaum, M.L. & Auerbach, C. (1994). Group work in graduate social work education: The price of neglect. *Journal of Social Work Education, 36*(2), 347-356.

Council on Social Work Education (2008). *2008 Statistics on social work education in the United States*. Retrieved December 17, 2010, from http://

www.cswe.org/CentersInitiatives/DataStatistics/ProgramData/44876.aspx

Drumm, K. (2006). The essential power of group work. *Social Work with Groups, 29*(2), 17-31.

Garvin, C., Gutierrez, L. & Galinsky, M. (Eds.) (2004). *Handbook of social work with groups.* New York and London: The Guilford Press.

Goodman, H. & Munoz, M. (2004). Developing social group work skills for contemporary agency practice. *Social Work with Groups, 27*(1), 17-33.

Kurland, R., Salmon, R., Bitel, M., Goodman, H., Ludwig, K., Newmann, E., et al. (2004). The survival of social group work: A call to action. *Social Work with Groups, 27*(1), 3-16.

Middleman, R. (1990). Group work and the Heimlich maneuver: Unchoking social work education. In D.F. Fike and B. Rittner (Eds.), *Working from strengths: The essence of group work.* Miami: Center for Group Work Studies, 16-39.

Sheehan, K.B. (2001) Email survey response rates. *Journal of Computer MediatedCommunication, 6*(2). Retrieved April 19, 2011, from http://jcmc.indiana.edu/vol6/issue2/sheehan.html

Simon, S.R. & Webster, J.A. (2009). Struggle for survival. In A. Gitterman & R. Salmon (Eds.), *Encyclopedia of social work with groups.* New York, NY: Routledge, 33-38.

Simon, S.R., Webster, J. & Horn, K. (2007). A critical call for connecting students and professional organizations. *Social Work with Groups: A Journal of Community and Clinical Practice, 30*(4), 5-19.

Simon, S.R. & Stauber, K.W. (2009). Group work and technology: Embracing our future. Plenary Address, 31st Annual International Symposium of the Association for the Advancement of Social Work with Groups, Chicago, IL.

Strozier, A.L. (1997). Group work in social work education: What is being taught? *Social Work with Groups 20*(1), 65-77.

U.S. Department of Education, National Center for Education Statistics. (2008). *Distance education at degree-granting postsecondary institutions: 2006-07.* Retrieved January 8, 2011 from http://nces.ed.gov/fastfacts/display.asp?id=80.

8
Global group work: Honouring processes and outcomes

Carol S. Cohen, Mark Doel, Mary Wilson, Deirdre Quirke, Karen A. Ring and Sharima Ruwaida Abbas

Abstract: This chapter focuses on the *Global Group Work Project's* action research study to explore and identify essential cross-national and cross-cultural elements of social group work practice, and to provide a model for international research and collaboration. It details study methods, process and outcome findings, analysis and recommendations. The key finding of the global themes of *being together* and *doing together* in social work groups, as well as the identification of local, indigenous practices contribute empirical knowledge about group work's international nature, with implications for teaching, research and practice.

This chapter is based on the Sumner Gill Memorial Plenary Address 31st Annual International Symposium Association for the Advancement of Social Work with Groups, Chicago, Illinois, June 27th, 2009

Key words: group work (groupwork), international social work, action research, collaboration, being together, doing together

---

Editors' note: This multi-authored paper contains stylistic variations in word choice, spelling, and quotation styles which reflect cultural differences among its authors. These variations parallel the themes of the paper.

Introduction

On June 27, 2009, we had the great pleasure of being together with our AASWG community, and were very proud to deliver the Sumner Gill Memorial Lecture at the 31st International Symposium on Social Work with Groups. Jean Gill described her husband, Sumner Gill, as a highly intelligent, loving and compassionate man. Through this presentation, it was our hope to honor his legacy.

The focus of our paper is the *Global Group Work Project's* action research study to explore and identify essential cross-national and cross-cultural elements of social group work practice, and to expand international networking. This paper includes the content of our presentation, and places the *Project* in the context of international social work and group work. We believe that our findings concerning important local practices and global features contribute empirical knowledge about group work's international nature, with implications for teaching, research and practice.

We begin with pride and belief in group work as a central methodology in the social work profession. The scholarly literature and daily experience of group participants suggest that members and their communities desire the connections promised by collective experiences of social work groups, and that group membership appears central to human experience. Reports of group experience across nations and cultures suggest that a social work group can serve as a *reservoir of power resources where individual participants can get help and receive support.* (Hirayama & Hirayama, 1986, p.124). Over 50 years ago, Lewis Lowy observed that *individuals want to gain satisfactions from group participation; they want to learn and to feel that they are part of a larger whole to which they can make a personal contribution* (1955, p.62). As an enterprise of mutual aid, William Schwartz (1971) placed the source of growth and social action through groups in the membership, and with its dual focus on individuals and communities (Cohen, 2002), group work demonstrates application as a tool of social inclusion (Wilson & Quirke, 2005). In these many respects we can talk meaningfully of *the essential groupworker* (Doel & Sawdon, 2001).

However, while the power of groups is indisputable, there has not been large scale research and international collaboration to study local variations and universal themes in diverse contexts, until the *Global Group Work Project,* founded in 2005, undertook this challenge. The *Project's* overall mission is to advance social group work knowledge, education and practice internationally through research, dissemination and collaborative development of globally and locally meaningful group work strategies. Within this context, the international partners of the *Global Group Work Project* recently completed a three-year action research project, funded by the International Association of Schools of Social Work and supported by the Association for the Advancement of Social Work with Groups. Our dual purpose was to:

1. Explore and identify 'global' (universally essential) concepts and practices and 'local' (geographically and/or culturally important) concepts and practices; and
2. Facilitate international networking and collaboration in group-based research and practice methods.

This paper presents the rationale, process, methods, findings, implications, recommendations and future directions of the *Global Group Work Research Project.* Our research methods, including cross-cultural facilitation and data collection from small deliberation groups at a wide range of international venues, have found essential common elements and sophisticated differences in the practice of group work. We also highlight the parallel process between the dynamics of our partner group conducting the study, and the experiences of the respondent groups. The study strongly suggests that exploring the interface of global and local elements of groups serves to broaden thinking about teaching and practicing with groups, and has implications for international research. We invite you to approach our *Project* from your own perspectives, and to join international networks developed through the *Project.* We anticipate that this paper will spark thinking about practice, education and research that is useful both locally and internationally.

International social work

At this point, it is important to place the *Global Group Work Project* in the context of international social work, and address three key contemporary concepts, drawn largely from the work of Mel Gray and her colleagues: Universalism, Imperialism and Indigenization (Gray,

2005; Gray & Fook, 2004; Gray & Webb, 2008). Universalism relates to the trend of colonization of global social work practice by western, developed countries. Over the last 100 years, many leaders from North America and Western Europe held the view that social work practice and education was based on a single, common set of principles and practices, regardless of location around the world. Imperialism in social work is a related concept, exemplified by western social work professionals promoting only their dominant world views over diverse, local perspectives. This oppressive practice assumes that there is only one way to practice, which should be applied universally around the world.

Indigenization refers to understanding international social work by working with people 'where they are' and seeking to understand locally developed and syntonic practices, goals and values that are rooted in the environment. For example, social work practice and education in Malaysia has been greatly influenced by western social work ideology, but social workers there are earnestly trying to learn and incorporate local perspectives that have emerged in the course of community work, and then integrate those values into local social work curricula.

The *Global Group Work Project's* goals are closely aligned with indigenization, and the theme of the 31st AASWG Symposium. 'Honoring our Roots' in this context means learning from the experience of others, broadening global social work development to include all local voices and local responsibility. We are committed to working vigilantly towards anti-universalist, anti-imperialist, and pro-indigenous approaches, by which we can acknowledge and honor both global similarities and local differences. We envision *Global Group Work* as a bridge, a connection that provides a flexible framework for sharing multiple international perspectives.

Methodology

A framing belief of the *Global Group Work Project* is that research is done *with* people – rather than *on* people. Our methods are rooted in group work, including both the organization and process of our research team, and the methods of collecting data and analysing findings. Action research, the qualitative methodology used in this study, is a form of inquiry through which participants reflect systematically on their practice as a means of contributing new knowledge, and researchers adjust the study protocols accordingly as they move forward. It is practitioner-based, collaborative and cooperative. Action research has been historically linked with working with people who were seeking social change (Garvin et al., 2004). This participatory approach acknowledges potential power differentials in research methodology and enables joint exploration of theoretical knowledge and knowledge from practice and experience (O'Brien, 1998; Healy, 2001). Other types of action research include community-based, feminist, action learning, and empowerment evaluation, which vary according to the functions of the participants and researchers and the ways in which the goals of the research process are achieved. (Alliance, 2010).

The participatory action research cycle of planning, acting, observing, reflecting and revising throughout the data gathering process gives participants and researchers opportunities for open discussions, group identification, and sharing information and experiences (O'Brien, 1998). Jacobson and Rugeley (2007) conceptualize participatory research as social justice-oriented group work in their discussion about their USDA funded project, *Finding Solutions to Food Insecurity.* This orientation connects to knowledge development, education and informed action. They emphasize the social work profession's 'rich heritage of social investigation that includes participatory research practices,' and trace this history to Jane Addams, calling the research method 'fundamentally a group work process.' (pp.24-25). Another example from the social group work world is the Wakefield Project, which sought both to establish a major group work service in participation with large groups of practitioners and to evaluate the process as it unfolded (Doel and Sawdon, 2001)

Through the development of the research methodology, the international *Global Group Work* research team encountered some interesting differences lying beneath commonly used terms. We consider the research team's processes in more detail later, but the differences in the interpretation of *action research* are illustrative of our general theme. For some in the team, *action research* was synonymous with *participatory research,* while for others the term action research was a more specific term in which the research itself changes the social reality (Shaw et al., 2010), and those who do the research also do the action (Dick, 2007). These differences – in the interpretation of *action research* – are not in themselves problematic as long as they are made explicit, as they were with the *Global Group Work* team; it is when there are implicit assumptions of sameness that difficulties can arise.

The qualitative study conducted by the *Global Group Work* partners obtained information predominantly from social group work practitioners and educators, along with other social work and human service professionals, at ten social work conferences and convenings over a three year period (2006-2008). Sessions took place in Germany, Italy, South Africa, Trinidad and Tobago, the United Kingdom and the United States. As the following Table indicates, the number of facilitators ranged from 1-5 and participants from 5-50.

Table 1
Global Group Work workshop venues

1. 27th International Symposium of AASWG, Oct. 2005 (Minneapolis, US); Facilitators: 3; Participants: 30
2. 28th International Symposium of AASWG, Oct. 2006 (San Diego, US); Facilitators: 3; Participants: 20
3. Mental Health Committee of DPINGO Affiliates to the United Nations, March, 2007 (New York City, US); Facilitators: 2; Participants: 20
4. Conference of European Schools of Social Work, IASSW & IFSW, March, 2007, (Parma, Italy); Facilitators: 3; Participants: 7
5. 50th Anniversary Conference of Wurzweiler School of Social Work, May 2007, (New York City, US); Facilitators: 1; Participants: 5
6. 29th International Symposium of AASWG, June, 2007 (Jersey City, US); Facilitators: 3; Participants: 20
7. Association of Caribbean Social Work Educators Conference, June, 2007 (Port-of-Spain, Trinidad and Tobago); Facilitators: 1; Participants: 11
8. European Groupwork Symposium, September, 2007 (York, England); Facilitators: 3; Participants: 20
9. 30th International Symposium of AASWG, June, 2008 (Cologne/Koln, Germany); Facilitators: 6; Participants: 50
10. 34th Biennial Congress of IASSW, July, 2008 (Durban, South Africa); Facilitators: 5; Participants: 22

The research participants were recruited through a convenience, opportunistic sample, with the participants making a choice to attend the workshop described in their conference programs or organizational invitations. Ethical issues and standards of the study were addressed through the Adelphi University (New York) Institutional Review Board.

According to O'Brien (1998), one principle of action research is the dialectical critique, where the social reality of those involved is shared through language and through dialogue; elements are seen in relationship to one another or in opposition to one another. A second principle is that participants are co-researchers and 'each person's ideas are equally significant as potential resources for creating interpretive categories of analysis, negotiated among the participants' (p.6). Some of these core principles of action research can be identified in the administration of our research. For example, we collected the data for this study in structured workshops using small group variations and exercises framed by opening and closing activities. Most sessions began with asking each participant to contribute a word that encapsulated their experience of social group work. After sharing these words in a variety of languages, participants engaged in an activity to identify the people in the room that were most geographically distant from them. Through this process, trios of participants formed and deliberated on items they thought were essential in their group work practice. The trios were asked to identify common or possibly global elements (those that everyone agreed upon) and unique or possibly local elements (those that were not shared, but thought important by at least one group member). Then, combining into second-level, larger groups of 6 or 9 members, participants were asked to reconcile their lists of local and global elements, and put together a new list of common and unique elements from those originally identified. Finally, with all participants back in a single group, we asked the second-level groups to share their lists, and all participants to collectively reflect on the process and engage in a closing activity. Following the session, the lists were inventoried and analyzed, and qualitative findings of the workshops' content and processes were examined for similar and dissimilar themes.

In addition to the structured workshops for data collection and analysis, narratives by individual group facilitators were written to record their reflections on the sessions. This documentation of the parallel process provided another source of data, informing and enriching both the content and the process of the research study. This process further illustrates the 'reflecting' phase of the participatory action model (O'Brien, 1998).

Some of the limitations of the study were the varying levels of expertise and experiences of the participants, and that most of the workshops were presented in English only, although participants used their language of choice in the word exercise of the opening activity. Lastly, as mentioned earlier, the participants were self-selected, and had the opportunity and resources to choose to attend a conference or organizational meeting.

Process findings and analysis

In this section, we focus on the narratives of the research process, and share how the process of the research yielded rich and sometimes unanticipated findings. As already mentioned, at the beginning of each workshop participants were asked to contribute one word that captured what group work meant to them. The word was reviewed and sometimes changed by the same participant at the end of the session. This activity acted as an ice-breaker and a bench mark for identifying outcomes. We felt that it was important to encourage participants to use a word in the language of their choice. This was also a way of engaging participants in the process of recognizing commonalities and differences.

It was essential, we believe, to spend time at the beginning of the session to give information about the research and to summarise the work undertaken to date. We believe that the first point of contact with the group must include an exercise in clarifying values. Not only is this good group work, but it also provides an opportunity for discussion about ethical issues that arise in the research. Participants were made aware that they would have an experience of group work, while also contributing as subjects in the research. In some instances this was different than their original expectations of a didactic presentation, and participants had the choice to remain or leave in light of this information. No participants left the session after this orientation to the session.

Participants in the workshops were mostly social workers, and some did not consider themselves group workers. It was important to afford them the opportunity to choose their point of entry into the research process. As a result, we found that participants at group work symposia engaged most readily with the data gathering process. Subjects from non-group work traditions had different expectations and therefore needed more time and active facilitation to encourage their participation in the data gathering process.

We found that sequencing was an important factor in promoting engagement with the research process while providing a positive group work experience for participants. In terms of timing, we found that the workshop was most useful in promoting international networking if scheduled towards the beginning of the programme, since the workshop served to build group relationships and effectively set the scene for engagement with the conference overall. Another finding concerned the process of conducting the research within a limited time in a conference programme. We know that the time constraints were often a concern to participants, and we continue to explore the question of the extent to which it had an impact on the quality of the work undertaken and the depth of the findings.

While not explicitly instructed to do so, participants often shared their educational background in social work. It appeared that course content is influenced by national traditions which reinforce the dominance of a particular social construction of reality. This determines the range of social work practice interventions taught and ultimately has an impact on constructing dominant forms of service delivery. For example, in the United States, where group work is most often delivered as an integral part of social work education and training, the findings showed that it became part of participants' skills sets. In contrast, in the European Union, group work tends to be viewed as a specialism, unique, and standing alone; it was also sometimes available as a separate and additional qualification, usually at post qualifying level. Another issue that arose through workshop discussion concerned the process of constructing professional identities, and who is responsible for their definition. Participants shared diverse experiences of the roles played by educational institutions, professional associations, work contexts and self-perceptions in the formation of their professional identities.

The workshops also provided extensive data regarding how needs are articulated and how group interventions are framed in the field. The research found that responses, and perhaps world-views of respondents, tended to be more individual (as in *membership criteria* and *every group is different*) or more collective (as in *network* and *relationship*). Descriptions of interventions appeared to be influenced by dominant discourses (as in *social justice, cultural diversity,* and *professional leadership*), and thus determined the range and possibility of social work practice interventions.

In all of the venues/contexts in which the research was carried out, English was the principal language used. Where it was not the first language of most participants, translation facilitated the process of data gathering. Regarding *Global Group Work* workshops in the European Union, the language of communication was English and this was made clear at the outset, but informal (Parma) and formal translation (Cologne) was used. In Cologne, one young American commented (in wonderment) on this experience in the workshop with the remark:

This is the first time I've been translated! We feel that we could have done more in inviting the use of other languages, especially in the US, where there was little formal recognition given to other languages. The AASWG also appears to be increasingly aware and concerned about this phenomenon, moving to a more inclusive approach to languages.

Facilitation was a key issue throughout the research process as both a means and method of conducting the research. Facilitation between the various 'actors' (i.e. the *Global Group Work* partners) engaging in data collection in a variety of locations, required ongoing reflective dialogue for critical review and revision. In order to maintain coherence it was necessary to accommodate the diversity of facilitation styles while processing the needs arising from the research participants. Facilitation of ten workshops, with a range of partners and participants required creative responses from the research team to ensure that those engaged in conducting the research did so in keeping with the overall aims and objectives of the project. This also required reflection post-group and ongoing consultation by telephone and email.

In workshop sessions where participants designated themselves as social workers/social pedagogues, their approach to the research process included an interrogation of the researchers about process and outcomes. Questions posed to us included: *how do you think it went?, how did we do?,* and *what do you think?* Participants asked for feedback and evaluation on performance, and in this process engaged the researchers in dialogue. This changed the dynamic of our roles from outsiders to insiders and required more active facilitation. In contrast, when participants identified themselves as group workers, a different facet of group behavior was apparent. Participants actively engaged with the task from the outset and 'knew' how the process would unfold. They were in a position to trust the process and just got on with it! In terms of roles, the researchers remained on the outside of these groups and participants took increasing ownership of the research process. This difference at this level was summarized by the comment: *One word is not enough for me! I could own all those words* [on the wall]; *they all belong to me.*

Outcome findings and analysis of common and unique aspects of *global group work*

As already demonstrated, our research findings include data regarding the process of group facilitation, small group dynamics, decision making strategies, worker orientations, environmental constructs and group research development, in addition to data regarding our central questions about global similarities and differences in social work with groups. Clearly, we found more than we were explicitly looking for, and much more than we expected. This section focuses on specific findings related to deliberations of the small groups in itemizing common and unique qualities of social group work.

In order to set the stage, a brief review of the process of small group deliberation is useful. As we have already described, after individually sharing an opening word in one's own language to characterise group work, participants formed the most geographically diverse trios possible. In the trios, members shared what was essential in their practice of social group work and most of the identified items fell in categories of strategies, skills, interventions, techniques. At the first level of the trio, participants agreed on what was common and different among them. Three examples of the lists made by trios of common elements are:

> Example A: *Working with conflict, Fun, Purpose is critical, Experience being 'the other'*
> Example B: *Group works itself, Members giving and accepting feedback, Emotional release*
> Example C: *Use of activity, Education as part of group work, Keeping numbers manageable*

In the next stage, when two groups (or sometimes, three) combined for a group of six or more, they were charged with reconciling their lists by consensus. At that level, few items were considered common after the reconciliation process, and those that were listed as common and essential to all group work practice were primarily those that we identified as values or meta-themes, such as *passion for groups, social change, group as microcosm, understanding culture and context, activity* and *mutuality and relationship.* In our analysis, we looked first at items that we categorized as strategies and techniques (such as *working through conflict, releasing emotions, sharing experiences,* and *keeping numbers manageable*. We examined which of these items remained on the lists of combined groups through the deliberation process, and then, we examined combined lists from all ten study sites.

What remained after this process of analysis is perhaps quite surprising. Some of our most commonly used strategies did not survive this full reconciliation process. Altogether, the respondents ultimately did not reach consensus around a single items of strategy or technique, and did not identify any such items as universal. Some may find this disturbing, and our *Global Group Work* team continues to consider this finding in the context of our research process. There are multiple interpretations for this outcome, including possible limitations of the research design. However, in addition to considering such limitations, we interpret this outcome largely as a positive sign of the great diversity in group work internationally and cross-culturally. We found that at the level of strategies and techniques, respondents did not agree on the universality of a specific set of skills, and we see this as an important reminder to work towards non-imperialistic and non-universalistic practice.

As noted earlier, while there were no single items of universal agreement, there were items that appeared in numerous reports by the workshop groups. Based on this, our research team made the decision to look at those items, especially meta-themes or values that were identified frequently, but not universally. After reviewing these items, we have attempted to identify broader concepts that encompass the frequently identified qualities. Through this extensive review process, we propose the following two common cross-national and cross-cultural themes: *Being Together* and *Doing Together*.

The first common, global theme, *Being Together*, suggests a sense of belonging to a group, building on ideas about group membership as a context of life. *Being Together* also accommodates ideas about the differences among members and between groups and cultures, and includes strategies related to mechanisms to facilitate joining the group and connecting members with each other and the group as a whole. The second theme, *Doing Together*, is also related to group participation as a part of life, through action undertaken in the group. *Doing Together* does not mean that members do the same thing at the same time (although they may), and focuses on members acting in ways that are related, but not necessarily simultaneous or synchronous. Concepts and strategies of activity in group work are included in this theme, as well as strategies that relate to what our team sees as *interplay*, or the inter-relational aspects of action and activity in the group.

In order to explain these themes further, it may be helpful to look at two widely held concepts that were not identified as universal in our study. First is the initial strategy of *establishment of a collective purpose,* a near-sacred concept in North America. We contend that *establishment of a collective purpose* is a critical, but ultimately local strategy for helping groups to coalesce and *be together* in geographic or cultural contexts where individualism is a predominant ideology. In contrast, in places where there is a predominantly collective oriented culture, the group work strategy of *helping members find their own voice* is seen as a very important local (but not universal) concept in the early phase of group formation. These examples highlight the importance for all of us to look beyond our cherished strategies, and to step back and consider the processes we hope they will set into motion. Globally, we believe that each locale and culture develops a particular set of skills that best meet the needs of members and specific communities. We recognize and share the difficulty in reconceptualizing our skill sets as local or indigenous strategies to actualize *Being and Doing Together* in groups, yet that is what our study and the current literature in international social work suggests.

Observation, analysis and narrative of the parallel process

In this section, we focus on the parallel process that we have experienced as a result of our ongoing involvement in the *Global Group Work Project.* We begin by noting that we are often asked a set of similar questions in the many locations in which the research has been conducted. They are as follows:

- How did such a diverse group of people/facilitators come together?
- Is it possible to identify and reflect upon the parallel processes at work?
- How do we continue to develop and sustain ourselves over such a long period?
- Can we capture and share the narrative of the group research process in action?

Some of us met initially at the annual Symposium of the AASWG in Denver, Colorado in 1999. We found ourselves together enjoying, in what later became one of our mantras, *professional fun.* From this genesis of conviviality, the decision to work together was taken and our group expanded over the next few years. This process encapsulates the essential elements from the findings, that of *Being and Doing Together.*

Regarding the second question, the possibility and efficacy of looking at the parallel process, we feel that our research team reflects many of the process and outcome themes found in the small groups in the workshops. Our stated purpose was to contribute to international group work research in order to profile and reclaim social group work's role as a principal method of social work for education, training and intervention. Participants engaged in a single workshop event in which the processes of giving and receiving became integral components of the experience in keeping with the ethical perspectives of the research team. Just as the workshop groups discovered their strengths, our research team discovered that our strengths, values and different styles of working were significant in accomplishing our tasks and building cohesion. We found that there needed to be a *fit* between how we practiced as group workers and how we carried out the research. Good group work practice became a focus and the means by which we continued to organize and deliver the research process. The reflective component dictated by participative action research posed challenges to the cohesiveness and creativity of the research group, while remaining central to shaping *what, why and how* to achieve the objectives of the *Global Groupwork Project.*

The development and sustainment of our group merits further discussion. In addition to the enjoyment that we gained from being together, it emerged very early that we held shared values, briefly summarized as a commitment to social justice and inclusion. We have a shared view of social work as having a responsibility to challenge dominant discourses, and give voice to alternative voices. This perspective is predicated on the notion of on-going professional development and the valuing of lifelong learning in the personal, professional and global spheres.

Group composition is an important element in the success of the *Global Group Work Project* research team. In order to understand this we believe that it is necessary to identify some commonalities binding the group. All members of the group are members of AASWG, and a majority have presented and attended its Annual Symposia, thus fostering the connections for the collaboration. All members of the group are professionally qualified social workers. Areas of practice represented by members cover a wide diversity of contexts in the non-governmental and statutory sectors, including learning disability, family support, children services, youth and community work. All members of the project are also social work educators and trainers. We share a belief in the importance of group work as a method of social work education which we promulgate in our teaching, practice and research.

The research has contributed to an expansion of our world reach and we have become globetrotters as a result. The opportunities to carry out the research in a variety of locations and contexts around the world gave us permission to travel and, therefore, direct opportunities for critical dialogue and reflection with others. We believe this process is central to developing the discourse of international social group work practice. An outcome from these experiences is an enhanced national and international profile of research group members, significant in this era of greater scrutiny and accountability.

The challenges inherent in collaborative ways of working (*doing together*), informed new ways of being and doing for the researchers. The collaboration paradigm that emerged required on-going communication and assigning equal value to process and outcome. In the doing we re-discovered an 'old' model based on parity of esteem, working to strengths and valuing diversity, dynamics that were modelled in our approaches to the research populations. In our experience, cultural and other differences that are apparent, such a skin color or religious affiliation, appear to be relatively easy to recognize and accommodate. With less obvious cultural differences, the possibility for conflict, miscommunication and misunderstanding is greater. These subtle differences were often evident in our use of an apparently *common language* (such as with the meaning of *action research* described earlier), and we made a concerted effort to seek clarification when the need arose. We had a strong commitment to parity of esteem in honouring the various dialects in the process.

Power is a constant issue in collaboration and requires on-going interrogation. In any collaborative endeavor, there will be differences in terms of leadership styles, power, culture, roles and responsibilities, communication and the ways in which conflict and uncertainty are managed. The most obvious differences are that members of the research group come from different countries and continents, cultures, religions and ethnic backgrounds. We have been asked: *What are the implications, benefits and challenges of working in this diverse group?* In response, we can report that it was up to us to choose to ignore or explore our differences. We chose dialogue and critical conversations about our own experience as a research team – debriefing, immersing ourselves in post-workshop reflective writing, mutual exchange, and new dialogue though technological media as well as face-to-face.

This process enabled us to build and sustain the research group while fostering adherence to our core values. One of our central practice issues is how to build trust between people who have not previously worked together. In order to be inclusive and encourage new ideas some prior knowledge and experience of being "other" is an important factor in the decision to co-work, as is being able to accommodate difference in leadership style. The value of bringing these ingredients and skills together is that new possibilities and networks result. Risk taking was a necessary part of this process. From it we found a community of interest and care. Through sharing our vision we experienced the support to examine, understand and overcome conflict and difference. This proved to be a valuable experience for facilitation and has enabled us to make a 'grounded' contribution to scholarship, knowledge building and practice wisdom. In essence, we charted new ways of *being and doing together.*

Implications and recommendations from the *Global Group Work Project*

In this section, we look at the implications of the research in three areas: Practice, Education and Research. Regarding group work practice, our study findings raise the central question of: *What is a group worker?* The diverse responses from the *Global Group Work* workshops suggest that there is not one, single method of defining or practicing group work, nor a single group work identity. The research also has implications for how group work practice should and could be supervised. Participants reported highly divergent supervisory practices, ranging from nothing at all to mentoring and co-working, suggesting both informal and formal supervision as an area for further inquiry and development. Our research indicates that we need to ensure that the forms of supervision are indigenous, while honouring our roots and beliefs about group work supervision. In addition, the findings direct our attention to question what peer support could be available for the supervisors as well.

Also, coming from our qualitative analysis of the data, comes the notion that group work practice has something important to contribute to ideas about *social capital*, highlighting social group work's potential to bring communities together, in which the sum of the whole is greater than the parts. This is not a new idea in social work, and the group work contribution to social justice and change merits further attention.

We have earlier emphasised the importance of local context. Our analysis suggests exploring this context at an even more localised level – that of individual organizations and institutions. Questions along this line of inquiry include:

- What role can we play in helping make organizations become more responsive to group work?
- How can we influence the way group work is perceived by social work educators, by the agencies in which social work placements occur, and more widely in the local cultural context?
- How is group work perceived by students and practitioners – as core or an add on?
- How can we reveal and highlight group work's relevance to other activities, such as teamwork, classwork, social and family groups, etc.?
- Are there prospects for some kind of international licensure? (Perhaps it could be based on the AASWG group work standards?)
- Can any international quality standards be relevant across countries and cultures, given the findings of this study?

Regarding group work education, the research findings raise questions about the level at which group work enters the social work curriculum. Specific findings and the process of workshop deliberations suggest the need to think further about what is needed, and where group work education and training might best appear in the social work curriculum. Of critical importance is the need to further examine the interplay between class-based and field-based teaching and learning. We wonder if there are prospects for international collaboration at the educational level (an international group work course and award, for example), and ways to enhance continuing professional development in group work.

Regarding future research, this *Project* suggests that there is a strong need to move from *anecdote* to *archive*; that is, to build on existing good practice and find systematic ways to publicise the experience of group workers and members (such as the group work portfolios of practice reported in Doel, 2006). Anecdotal knowledge enriches practice wisdom; whilst this can be of great value, it is accessible to relatively few. In order to broaden global accessibility, it will be important to find ways to *archive*, or collect it into something like an open access, international portfolio that expands knowledge whilst respecting confidentiality.

A number of recommendations emerge from this research. First, the *Global Group Work Project* is committed to help in the process of systematic archiving and dissemination of our knowledge of group work practice. The web, including our page at www.AASWG.org, is an important part in this effort, where we have the potential to post data about *Global Group Work* research, and local partner activities. We will be launching the *Global Group Work Network*, with an international list to promote collaboration, share news of projects, and campaign for group work and the development of its global evidence base.

Second, there is a need for further cross-national, cross-cultural study to develop and refine the findings from this first *Project.* This next phase of work will include the encouragement and dissemination of international reports of group work in action internationally, and opportunities to assess how the concepts of *being together* and *doing together* serve in a process of cross-national, cross-cultural analysis and knowledge sharing. Third, in the area of education and training, we recommend the development of cross-national group work education modules, which could draw from an expanded collection of literature on international group work, and be used in academic, workplace, and continuing education settings.

Finally, we recommend publishing more cross-national group work articles in peer-reviewed journals, since there are remarkably few of these involving people across countries. As evidence, an analysis of the authorship of articles in *Groupwork* journal between 2000-2009 showed that none of the 51 co-authored articles in this period had authors from different countries (Editorial, 19.3). In general, we wish to encourage and facilitate cross-national and cross-cultural collaboration.

Conclusion

In bringing this presentation and paper to a close, we wish to thank the people (over 200) who participated in the *Global Group Work* workshops – without them this research would have been impossible. We also want to acknowledge our colleagues Roni Berger, who co-facilitated the first workshop, and Carol Irrizary and Ingrun Masenek, who have been partners in the *Global Group Work Project.* The International Association of Schools of Social Work funded this *Project* through its small grant program and the Association for the Advancement of Social Work with Groups has been a consistent and early supporter of this effort.

The work of the *Global Group Work Project* is ongoing, and through this research we have begun to build a network of practitioners and educators who are committed to the diversity and power of group work internationally. Our study has taught us about working in a group through an extraordinary *in vivo* experience, and has reminded us to stay open and flexible in our relationships with others, in collaborative research, and in practice. Whatever we have accomplished, it has come by *being together* and *doing together.* Our charge, to expand group work practice internationally with an expanded knowledge base of local and global elements, is ambitious; we know it is shared by many.

References

AASWG (2005). *Standards for social work with groups.* (2nd ed.) Association for the Advancement of Social Work with Groups. Retrieved April 12, 2010 from: http://www.aaswg.org

Alliance (2010). *Factsheets: Models of participatory research.* Retrieved November 12, 2010 from *http://www.svfreenyc.org/media/factsheets/fsht_119.pdf*

Cohen, C.S. (2002). Putting principles into practice: Strategies for successful social work practice. In: M.O. Zubiri & J.H. Aristu (Eds.), *Trabajo social: Cuestiones sobre el que y el como.* Zaragoza, Spain: Libros Certeza.

CSWE (2008). *Education policy and accreditation standards.* Council on

Social Work Education. Retrieved February 12, 2010, from http://www.cswe.org/NR/rdonlyres/2A81732E-1776-4175-AC42-65974E96BE66/0/2008EducationalPolicyandAccreditationStandards.pdf

Dick, B. (2007) Action research as an enhancement of natural problem solving. *International Journal of Action Research, 3*, 149-167.

Doel, M. & Sawdon, C. (2001). *The essential groupworker: Teaching and learning creative groupwork.* (2nd ed.) London, Philadelphia: Jessica Kingsley.

Doel, M. (2006). *Using groupwork.* Abingdon, Oxon: Routledge.

Garvin, C.D., Gutiérrez, L.M. and Galinsky, M.J. (2004). *Handbook of social work with groups.* New York: Guilford.

Gray, M. (2005). Dilemmas of international social work: Paradoxical processes in indigenisation, universalism and imperialism. *International Journal of Social Welfare, 14*, 231-238.

Gray, M. & Fook, J. (2004). The quest for a universal social work: Some issues and implications. *Social Work Education. 23*(5), 625-644.

Gray, M. & Webb, S.A. (2008). The myth of global social work: Double standards and the local-global guide. *Journal of Progressive Human Services, 19*(1), 61-66.

Healy, K. (2001). Participatory action research and social work: A critical appraisal. *International Social Work, 44* (1), 93-105.

Hirayama, H. & Hirayama, K. (1986). Empowerment through group participation: Process and goal. In M. Parnes (Ed.), *Innovations in social group work: Feedback from practice to theory; Proceedings of the Annual Group Work Symposium.* New York, London: The Haworth Press, 119-132.

IASSW & IFSW. (2004). *Global standards for social work education and training.* International Association of Schools of Social Work & International Federation of Social Workers. Retrieved May 15, 2010, from http://www.iassw-aiets.org/.

Jacobson, M. & Rugeley, C. (2007) Community-based participatory research: Group work for social justice and community change. *Social Work with Groups, 30*(4), 21-39.

Lowy, L. (1955). *Adult education and group work.* NY: Whiteside, Inc, and William Morrow & Co.

O'Brien, R. (1998). An overview of the methodological approach of action research. Retrieved May 20, 2010: http://www.web.net/~robrien/papers/arfinal.html

Schwartz, W. (1971). On the use of groups in social work practice. In W. Schwartz and S.R. Zalba (Eds.), *The practice of group work.* NY: Columbia University Press, 3-24.

Shaw, I., Briar-Lawson, K., Orme, J & Ruckdeschel, R. (2010). *The Sage handbook of social research.* London: Sage.

Tribe, R. and Shackman, J. (1989). A way forward: a group for refugee women. *Groupwork, 2*(2), 159-166.

Wilson, M. & Quirke, D. (2005). *When words are not enough: Facilitating angels in the funzone!,* International Symposium of the Association for the Advancement of Social Work with Groups, Minneapolis, MN.

9
The 'Rainbow Nation' way of teaching sensitivity to diversity for social work with groups

Reineth Prinsloo

Abstract: Because social work clients are often members of oppressed, vulnerable and disempowered groups, teaching sensitivity to diversity and empowering social work students to be culturally competent is of the utmost importance. South Africa's history of *apartheid* has had detrimental effects on personal, social, economic, and political development. A department of social work at a university in South Africa introduced specific study units within its BSW programme to address the influence of this particularly vicious form of discrimination. The units help students to confront their own prejudices, enhance their self-awareness, and obtain knowledge of and exposure to diverse client populations. This paper discusses the need for coursework in this area, and describes the process of teaching these study units.

Key words: Social work intervention with groups; diversity education; South African group work.

'I am glad for the word *apartheid*'. The audience falls silent. How is it possible for a white South African woman to state this at an international symposium in the United States of America?

The liberation of South Africa from apartheid in 1994 has resulted in changes which have forced the people of this 'Rainbow Nation' towards greater tolerance and accommodation. It is the author's opinion that by openly *naming*, discussing, criticizing, judging, and eventually addressing apartheid, discrimination and insensitivity to cultural diversity are finally being confronted in South African society.

South Africa has eleven official languages and as many and more different cultural groups. This diversity creates many wonderful opportunities to learn about other cultures and overcome conscious or unconscious discrimination. This paper describes the specific study units developed by a department of social work at a university in South Africa to prepare their BSW students to address the influence of apartheid.

The effects of apartheid

The former National Party of South Africa, consisting mainly of white South Africans, implemented and maintained a system referred to as 'apartheid' – an extreme form of discrimination and insensitivity to diversity – from 1948 until 1994. This political party used their immense power to influence people and decide on the distribution of resources. As Mamphiswana and Noyoo (2000, p.31) emphasize, apartheid was a brutal form of colonial domination that sapped the energies of the people and eroded their self-worth. Apartheid had detrimental effects on personal, social, economic, and political development. Poverty and inequality in South Africa result from centuries of colonialism and apartheid during which indigenous populations were oppressed and their lands, productive assets, cultural heritage and self-respect severely impacted (Hölscher, 2008, pp.120-121).

South Africa has been faced with many challenges with regard to a 'new' way of functioning since the democratization in 1994. All spheres of life and social relations have been affected. While the nation has reached higher levels of liberation from apartheid since 1994, poverty, structural oppression, and power imbalances continue (Smith, 2008, p.371).

Sensitivity to diversity in social work

Cultural diversity refers to the variety in human society and culture in a specific region – seen in aspects such as language, dress, tradition and the way people interact with their environment. Unfortunately, human beings often respond to diversity with conscious or unconscious discrimination. Discrimination and abuse of power are worldwide phenomena. As defined by Zastrow (2009, p.198), discrimination means taking action against people because they belong to a specific category of people. Such behaviour is unethical. Although there are different views about specific social work values and principles, most reflect the acceptance and positive evaluation of diverse ways of life (Wilson *et al.*, 2008, p.83).

Failing to recognise the reality of all people, but especially a disadvantaged or socially excluded person, may in itself be regarded as oppression (Wilson *et al.*, 2008, p.83). Miley *et al.* (2009, p.94) regard oppression as the injustice that results from domination and control of resources by favoured groups. Social work deals with clients that are oppressed, disempowered and vulnerable. This necessitates that social workers should confront the multiple dimensions of oppression (Miley *et al.*, 2009, pp.95-96), understand the world of the powerless, and not contribute to oppression in any way.

Populations served by social workers cut across diverse socio-cultural contexts. Social workers need a depth of knowledge and skills to intervene with sensitivity (Carter-Black, 2007). Cultural competence and a practical familiarity are of the utmost importance to maintain high standards in service delivery (Corey & Corey, 1996, p.28; Carter-Black, 2007, p.31; Allen-Meares, 2007, p.83). Social workers with a culturally sensitive approach appreciate clients' uniqueness (Miley *et al.*, 2009, p.70). Acceptance of and respect for this uniqueness are necessary for competence.

Sensitivity to diversity in group work

Konopka (1983) suggests that the following values related to diversity are important in group work practice:

1. positive relations and participation among people of different colour, creed, age, national origin and social class;
2. a high degree of individualization so that every member's unique concerns are addressed.

Group leaders often work with group members from diverse backgrounds. The *Standards for social work practice with groups,* developed by the Association for the Advancement of Social Work with Groups, Inc. (1998) emphasizes that a core value of group work practice is respect for persons and their autonomy. Group workers must place a high value on respect for diversity in all its dimensions, including culture, ethnicity, gender, sexual orientation, physical and mental abilities, and age (Johnson & Johnson, 2003, p.479). They should appreciate and understand the differences among members, and between members and the group worker, that may influence practice. Effective group work practice calls for cultural competence.

No matter how stigmatized group members may be by society, they deserve to be treated with respect and dignity. Group work should facilitate understanding and camaraderie among people from diverse backgrounds (Toseland & Rivas, 2009, p.8). Effective counsellors learn how to recognize diversity and shape their intervention according to the world of a group member. Lordan and Wilson (2002, p.11) emphasize the importance of naming differences as a first step to understanding them. Identifying and engaging differences from the beginning of the group create opportunities for better understanding and intervention. Doel (2006, p.143) emphasizes that it is likely that there will be different values within every group and that denying or suppressing differences will not make them disappear.

Not only should group workers help members to recognize differences and understand them, but they should also recognize and understand their own values and differences. As Marsiglia (2003, p.84) points out, group workers' world views, beliefs and values influence their practice. A group worker has to be clear about his or her own values and perceptions before attempting to engage with others.

Culturally skilled group workers will move away from their own values and prejudices to understand the world of their group members. It is, however, not possible to do so without understanding their own cultural conditioning and family of origin beliefs, as well as the socio-political systems that they are part of. Family of origin provides the foundation of culture, gender expectations, and general perceptions of society (Waldegrave, 2009, p.86). For example, the political system in South Africa dictated and ascribed certain values and prejudices to difcrferent groups, regardless of individual differences, and this was conveyed in the context of the family of origin.

If group workers are not aware of their own values, they will have difficulty when faced with value-laden situations. Exercises to clarify values can help group workers to identify personal and professional values that may influence their group work practice. Supervision can also help group workers to become aware of their own values, and to modify or change values that are neither consistent with the values of the social work profession nor helpful in their group work practice.

Members who reflect on and recognise their own culture are more likely to participate and to benefit from intervention (Marsiglia, 2003, p.85). Group workers should be aware of the cultural backgrounds of group members, and how their backgrounds affect their attitudes about sharing personal information with persons outside the family or their culture (Henry, 1992). Group workers also need to be sensitive to the effects that cultural diversity have on valued behaviour in the group. Culture influences beliefs about social distance, the appropriate way to speak, the proper treatment of persons in authority positions and certain age groups, and the correct way to address persons from other cultural or age groups.

Sensitivity to all of these factors requires knowledge with regard to the values of different cultural groups. A group leader should understand the different cultures of group members as well as how these cultures affect participation in group contexts (Jacobs *et al.*, 2009, p.140; Zastrow, 2009, p.215).

The role of social work education

Preparing social work students to conduct their practice with respect for diversity and sensitivity to discrimination has been a long-standing objective of social work education. Social work programs across the globe have a responsibility to teach sensitivity to diversity in order to prepare social workers to address inequality and help vulnerable groups affected by skewed power and racism. This holds especially true for teaching social work in post-apartheid South Africa.

Collective social responsibility is necessary in order to overcome the legacy of apartheid. Social work holds an excellent position in such collective efforts.

> Social work has ... a major role in rejuvenating the spirit of self-worth, especially amongst the African communities who were brutalized both physically and mentally by apartheid for many years (Mamphiswana & Noyoo, 2000, p.31).

Erasmus (2006) in Leibowitz *et al.* (2007, p.703) argues that race, as well as identity based on racial perceptions, influences the lives of South African students. Since social work students enter the field of study from a specific historical and rational context of racial discrimination, it is imperative that social work teachers stimulate the process of critical reflection (Smith, 2008, p.374).

The department of social work in a university in South Africa has developed a program to teach sensitivity to diversity. The department has a diverse student population, including individuals from the different cultural and ethnic groups. These students are exposed to equally diverse client groups in their social work practice. Cultural sensitivity is thus of the utmost importance.

Teaching diversity in a South African BSW programme

This paper describes the activities used for teaching sensitivity to diversity in a BSW programme within a department of social work in a South African university.

The first year practice module aims to enhance understanding and sensitivity to diversity. In order to accomplish this goal, lecturers purposefully divide students into small groups, based on gender and cultural/ethnic diversity. They attempt to ensure that practice groups include both male and female students from different ethnic backgrounds. Within these groups, students identify and discuss their individual cultural practices, with an emphasis on being sensitive and respectful to fellow learners. The importance of cultural sensitivity in social work practice is discussed.

Social work students receive the opportunity to gain knowledge in group supervision and discussion classes when talking about rituals and practices in their cultures. Dating and mating rituals, wedding practices, funeral rituals and methods of communication are discussed. Students become aware of dowry practices in modern times; the management of marital conflict in traditional families; extended family practices; the use of eyes in communication to reflect respect; and norms for addressing someone older than oneself.

A handshake is very important in African greetings and is done in a specific way. Students unfamiliar with the handshake learn how to greet in the appropriate way, while the students teaching their peers feel privileged to do so. Greetings in the different languages are practiced. This exercise results in laughter and bonding at the same time, as students struggle to pronounce the words correctly. Students are encouraged to greet each other in the different languages outside the classroom setting. It is clear that they enjoy learning how to greet in a different language, but what is even more important is that the students being greeted in their own language feel valued and understood. Students are also encouraged to enquire about the origin and meaning of each other's names. Showing interest in another's name makes a person feel respected and valued.

Animals have many meanings in Africa, and certain animals signify certain character qualities. Some cultures view owls as bad omens, rather than as embodiments of wisdom and intelligence. A baboon may be regarded as an evil spirit and even be linked to witchcraft. A chameleon may be associated with witchcraft because of its ability to change colour. Students need to have knowledge of these meanings in order to intervene in a sensitive way. In conversations, exercises, and classroom discussions they learn to be sensitive to the use of animal metaphors.

Exercises to discuss the above cultural practices and meanings are included in the study units. Experiences are reflected in narrative reports and, where necessary, discussed in supervision. Students openly admit their ignorance about other cultures and aspects of diversity and are excited to learn about each other's cultures.

Feedback from students includes the following comments:

1. 'I now understand the emphasis on getting engaged and having an engagement ring. I thought it was just to show off and never knew that it was an expectation.'
2. 'I am glad that I do not have to be present when the bridegroom slaughters a cow but now understand that it is a cultural ritual. The

colourful wedding process to incorporate western and traditional practices amazes me. I wish that I can have the opportunity to be invited to such a wedding.'

Teaching sensitivity to diversity intensifies in the second year of the programme and focuses on self-development. Within small groups, students further identify diverse cultural practices amongst themselves and in the community. These groups are again purposefully composed to be culturally/ethnically diverse. Students are asked to confront their own personal stereotypes and prejudices. Lecturers facilitate the development of awareness and mutual understanding of group members' cultural practices.

Class exercises to clarify values can help students to identify personal and professional values that may influence their practice. They examine their own personal backgrounds and socialization experiences, consider personal manifestations of prejudice, and then list ways to overcome their prejudices.

Students discuss specific scenarios where cultural and religious diversity are prominent. An example of such a scenario is one in which a black farm worker is killed by both a white and a black man and then fed to a lion on the farm. What do students see when they first read the headline? A white man killed a black man? A white man and a black man committed murder? Just a brutal murder?

A second example involves a single sex white couple wanting to adopt a black AIDS orphan. Do students first see that this couple is single sex? Do they see a white couple wanting to adopt a black baby? Do they see the selfless act of providing a home to an orphan?

In response to these scenarios students, within two-hour classes, identify and reflect upon their own prejudices and identify areas for change and growth. Their responses include:

1. 'When I first read the scenario I saw a black farm worker killed by a white man. When I read it again and we discussed it in class I realised that it was murder and had nothing to do with race. I realise that my family background and the way I was raised make me to sometimes respond with the looking glass of prejudice, induced by my family that suffered because of apartheid. I have to change my own way of thinking. I cannot react this way as a social worker.'
2. 'Perhaps the white man used the black man to do his dirty work. No, they both killed a man. This has nothing to do with skin colour

and I may not think this way. Murder is wrong!'

3. 'HIV/AIDS is such an enormous problem and children do not ask to be influenced. Anyone that can provide a home, love and care should do so. Sexual preferences and ethnic group play no role.'
4. 'I will gladly assist in facilitating adoption of orphans because of the pandemic, regardless of diversity.'
5. 'How can I be so stuck on skin colour? Are we not all the same human beings with similar feelings? Apartheid was so wrong.'

Students indicate that confronting and discussing these scenarios, although disturbing, forces introspection and change. They report enhanced awareness of their own beliefs, prejudices, and values.

Each second year student is required to conduct and record an interview with a person who has a sexual, cultural or religious orientation, which is different from his or her own. Lecturers assess the contribution of the interview to the student's own sensitivity to diversity. Student comments include: 'I have never thought that a person of that religion experienced so much stigmatization, even here on campus. The interview made me realise that I should not do the same and never judge. I have to respect people's preferences' and 'The person from the interview could not thank me enough for asking and showing interest. He thinks that everyone should be willing to gain knowledge to understand and not to judge without knowing.'

During the second year, students reflect on their self-development in reports of their growing awareness, insight, and self-confidence. They are also expected to demonstrate the ability to internalise their new skills and knowledge in everyday practice and in professional conduct during class exercises.

The theory module for social work intervention with groups provides the basis for the practice training which follows. Students work in task groups and discuss approaches to multi-cultural group work, as well as ways for the group worker to intervene with sensitivity to issues of diversity in the group. All students in the task groups, in turn, discuss their ethnic backgrounds. They discuss how their heritage might influence participation in a group. They also discuss how demographic variables such as age, gender, education, or socio-economic status influence the behaviour of group members. A volunteer within the task group discusses an incident in which he/she experienced prejudice or discrimination (prejudice could occur because of many characteristics, such as age, race, gender, or disability).

The study unit on self-development comes together in a practice experience in which students demonstrate their sensitivity to diversity by conducting life-skills groups with first year students from diverse backgrounds.

Finally, students complete an assignment involving sketching a possible diversity scenario for a treatment group. They are required to discuss one of the eight ways proposed by Toseland and Rivas (2009, pp.139-146) in which the group leader can intervene with **sensitivity to issues of diversity** in the group:

1. Using social work values and skills
2. Using a strength perspective
3. Exploring common and different experiences among group members
4. Exploring meanings and language
5. Challenging prejudice and discrimination
6. Advocating for members
7. Empowering members
8. Using culturally appropriate techniques and program activities

This final assignment contributes to students' ability to make connections between theory and their practice experience. Second year social work students consistently reflect that the learning modules just described empower them to broaden their frame of reference and knowledge base.

Conclusion

Diversity provides many opportunities for the enrichment of society, but we can only take advantage of these opportunities if we embrace it with sensitivity and respect. In every society, social work plays a major role in contributing to an environment that works toward this goal. The study modules discussed in this paper are one attempt to address the need to prepare social work students in South Africa to address the critical issues of diversity in a post-apartheid society. In an increasingly global world, it is imperative that we share our strategies for teaching this critical aspect of social work and group work practice with the next generation. If we embrace diversity with the necessary sensitivity and respect and humbly acknowledge our differences, we realise that these differences create a unique rainbow.

References

Allen-Meares, P. (2007). Cultural competence: An ethical requirement. *Journal of Ethnic and Cultural Diversity in Social Work, 16*(3), 83-92.

Association for the Advancement of Social Work with Groups. (1998). *Standards for social work practice with groups*. Akron, OH: AASWG.

Carter-Black, J. (2007). Teaching cultural competence: An innovative strategy grounded in the universality of storytelling as depicted in African and African American storytelling traditions. *Journal of Social Work Education, 43*(1), Winter 2007, 31-50.

Corey, M.S. & Corey, G. (2006). *Groups. Process and practice.* USA: Brooks/ Cole.

Doel, M. (2006). *Using groupwork.* London: Routledge.

Henry, S. (1992). *Group skills in social work. A four-dimensional approach.* (2nd ed.) Pacific Grove: Brooks/Cole.

Hölscher, D. (2008). The Emperor's new clothes: South Africa's attempted transition to developmental social welfare and social work. *International Journal of Social Welfare, 17,* 114–123.

Jacobs, E.E., Masson, R.L. & Harvill, R.L. (2009). *Group counselling. Strategies and skills.* (6th ed.) Belmont: Thomson Brooks/Cole.

Johnson, D.W. & Johnson, F.P. (2003). *Joining together. Group theory and group skills.* (8th ed.) Boston: Allyn & Bacon.

Konopka, G. (1983). *Social group work: A helping process,* (3rd edn). Englewood Cliffs, NJ: Prentice-Hall.

Leibowitz, B., Rohleder, P., Bozalek, V., Carolissen, R. & Swartz, L. (2007). 'It doesn't matter who or what we are, we are still just people': Strategies used by university students to negotiate difference. *South African Journal of Psychology, 37*(4), 702–719.

Lordan, N. and Wilson, M. (2002). Groupwork in Europe: tools to combat social exclusion in a multicultural environment. In S. Henry, J. East, & C. Schmitz, (Eds.), *Social work with groups. Mining the gold.* New York: Haworth Press, 9-30.

Mamphiswana, D. & Noyoo, N. (2000). Social work education in a changing socio-political and economic dispensation. Perspectives from South Africa. *International Social Work, 43*(1), 21–32.

Marsiglia, F.F. (2003). Culturally grounded approaches to social justice through social work with groups. In N. Sullivan, E.S. Mesbur, N.C. Lang, D. Goodman, & L. Mitchell (Eds.), *Social work with groups. Social justice through personal, community, and societal change.* New York: Haworth Press, 79-90.

Miley, K.K., O'Melia, M. & DuBois, B. (2009). *Generalist social work practice. An empowering approach.* (6th ed.) Boston: Pearson Education.

Smith, L. (2008) South African social work education: Critical imperatives for social change in the post-apartheid and post-colonial context. *International Social Work, 51*(3), 371-383.

Toseland, R.W. and Rivas, R.F. (2009). *An introduction to group work practice.* (6th ed.) Boston: Allyn & Bacon.

Waldegrave, C. (2009). Cultural, gender, and socioeconomic contexts in therapeutic and social policy work. *Family Process, 48*(1), 85-101.

Wilson, K., Ruch, G., Lymbery, M. & Cooper, A. (2008). *Social work. An introduction to contemporary practice.* Essex: Pearson Longman.

Zastrow, C.H. (2009). *Social work with groups. A comprehensive workbook.* (7th ed.) Belmont: Thomson Brooks/Cole.

10

Alzheimer's disease and dementia sufferers access their inner artist:

Maintaining connections rather than becoming strangers

Lorraine Ruggieri

Abstract: Alzheimer's disease and dementia consume the mind, obliterate memory, and render the sufferer alienated and totally dependent on a caregiver. As the illness progresses and memory and the ability to connect fade away, the sufferer and caregiver's relationship loses its intimacy and the two become strangers to each other. With the number of those afflicted by Alzheimer's disease and dementia increasing dramatically, the number of caregivers, the second victims of this illness, will rise proportionately. To face this new reality, exploration is developing creative ways to mitigate the alienating consequences of dementia for the sufferer and the caregiver. There is an innovative trend in dementia care to connect both caregiver and care recipient via group interventions involving arts-based programs. This paper explores the theory and practice of these group interventions utilizing the following creative arts or arts-based programs: Meet Me at MoMA, Met Escapes, Support Group and Art Workshop at The Met, and Time*Slips*.

Keywords: Alzheimer's disease, dementia, caregiver, dementia care, creative activities, arts-based group programs

Introduction

'Becoming strangers' is the term used by Wuest, Ericson and Stern (1994) to describe the transition from intimacy to alienation that occurs between Alzheimer's disease and dementia sufferers and their caregivers. It might also be metaphorically interpreted to mean the alienation of the sufferer from the self. Alzheimer's disease and other dementias[1] are progressive, non-reversible, degenerative diseases that attack the brain and cause impaired memory, thinking and behavior. Simply put, for dementia sufferers, meaningful thought fades away as if the plastic page on a magic slate slowly lifts and all memory of life and self disappears. Dementia sufferers experience physical and emotional impairments as well as motor and visual changes. Medicare spends three times as much on the care of a person afflicted with dementia than on a person without this diagnosis (Alzheimer's Association, 2008).

Projected magnitude of the problem

Alzheimer's disease is not a disease only affecting the aged; 10 per cent of the sufferers, half a million people, are 60 years old or younger due to a genetic form of the disease. Currently, this disease afflicts 5.2 million Americans and it is estimated that one in three of us will face this disease in an older relative. By 2050, that number will rise to 16 million sufferers. Alzheimer's disease is the sixth leading cause of death among adults, having recently replaced diabetes in ranking, and the numbers continue to increase each year (Alzheimer's Association, 2008). Beginning in 2011, when the first of the baby boomers turn 65, the epidemic of cases is expected to accelerate, reaching about 16 million people in 2050, with an annual cost of about $700 billion dollars (Shenk, 2001, p.5). Collectively, all the dementias will have a seismic impact on sufferers and their caregivers as their numbers continue to grow.

The caregiver becomes the second victim

Dementia also claims a second victim, the caregiver, without whom a person afflicted with dementia could not survive. This disease creates a unit consisting of caregiver and care recipient because the sufferer becomes totally dependent on a caregiver, who provides 24-hour care and supervision and who, subsequently, suffers his or her own decline due to mental and physical stress. Recent studies suggest that psychological systems suffer 'cumulative wear and tear following chronic stress leading collectively to poor health' (Clark, 2007). Caregiving for dementia sufferers is extremely taxing and exhausting (Pratt *et al*, 1985). Caregivers suffer a subjective sense of burden (caregiver burden), that manifests itself as feelings of depression, anxiety, and loneliness. They are also vulnerable to physical illness and accidents, have time constraints and financial limitations, and may experience low life satisfaction. Caregivers are also known to suffer impaired immune function and an increased susceptibility to disease.

> Caregiving may increase the stressfulness of already stressful events, such as health problems, and may cause previously non-stressful events, such as going to the grocery store with a spouse or going for a walk alone, to become stressful (Gallagher-Thompson & Powers, 1997, p.253).

Clearly, when proposing interventions, group or otherwise, there are two sufferers to consider: the caregiver and the care recipient.

Day care programs, creative activities and support groups as interventions

Day care programs

Not long ago, people in medical facilities or nursing homes who suffered from dementia were tethered with restraints in geri-chairs to prevent wandering and difficult behaviors such as pacing, angry outbursts, grabbing, reaching and pulling at others that may arise from anxiety, inactivity or an inability to connect with others.

In the 1990s, day care programs were launched to provide supervised social opportunities and activities for people with dementia while offering respite for the caregiver. In the words of Paul Arfin, President of the NYS Adult Day Services Association:

> Just being in a social setting can reduce the deterioration that people have in their physical and mental health. For many, social day care can help delay or avoid placement in a nursing home (*New York Times*, 3/28/99).

In these early day care programs, interventions involved socialization, music and therapeutic arts activities which, while an obvious advance over the use of restraints, did little to forestall the alienation between caregiver and care recipient.

Creative activities

Progress in methods of interventions has resulted in the development of new arts-based groups over the past decade, bolstered by research that has confirmed the benefits of creative activities developed for dementia patients. Hanneman (2006) affirms that creative activities can be stimulating to dementia patients and that older people, in general, are capable of developing their abilities of improvisation and imagination to a higher degree than younger people. The author also states that, because divergent thinking is favored over analytical thinking in the process of creativity, arts-based activities are more readily accessible to persons with dementia. The results of this study demonstrate that creativity can increase well-being, sharpen the senses and decrease depression and the sense of isolation. The elderly, and some dementia patients who are non-verbal, are able to use creativity in the arts to express their feelings in other matters: 'There is an opportunity to recognize the beauty of existence and improve one's sense of life by getting more independent' (p.65).

Anne Davis Basting (2006), the founder of the Time*Slips* Creative Storytelling Project (described later in this paper), defines 'the arts' as any medium (also described as a *tool*) that is used for creative expression to convey meaning. Basting feels that people with dementia who:

> ... edit themselves into silence for fear of saying the wrong thing, or shut themselves down to avoid contact they cannot understand, can use the arts to reconnect with themselves and the people who care for them...the

> arts offer great value to people with dementia and warrant tremendous hope for the future (p.16).

Whether they take the form of a poem, a painting, a story or a dance, the arts and the feelings they inspire provide tools of expression that operate on an emotional level when memory and factual language have failed. Through assessment of facial expression, degree of interest and engagement, and decrease in difficult behaviors, observational research has concluded that the arts work effectively as an intervention (Basting, 2006). Therefore, creative activities and accessing one's inner artist may provide satisfaction and increase well-being for dementia patients.

Support groups

As stated above, there is another victim of dementia, the caregiver, who also becomes alienated and isolated. Ballard (2007) discusses the role of caregivers' support groups in: (1) helping the caregiver, 'the hidden patient,' manage and accept the challenges of caregiving; (2) normalizing patient and family reactions to the disease; (3) relieving *caregiver burden;* (4) linking the caregiver with professionals for both practical and emotional support; and (5) easing isolation. Ballard also cites reasons why spouses/caregivers do not participate in support groups. These include resistance to the role or label of caregiver; viewing participation in a support group as betrayal to a spouse; feeling uncomfortable or embarrassed sharing personal problems with strangers; fearing the predictions regarding the progression of the disease; unavailability of time; lack of access to a group; and lack of respite time for the caregiver, who is without help and must remain with the care recipient. The possibility exists, however, that the chances of success are improved if support group interventions are arts-based and involve both caregiver and care recipient.

Arts-based group programs for dementia sufferers with their caregivers

While daycare programs, creative activities and support groups may have beneficial effects, the fact that caregivers and care recipients participate separately from one another does little to alleviate their alienation from one another. Emerging evidence suggests that arts-based group programs for dementia sufferers with their caregivers are able to provide a connection between caregiver and care recipient and a mutually enjoyable experience for both. Meet Me at MoMA, Met Escapes, The Met – Support Group and Art Workshop and Time*Slips* are four creative arts-based programs that allow the dementia sufferer and caregiver such an experience.

Dr. Mary Mittelman, Director of Psychosocial Research and Support at the Center of Excellence on Brain Aging and Dementia at New York University (NYU) and principal investigator of a study commissioned by the Museum of Modern Art (MoMA) on the effects of the newly initiated Meet Me at MoMA program, reports:

> The first time we went [to MoMA], we were overwhelmed by how involved the participants were. It spoke to the fact that people with dementia in the early stages are people first. They have an illness, and it affects certain areas of their functioning but not all. It is obvious they are enjoying the art and responding to the educators (Jones, 2009, p.F3).

Dr. Mittelman also cites the first evidence-based study conducted by NYU[2] as providing scientific proof that dementia patients in the MoMA program experienced an improvement of mood, as well as intellectual and social stimulation. Caregivers also benefited from this sharing and viewing of art because they, in this 'accepting environment,' connected with their care recipient in a positive and enjoyable experience (Jones, 2009).

When these caregiver-care recipient pairs join together in the company of other pairs who are in similar circumstances there is a likelihood of social engagement and a climate of openness and understanding. Exploration of the arts in this climate allows caregivers and care recipients to experience respite and camaraderie.

Field research was conducted by this author to observe the effects of these arts-based group programs. The findings of this research follow.

Meet Me at MoMA

Begun in 2006, the *Meet Me at MoMA* program is an attempt by the Metropolitan Museum of Art in New York City to reach out and make its collection available to people with Alzheimer's disease and their caregivers free of charge. It grew out of certain research and literature that suggested that involvement with the arts, whether through viewing, discussing or creating art in a group experience, could provide dementia victims with an opportunity for social engagement, self- expression and sensory stimulation. Groups consist of those who call the museum to pre-register for the tour and show up on the designated Tuesday each month when the museum is closed to the public. On arrival, the dementia participant and care partner are welcomed and receive name tags color-coded to a group leader/educator. Wheelchairs or very-lightweight stools are provided for comfortable seating while viewing and discussing the art works. Groups of about sixteen participants are led by a museum educator who has received special training in Alzheimer's disease and who engages participants in a lively and interactive discussion focused around the great masters of art.

When this author, a support group facilitator and graduate student doing field research, toured on a recent Tuesday afternoon in March, she was part of the *purple* group that visited the fifth floor of MoMA. Two of the paintings chosen for the tour were Pablo Picasso's *Girl with a Mandolin* and Gustave Klimt's *Vision*. Museum educators offered information about the paintings and encouraged expressions of thoughts, feelings, and preferences: 'How does this painting make you feel...Would you hang this in your home?' The pairs of dementia participants and care partners became art appraisers, allowing both to share a rich experience in an accepting environment. Jed Levine, Executive Vice President and Director of Programs and services at the New York City Chapter Alzheimer's Association, refers to the program as 'exquisitely well run' and 'emblematic of the changing perceptions toward people with dementia... [W]e are finally looking at all the residual strengths, like participating in art and enriching activities, rather than focusing on the multiple losses' (Jones, 2009, p.F3).

MoMA has now expanded this museum program and arts-based group intervention into a nationwide outreach and initiative known as The MoMA Alzheimer's Project. This project has been initially funded by a two-year, $450,000 grant provided by MetLife Foundation and is currently conceptualizing program models for use by other museums, assisted living facilities, nursing homes, and Alzheimer's Association chapters across the country (Metropolitan Museum of Art, 2009)[1].

Met Escapes

In 2008, the Metropolitan Museum of Art (the Met) initiated Met Escapes in consultation with MoMA. The Met Escapes program, which was developed in accordance with the Meet Me at MoMA model, was incorporated into the Met's Access Programs for Visitors with Disabilities. Similar to Meet Me at MoMA, the Met Escapes Program is offered to visitors with dementia and their family members or care partners free of charge. The Met's website invites these individuals:

> ... to take a break from the everyday with the Museum's Met Escapes Program. Through discussions, handling sessions, art making, and other interactive and multisensory activities in the galleries and in the classroom, we will travel through time, using the Metropolitan's collection spanning five thousand years of world culture (Metropolitan Museum of Art, 2009).3

Met Escapes programs are scheduled on Wednesdays as well as on Sundays for the convenience of care partners who may be working. Groups consist of four dementia participant-care partner pairs, an educator, and a helper; each tour consists of four to five groups that are conducted individually. Wheelchairs and walkers are utilized and lightweight stools are carried about by helpers for sitting convenience. This program engages the participants in several ways: gallery tours, studio discussion before or after tours, arts-based discussion groups, support groups, and touch collection groups.

This author joined a Sunday morning tour which visited the Arms and Armor Gallery. In the pre-tour discussion, one participant stated in a jocular way, 'I'm into machine guns.' A lively discussion followed on this topic because, on this particular day, heavily armed police were stationed outside the Met and the assumption was that there was a visiting dignitary. This information gave added interest to the day's tour. As the tour progressed from German armor to Italian armor, all became absorbed in the displays. Many leaned in towards each other and focused on the facilitator or the exhibit, while others held hands and shared an 'in' joke. Some members of the group participated in a 'handling session' which allowed them to handle and inspect a medieval gauntlet similar to those found in the exhibit. Others in the group engaged in sketching the armor. At the end of the tour all left with a colored picture from the exhibit to extend the experience.

According to Deborah Jaffe, Associate Museum Educator and Access Coordinator, Met Escapes considers their groups to be a 'laboratory for future group development' for dementia victims and their care partners to provide new pathways for socially and culturally rewarding experiences (Jaffe, personal communication, 2009).

The Met: Support Group and Art Workshop

The Met has also offered time and space in its classrooms to the Taub Institute for Research on Alzheimer's Disease and the Aging Brain, Alzheimer's Disease Research Center at Columbia University, for a parallel program to engage dementia sufferers in arts-based groups and workshops for socialization, stimulation and support. According to Jaffe, 'there is a link between the two programs, but they are separate.'

This author recently attended one of these groups, a poetry discussion, and became a participant in a discussion of Emily Dickinson's poem #1242:

To flee from memory
Had we the Wings
Many would fly
Inured to slower things
Birds with dismay
Would scan the cowering Van
Of men escaping
From the mind of man

This poem proved to be an interesting choice for the nine participants in the group who decided that they would rewrite the first line as: *To flee from bad memory,* albeit with apologies to Emily Dickinson. The mutual aid benefit of the group was apparent as participants engaged in banter about their lack of facility with poetry or language, in general. The poem, like a painting on the MoMA tour, became a tool for inspiring imagination and communicating in-the-moment feelings.

Even those members who had limited verbal capacity appeared engaged and were able to contribute to the discussion without appearing embarrassed. At the end of the meeting, participants left with a copy of the poem to extend the experience at home.

Time*Slips*

Like programs initiated at MoMA and the Met, the Time*Slips* Creative Storytelling Project presupposes the creative potential of dementia patients in a group situation. This project was founded in 1998 by Anne Basting, Director of the Center on Age and Community at the University of Wisconsin Milwaukee and Associate Professor in the Department of Theatre at the Peck School of the Arts, who has produced plays and art exhibits across the country. Time*Slips* itself is a non-linear storytelling method and group activity for dementia sufferers and caregivers that generates creative expression and social connections. In this method, there is a shift of focus from reminiscence and factual knowledge to images and in-the-moment thoughts that are woven together to create stories among group participants (Basting, 2006).

The 'storytellers' – the dementia sufferer and care partner – usually sit in a circle and are welcomed by two facilitators, trained workers disciplined in the humanities or the arts and dementia care. A 'fantastical' image is handed out to storytellers and one facilitator asks well-crafted, open-ended questions, while another (the scribe) writes down responses on a sketchpad large enough for all to see. All responses, whether they are nonsensical or unrelated, such as the lift of an eyebrow or the wandering of a storyteller, are incorporated into the context of the story for validation of all storytellers. At the end of the story, or when attention drifts, the story is reread by the scribe facilitator and all are thanked. This free-form method of storytelling runs counter to preconceived notions of what constitutes a story and allows for the possibility of interaction among all storytellers who contribute to the expressive and controlled chaos.

In order to increase awareness of the creativity of dementia patients, and with the help of professional actors, Bastings produced a play in SoHo, New York inspired by the stories resulting from these initial storytelling circles. Basting designed a study to research whether or not the play production generated a change in viewers' perceptions of the potential of creativity in participants with dementia (data collection was by means of questionnaires inserted into play programs). In 2001, as a post-show evaluator for the Time*Slips* Play project, this author recorded the feedback of playgoers from the facilitated group discussions that followed each performance. At that time it was novel to recognize the creative storytelling potential of dementia sufferers. A blurb in the *Village Voice* touted:

> This play is inspired by [Anne Basting's] work with a group of Alzheimer's patients in a storytelling circle. The piece is simply an enchantment. Like a lullaby, it shows a poetical and musical universe where afflicted people create fantastical characters. A good lesson for those who think that our reality is the only one, and the only one to impose on people (Poitrasson, 2001, p.93).

The data collected from a sample of 539 respondents indicated that the play had a significant and positive impact on the perception of the creative ability of participants with dementia. Analysis of the responses before and after the play showed an increase by several points in the belief that people with dementia could connect and be creative as demonstrated in the storytelling circle presented in the play (Basting, 2006). Additionally, the Time*Slips* storytelling method was recognized as a tool to connect all group participants – dementia patients as well as caregivers.

Blending group work practice and the creative arts in dementia care

Drawing from the programs and project described above, this author proposes that group work practice blended with the creative arts, as in arts-based programs, may provide a gold standard for intervention with the unit of dementia patient and caregiver. Group work practice focuses on a glass-half-full perspective and on the abilities that a client retains to meet challenges and to engage in the processes of problem-solving. The worker, as a facilitator of a group intervention, provides an environment conducive for group members to validate and share experiences; this helps uplift the individual to attain a sense of well-being and social engagement. The creative arts or arts-based programs involve individuals in a creative process that stimulates the brain and helps to alleviate stress and emotional problems. Blending these two interventions in group work practice can be a valuable addition to the existing supports for dementia sufferers and their caregivers. Both the patient and the caregiver participate in the process together and reap benefits mutually and individually.

Proposing a beneficial model

Group work practice, as offspring of social work practice, can be synthesized with the creative arts to provide a beneficial dementia care model that builds on an art infusion approach to practice. Damianakis (2007) highlights the intersection of the creative arts and social work practice according to four themes: (1) the arts and social work stir physical, emotional and spiritual feelings; (2) both are involved with constructing a language to connect people and their experiences; (3) the arts inspire self-reflection, as does social work, which inspires us to think about things from different perspectives; and (4) the arts integrate mind-body-spirit connections that social work practice is also willing to embrace. As stated in an earlier study by Goldstein (cited in Damianakis, 2007, p. 527):

> The arts have the potential to impact social work at multiple levels: in bridging theory with the practical wisdom; by infusing reflective, critical, and ethical inquiry in social work education; and by locating social work relations as central to a dialogical process within the clients' constructed and experienced world.

In the models of arts-based group interventions described above, a joining of the creative arts and social work practice allows group participants to be stirred by the art form (painting, art work, poetry, or storytelling), and to reflect on any and all possible meanings – experiencing it without confinement to realism or intellectual explanations. There then exists a domain where the principles of art and the principles of social work – group work, in this case – fuse into constructs that enable the dementia sufferer and his or her caregiver to connect via the greater world of arts-based expressions. Educators, psychologists, gerontologists, and social workers observe in practice (see addendum) that the act of looking at art, speaking about art, or stimulating creative expression in storytelling can be satisfying experiences for people who are memory-impaired as well as for the caregivers who join them in participation.

Recommendations

The prospect of incorporating the creative arts and arts-based programs and group work interventions into practice is extremely promising. Group workers who work with this population might:

- *Plan the development of programs within local museums for people with dementia*
  Check out http://www.moma.org/meetme/index for more information about the MoMA Alzheimer's Project and a guide to design your program.

- *Visit the New York City Chapter of the Alzheimer's Association web page*
  See http://www.alz.org/nyc.in_my_community_21017.asp for information on Greet Art workshops to educate family and professional caregivers to use works of art to generate conversation with people with memory loss.

- *Consider training to become a certified Time*Slips *facilitator or attending an intensive training workshop that can be arranged at your facility.*
  Check out http://www.timeslips.org/training.html for information.

- *Explore strategies for artistic expression or art programming that might be incorporated within programs at day care, assisted living and long term care facilities*
  Contact Elders Share The Arts (ESTA) at http://www.eldersharethearts.org/core_programs/overview.php for information on the Arts in Dementia Care. Programs are available in both direct service and training formats.

- *Encourage caregivers to participate in arts-based programs for stimulation, socialization and stress relief*

- *Engage in research to evaluate the effects of creativity and the use of creative art forms on patients' long-term care.*
  In order for arts programs to successfully compete for time and money, evidence-based research must be provided to demonstrate the benefits of these programs on quality of life of people with dementia and their caregivers. Thus, funding may be appropriated if favorable outcomes are predictable.

Conclusion

The creative arts and arts-based group programs demonstrate a model for beneficial group work practice to engage both caregiver and care recipient. Cultivating and encouraging the abilities of both dementia sufferer and caregiver to explore this art-infused domain together inspires connections and may prevent premature alienation. Utilizing these models of group interventions, group workers can facilitate access to *their inner artist* for those suffering from dementia as well as for their caregivers. Thus they may be able to forestall their *becoming strangers.*

Addendum

Additional information regarding the group programs discussed in this paper follows, including group processes, impacts on the members, the challenges faced by the leaders, and contact information. Data collection occurred through this author's participation in the programs, including interaction with and observation of participants; in-depth interviews with group facilitators and administrators of the programs; and content analysis of printed materials. Contact information was obtained through the administrators or websites for each program

Meet Me at MoMA

The process

The Meet Me at MoMA program consists of group discussion involving eight pairs (person with dementia and care partner) led by a museum educator/facilitator in front of an artwork in a process that combines: (1) general museum technique of observation, description, interpretation and connections; and (2) communication and group techniques used for people with dementia. The group discussion employs techniques taught by Anne Basting's Time*Slips* method of storytelling and by the Alzheimer's Association for people with dementia and caregivers combined with the education model used by museum educators/ facilitators. The facilitator asks open-ended questions, encourages participation, repeats and validates all responses, conveys levity, and listens and remains alert for cues from less verbal group members.

The impact on the members

- Camaraderie
- Connections
- Interest
- Fun
- Comfort
- Positive carry-over effect

The challenges faced by the leader

- Managing the logistics of coordination of the program
- Recognizing all participants' needs without having had the benefit of pre-selection of participants
- Coordinating check-in procedures for 100 people arriving at the same time
- Creating a relaxed atmosphere
- Knowing when and how to elicit a response when engaging in group discussions
- Balancing the responses among caregivers (who can manipulate because of need to communicate) with PWAs (who are reticent to speak and unsure of themselves)

For additional information: http://www.moma.org/meetme *or email* accessprograms@moma.org

The Metropolitan Museum of Art – Met Escapes

The process

Facilitators for each tour are educators at the Met who have received specialized training from the Taub Institute for Research and the Aging Brain, Alzheimer's Disease Research Center at Columbia University. These facilitators meet beforehand to choose exhibits that may be of interest to the person with dementia and care partner or inspire an engaging discussion among the participants. Each facilitator with the assistance of a helper leads his or her group to 4-5 locations for a sit-down discussion in front of artworks providing information and asking open-ended questions. Discussions are intended to be free-form and inclusive of all the participants. Each tour also consists of passing around an item from the touch collection and/or an activity such as sketching, engraving or some form of art expression. At the end of the tour, participants receive a picture from one of the exhibits viewed.

The impact on the members

- Engagement
- Connections
- Interest
- Relief from anxiety, depression and boredom
- Fun
- Positive carry-over effect

The challenges faced by the leader

- Adjusting to the tempo and pacing of the group
- Recognizing all participants' needs without having had the benefit of pre-selection of participants
- Allowing for silences without 'running on' through pauses
- Adjusting to the individual person with dementia and care partner; each one experiences the disease and symptoms differently
- Responding to participants who may be wandering, tired, losing

interest or hungry
- Maneuvering through crowded public space
- Managing the crush of time

For additional information: www.metmuseum.org/events/visitorsdisabilities *or email* access@metmuseum.org

The Metropolitan Museum of Art: Support Group and Art Workshop

The process

The ongoing support group/art workshop utilizes free-form discussion with open-ended questions combined with an arts-based activity. Group numbers can vary with the average being 8-10 participants with two facilitators. The facilitators allow topics to develop and inspire and motivate involvement in an arts-based activity. In social work parlance, facilitators must be flexible and *go where the client is.* Support group/mutual aid results by means of discussion and sharing experiences and stories, thoughts, and feelings in the moment.

The impact on the members

- Anecdotal responses by facilitators report a 'healing effect'
- Experiential process with positive reinforcement by facilitators gives a feeling of competence
- Initial resistance towards participating or creating art (in the form of a painting, poetry, collage, etc.) is overcome with encouragement; creating something individually compensates for the feeling of the loss of skills
- Interactivity and temporary relief of anxiety
- Development of trust with facilitators
- Interaction among group members who befriend each other
- Development of a sense of purpose – at least for the day of the group meeting
- Positive carry-over effect
- Fun

The challenges faced by the leader

- Inspiring trust
- Using arts-based interventions -- not *art therapy* but *art as therapy*
- Stressing encouragement and support
- Creating an accepting atmosphere
- Maintaining cohesiveness of group with new members joining and other members leaving due to illness or progression of the disease
- Communicating the effectiveness of a group without a fixed agenda to museum educators who typically select pre-arranged topics/ themes for group meetings

For additional information, email:
Jill Goldman at jg2673@columbia.edu

Time*Slips*

The process

Time*Slips* is a free form, non-linear method of storytelling and a 'group process that opens storytelling to people with cognitive challenges by replacing the pressure to remember with the encouragement **to imagine**' (from web site www.TimeSlips.org). The storytelling circles, consisting of people with dementia or memory loss and their care partners (the storytellers), are welcomed by two trained workers (the facilitators). A fantastical or provocative image is handed out to storytellers. One of the facilitators asks well-crafted, open-ended questions about the image and weaves all responses into a story while the other facilitator writes down these responses on a sketchpad large enough for all to see. All responses, whether they are nonsensical or unrelated or gestures, such as the lift of an eyebrow or the wandering of a storyteller, are incorporated into the context of the story for validation of all storytellers. Facilitators read aloud the responses periodically and weave them into a story. Storytelling sessions can last up to an hour with a final retelling of the story, a thank you and a farewell.

The impact on the members

- Teamwork develops among storytellers and among staff, be they direct care workers, housekeeping staff, chaplains, nutrition staff, activity staff, social workers, nurses, or administrators – all can contribute to the storytelling

- Improvement of the quality and quantity of interactions between staff and participants with dementia; and improvement of staff attitudes toward working with people with dementia
- Development of communication skills among people with dementia
- Fun
- Positive carry-over effect.

The challenges faced by the leader

- Being flexible, patient, and playful
- Allowing the storyteller to *lead* the story
- Responding to members' cues and knowing when to encourage and when to back off when a storyteller feels pressured
- Attuning to the participants, listening and echoing, and running around the group in order to incorporate all the responses.
- Creating a ritual process and a special event
- Accepting and validating all responses including gestures, sounds, and nonsensical answers
- Being imaginative and weaving responses into a story
- Sharing the stories beyond the group and amplifying the special event
- Inspiring fun

For additional information: www.TimeSlips.org

Notes

1. In this paper, the term dementia will stand for Alzheimer's disease and other dementias.
2. This study was designed by the Psychosocial Research and Support Program of the NYU Center for Brain Aging and Dementia in partnership with the Museum of Modern Art and done under the auspices of MoMA Alzheimer's Project funded by MetLife Foundation. The report findings

were subsequently incorporated in 'The MoMA Alzheimer's Project: Programming and resources for making art accessible to people with Alzheimer's disease and their caregivers' by Francesca Rosenberg, published in *Arts & Health*, 1 (1), 2009, 93-97.

3. See recommendation section for contact information for MoMA's Alzheimer's Project and guide to design a program

References

Alzheimer's Association, NYC Chapter (2008). Retrieved March 21, 2009 from website: http://www.alznyc.org

Ballard, E. (2007). Support groups: meeting the needs of families caring for persons with Alzheimer's disease. In C. Cox (Ed.), *Dementia and social work practice – Research and interventions.* New York, NY: Springer Publishing Co., 321-337.

Basting, A.D. (2006). *Arts in dementia care: 'this is not the end...it's the end of this chapter.'* Generations, Spring 2006, *30*(1), 16-20.

Basting, A.D. (2006). Creative storytelling and self-expression among people with Dementia. In A. Leibing & L. Cohen (Eds.), *Thinking about dementia: Culture, loss, and the anthropology of senility.* Piscataway, New Jersey: Rutgers University Press, 180-194.

Clark, M., Bond, M. & Hecker, J. (2007). Environmental stress, psychological stress and allostatic load. *Psychology, Health & Medicine, 12*(1), 18-30

Damianakis, T. (2007). Social work's dialogue with the arts: epistemological and practice intersections. *Families in Society: The Journal of Contemporary Social Services, 88*(4), 525-533.

Gallagher-Thompson, D. & Powers, D. (1997). Primary stressors and depressive symptoms in caregivers of dementia patients. *Aging and Mental Health, 1*(3), 248-255.

Hanneman, B.T. (2006). Creativity and dementia patients. Can creativity and art Stimulate dementia patients positively? *Gerontology* 2006, *52*, 59-65.

Jaffe, D. Personal communication, February 19, 2009.

Jones, K. (2009, March 19). Keeping those with Alzheimer's engaged. *New York Times,* p.F3.

New York Times (1999). Breaking barriers of Alzheimer's. Retrieved March 22, 2009 from web site: http://nytimes.com/1999/03/28/nyregion/breaking-barriers-of-alzheimer-s.html

Poitrasson (2001, November 13). Timeslips. *The Village Voice, Voice Choices,* 93

Pratt, C., Schmall, V., Wright, S. & Cleland. M. (1985). Burden and coping strategies of caregivers to Alzheimer's patients. *Family Relations,* 1985, *34*(1), 27-33.

Shenk, D. (2001). *The forgetting: Alzheimer's portrait of an epidemic.* New York, NY: Doubleday, 5

The Metropolitan Museum of Art, New York (2008). Retrieved March 28, 2009 from website: http://www.metmuseum.org/events/visitorsdisabilities/dementia

The Museum of Modern Art, New York (2008). Retrieved March 28, 2009 from website http://www.moma.org/education/alzheimers.html

Wuest, J., Ericson, P. & Stern, P. (1994). Becoming strangers: the changing family caregiving relationship in Alzheimer's disease. *Journal of Advanced Nursing, 20,* 437-443.

11
Group work and technology: Embracing our future

Shirley R. Simon and Kathleen W. Stauber

Abstract: This paper provides an overview of the evolution of online technology – how the technological revolution of the computer, the Internet, and mass access to new communication devices has impacted our lives with a speed and universality that is unprecedented. It discusses the natural and understandable resistance of many skilled and renowned group workers towards the use of these new modalities. It addresses the numerous benefits that technology has to offer us, and the critical and timely need for group workers to make the conceptual shift to embrace these modalities. A case is made for group workers' ability to take a leadership role in the development of effective, efficient and ethical online groups across disciplines and fields. Finally, an online resource center and a live meeting of educators interacting via online technology are demonstrated.

This paper is based upon the Joan K. Parry Memorial Plenary Address at the 31st Annual International Symposium of the Association for the Advancement of Social Work with Groups, Chicago, Illinois June 28th, 2009

Key words: Social group work, group work and technology, online education, online groups, distance education, social work education and practice

Introduction

During this 2009 Symposium we have looked back on our roots as group workers. We were touched by a spell-binding letter to Jane Addams, written and delivered by our beloved Katy Pappel in the very room where Jane conducted her settlement house activities. Our visit to Hull House offered a vivid, emotional picture of our heritage and contributions.

We also looked at the current state of group work via myriad papers, workshops and posters on contemporary group work efforts in education and practice. We heard about the cross-national and cross-cultural focus of group work in a plenary address by the members of the Global Group Work Project and recognized group work's wide-ranging contemporary impact.

In this plenary address, we ask you to look to the future, to consider a platform for group work that cannot be ignored if we are to continue our historical influence on social work practice. We ask you to look at group work and technology, and recognize and appreciate the inevitability of the melding of the two.

This address provides an overview of the evolution of online technology – how the technological revolution of the computer, the Internet, and mass access to new communication devices has impacted our lives and culture with a speed and universality that is unprecedented. It discusses the natural and understandable resistance of many skilled and renowned group workers to the use of these new modalities. It also addresses the numerous benefits that technology has to offer us, and the critical and timely need for group workers to make the conceptual shift to embrace these modalities. A case is made for group workers' ability to take a leadership role in the development of effective, efficient and ethical online groups across disciplines and fields. Finally, an online resource center and a live meeting of educators interacting via online technology are demonstrated.

Evolution and impact of technological communication

Communicating via technology has come a long way in a very short time. In the late sixties, we were excited by the electronic calculator which was then the size of a large cash register. In the seventies, many of us were thrilled to use an electric rather than a manual typewriter to complete our dissertations. Over the last thirty years, the Internet and the personal computer have completely changed how we communicate and seek information. Most of us use email daily and are familiar with Microsoft Office software. Global communication has become virtually instantaneous. PDAs, laptop computers, and Wi-Fi access at every Starbucks foster our perpetually connected society. Perhaps the most profound example of the power of harnessing this new technology is Barack Obama's 2008 presidential campaign. His use of online communication with its instant messaging and constant email has forever changed the process of U.S. election campaigns.

Today's youth have grown up with technology. They have never known a world without remote control devices, DVRs, or computers. Contrary to many of us, today's traditional age students are adept at using the myriad technological tools now readily available. They have worked with technology from pre-school through college, with curricula in virtually all disciplines integrating these new platforms. The rapidly changing technology does not bother these younger generations; rather, they embrace it. Everywhere you see young people on cell phones, talking, texting or twittering. With the increase of sites like Facebook, My Space, and LinkedIn, online social networking successfully vies with local social clubs and organizations for youth involvement.

Within academia, technology has become essential for all fields of study, from computer aided design in architecture to statistical programs in mathematics, to database management in medicine. Email, 'wired classrooms' and online research are now accepted components of higher education. Online courses and degree programs are growing exponentially as administrators recognize the untapped student markets, the economic benefits, and the competitive necessity of keeping up with other institutions' offerings in distance education. In addition, the increased speed and efficiency of student-faculty communication, the flexibility in format and time of instruction, and the innate demand for enhanced organization and accountability in teaching are enticing more and more schools to embrace this modality (Simon & Stauber, 2009).

In schools of social work, distance education is experiencing similar growth. With the exception of field practica and field supervision, the Council on Social Work Education (CSWE), the accrediting body for U.S. schools of social work, accepts distance education methodologies for all other courses. As the 2008 CSWE Educational Policy and Accreditation Standards (EPAS) state, all accredited programs are subject to the same accreditation standards and review criteria regardless of the curriculum delivery method. Accordingly, CSWE has accredited BSW and MSW programs that use distance education technology with the numbers increasing annually.

Within the practice community, technological applications are everywhere. Online communities for treatment, support, education, growth and socialization have been developed (Perron & Powell, 2009). The ready access to phones, computers and the Internet has led to a proliferation of non-traditional group interactions. Telephone support groups and online support groups (OSGs) are increasingly available. Whether it be a telephone support group for caretakers of the chronically ill, an online spirituality group for lay ministers, or one of the other myriad groups that populate the Internet, people are increasingly gathering in groups in non face-to-face situations.

Pairing group work and technology

Before further exploring the connection between group work and technology, we would like to know what you think when you hear the two terms linked. Please spend a moment reflecting on the one or two words that come to mind when you hear 'group work and technology'.

Authors' note: This exercise resulted in the following responses:

Oxymoron	Ethical issues	Potential
Resistance	Cold	User friendly
Impersonal	Speed	Not user friendly
Accessible	Confidentiality	Cutting edge
Dangerous	Identity stealing	Inexpensive

Rural access	Over-stimulating	Technophobia
Hacking	Exposure	Invasion
Greater connection	High risk	24/7 access
Less connection	Virus	

These words clearly capture the complex and dichotomous feelings and thoughts generated by linking group work and technology.

Challenges and resistance to technology-enhanced communication

'Technology!' The word alone can send shivers up the spine of many group workers. We pride ourselves on the face-to-face context of our work – the power of process without interference or artificial barriers. We speak to our students and interns about the important influence of environment and discuss the problems associated with distracting, uninviting, and impersonal settings. And yet, that is precisely how many of us picture online connections. We think of it as cold, distant and unfamiliar.

For many group workers, online communication requires a critical conceptual shift in perspective. In past decades, the very definition of small group work required face-to-face interaction. As communication options have expanded, however, new platforms for group interaction have arisen. Internet chat groups, telephone groups, online support groups, and other virtual groups no longer require face-to-face interactions. Understandably, many group workers have been less than enthusiastic about utilizing these newer formats (Simon & Stauber, 2009).

A large percentage of today's group workers were educated before the development of these formats. Learning about online communication can be perceived as an additional pressure. While email communication has become widely accepted, many skilled practitioners and educators may justifiably feel overwhelmed by the technical skills required to conduct online groups. Learning something new can be intimidating. We may fear the unfamiliar and imagine making critical mistakes, losing connections and data, or even blowing up the whole system. And frankly, these things can happen, albeit very rarely. In addition, there may be a sense of a dehumanizing process with the computer being in control. We may also recognize that we live in a litigious society and what we write can ultimately be used against us.

For many of us, adapting to and incorporating newer technological modalities can be deterred by a lack of time, interest, and patience. There is the initial investment of time required to learn a new technological process. Then, once you learn what to do, it all changes with new advances in software, so-called 'upgrades' and differing formats and systems. With online communication, there is a continuous need to adapt to all of these changes.

Technology can be frustrating. Push the wrong button and your data disappears. Where did it go? How do you retrieve it? What did you do wrong? What do you do next? Is the audio, video or text being clearly received by all participants? Technology and cyberspace can be intimidating, especially to those of us who grew up in the decades before the computer and the Internet.

Ethical concerns also abound. How protected are our online conversations? Who can access them and what are the realities of confidentiality in such groups? What safeguards are there regarding the composition of the group? Without face-to-face interaction, do we really know the identity of a group's members? Are there predators or imposters participating? These questions and many others are legitimate concerns when working in these new formats.

Finally, online communication with its 24/7 accessibility and instantaneous communication can be experienced as an invasion of one's privacy and personal life. Work time is no longer a Monday to Friday, nine to five schedule. Students and clients expect ready, sometimes round the clock availability. Setting boundaries becomes more difficult without the traditional barriers.

So why incorporate technology? Because despite all of the above, the benefits are significant and the opportunities great.

Benefits offered by technology-enhanced communication

The speed and efficiency of our communication is clearly facilitated by technology. We can interact with people around the globe virtually instantaneously. We even refer to the traditional postal mail services as 'snail mail', an inference about its lengthy process when compared to online communication. We can search for information with literally the push of a button. We can ask questions and receive responses with a speed that would have been unimaginable when many of us were young. And we can do all of this without great expense. Communicating via technology is generally extremely cost effective.

In our complex, over-committed world, technological communication offers convenience and scheduling flexibility. It allows us to do our work on our timeline – when the baby is sleeping, when dinner is cooking, when we feel inspired. We are not bound by the conventional nine to five schedule, and while there are the obvious drawbacks mentioned earlier, there is also a freedom and sense of personal control that many of us value. Without this flexibility, it would be significantly more difficult to accomplish the myriad tasks and responsibilities that so many of us undertake.

Technology also helps us reach underserved populations – the new mother in a rural household, the home-bound elderly widow, or the physically challenged caretaker of an ill spouse. These individuals can experience the therapeutic benefits of being part of a group even if this group is not the traditional face-to-face experience. With technologically supported communication, they no longer need to be isolated and alone in their struggles.

Within our educational communities, schools and universities can also reach new and underserved markets. The same rural mother, home-bound widow, or physically challenged caretaker can attend school, albeit virtually. Distance education is one of the fastest growing educational offerings, and social work education is quickly adapting to this new reality. Recent U. S. Department of Education findings indicate that students in online learning conditions performed better than those receiving face-to-face instruction (Means, Toyama, Murphy, Bakia, & Jones, 2009, p.ix). Furthermore, online education has been shown to facilitate more organized instruction (Means, Toyama, Murphy, Bakia, & Jones, 2009). Online instructors cannot come into a class and just 'wing it'. Materials need to be prepared in advance in a detailed, clearly organized fashion.

Finally, these new technological communication processes provide an opportunity to contribute to the resurgence of group work. Group workers' stock in trade is the development of cohesion and connection. We are the recognized experts in the process of helping individuals become a community, and we now have the opportunity to have our voice heard by assuming a leadership role in this new avenue for effective group work practice.

Are there issues, concerns and drawbacks to utilizing technology in conducting groups? Absolutely! As the word pairing exercise indicated, there are many potential deterrents inherent in the linking of technology and group work practice, and yet, at this point in time, we must do exactly that.

Technology and group work

Technology-enhanced communication with its good, bad and ugly qualities is with us to stay. It's time for group workers to truly embrace technology, incorporating it into our own practices and helping others use these newer platforms to create effective groups. Technology and group work cannot remain separate entities. It is no longer a choice; it is a mandate. We must not relinquish the leadership of online groups to those with technical expertise but little or no group work expertise. We are the ones who know about building community. We need to claim our heritage and collaborate with our colleagues in differing fields to develop and implement online groups with the safeguards, practices and processes essential to effective group work.

We also need to contribute to the research and scholarship on the creation of successful online communities. Much scholarly discussion and research is being conducted on best practices in online groups (Marathe, 2002; Palloff & Pratt, 2007; Parr & Ward, 2006; Simon & Stauber, 2009). We, as group work experts, need to become further involved in this area and raise our voices in this emerging literature. Group workers have a long-term heritage of developing effective communities, and it is precisely this expertise that needs to be shared and applied to this new modality of practice and education (Simon & Stauber, 2009). If this work is neglected – either by fear, indifference, lack of interest or competing priorities – group work as a contemporary modality is threatened. We have an opportunity to revitalize group work's role in today's environment. Let's grab this opportunity and restore group work to its rightful leadership place.

Demonstration of Group Work Faculty Resource Center

For the past fifteen years, there has been an ongoing group to support and empower the largely part-time faculty constituency that teaches group work courses at our school of social work. Using a theoretical base of social group work practices and procedures, including mutual aid, empowerment, cohesion, participation, and the developmental stages of groups over time, we developed an empowered constituency of faculty to enrich and highlight the importance of the school's group work offerings. (Bergart & Simon, 2004)

During the past two and a half years, this group of faculty has utilized Blackboard, the school's online platform, as a vehicle for increased communication. A dedicated group work faculty site was secured and is now the repository for all Committee material, including agendas and minutes of meetings, syllabi for all sections of group work courses, text and audio-visual resources, suggested exercises and assignments, administrative forms, professional association information, and group work faculty publications. The Committee began with traditional face-to-face gatherings, but gradually transitioned to alternating face-to-face and online meetings. During the past year, it has conducted most of its business on the Blackboard site via monthly Wimba Classroom audio meetings. This alternate format has been particularly effective in promoting the participation of the part-time faculty who have busy and diverse schedules that limit their on-campus availability. It also exposes these instructors to new technologies, encouraging the integration of these applications within their own teaching.

This Blackboard site, known as the Group Work Faculty Resource Center, opens with a welcome page and includes access to the following pages:

1. Announcements – a site for posting new information, updates and reminders. Announcements can be maintained as a permanent record or deleted by date. An email of the announcement can be sent to all members or select participants from this site.
2. Group work faculty information – a list of contact information for faculty. This is particularly useful for part-time faculty access.
3. Agenda and minutes of meetings – a repository for the agenda and minutes of each meeting. This minimizes the need for paper copies,

and provides a ready access to the history of the Committee.

4. Group work courses – a central location for the most current syllabi, assignments, readings, quizzes, copyright forms, and additional course material. This is the site most frequented by current faculty. Both full- and part-time faculty post their syllabi and related material, ensuring up-to-date and comprehensive records and accountability. Moreover, faculty new to teaching these courses have easy access to the course material.
5. Sample small group exercises – a list and description of the classroom exercises used in teaching the various group work courses. These exercises provide teaching tools for class experiences and connections.
6. Favorite course videos – a list of the videos and films used by class instructors. Links and comments on the videos can be indicated here.
7. Professional association information – a site where AASWG and other social work associations are identified. Information about the associations and their meeting dates, times, locations, and contact person(s) are posted here.
8. Conference information – a site for notices about upcoming professional conferences. Calls for proposals are also housed here.
9. Faculty scholarship – publications and presentations by the group work faculty are posted and shared in this location. Often faculty are unaware of their colleagues' professional work, and this central site allows for ready access to this information.
10. Meeting communications – the location of the links for group communication. The Discussion Board allows participants to connect around particular topics via text postings. These postings can be reviewed and revised by all participants. Members can respond to these communications in a threaded, chronological format. Wimba Classroom, a component of this page, allows for audio and text sharing by participants in a synchronous, real-time interaction from diverse locations.

Authors' note: The plenary address continued with a live online presentation of the Group Work Faculty Resource Center.

The presenters then used Wimba Classroom to demonstrate a live audio exchange among group work faculty. Two faculty members joined the presentation via the internet – one from his home in a Chicago suburb and one from her hotel room. The discussion focused on the sharing of information about upcoming continuing education workshops. The ensuing dialogue summarized the workshops and exchanged ideas about how best to market them. This discussion paralleled the process of a face-to-face meeting.

The live presentation provided a brief example of how the virtual meeting process can work in a task group setting. It is hoped that this presentation helped to diminish some of the mystique surrounding online communication groups and encouraged the increased use of technology. The complexities and potential frustrations of such applications are real, but the assets and opportunities are undeniable.

Conclusion

With regard to group work and technology, the future is now, and we can no longer resist the inevitable. We need to embrace all that technology has to offer, and use our group work skills to take a seat at the head of the table in creating effective, ethical online communities. We know how to develop groups. We can do this in an online format. Let's combine our group work knowledge, values, skills and practice wisdom with that of the technological experts to continue and enhance our group work legacy. It is time to embrace the inevitable!

References

Bergart, A.M. & Simon, S.R. (2005). Practicing what we preach: Creating groups for ourselves. *Social Work with Groups, 27*(4), 17-30.

Council on Social Work Education (2008). *Educational Policy and Accreditation Standards.*

Marathe, J. (2002). Creating online communities. Durlacher Research, Inc. Retrieved February 23, 2005, from www.durlacher.com

Means, B., Toyama, Y., Murphy R., Bakia, M. & Jones, K. (2009). *Evaluation of evidence-based practices in online learning: A meta-analysis and review of online learning studies.* U.S. Department of Education, Office of Planning, Evaluation, and Policy Development Policy and Program Studies Service, Center for Technology in Learning.

Palloff, R.M. & Pratt, K. (2007). *Building online learning communities: effective strategies for the virtual classroom.* San Francisco: Jossey Bass–Powell Higher and Adult Education Series.

Parr, J. & Ward, L. (2006). Building on foundations: creating an online community. *Journal of Technology and Teacher Education, 14*(4), 775-794.

Perron, B. & Powell, T.J. (2009). Online groups and social work practice. In A. Gitterman & R. Salmon (Eds.), *Encyclopedia of social work with groups.* New York: Routledge.

Simon, S. & Stauber, K.W. (2009). Group work education: The use of technology in teaching. In A. Gitterman & R. Salmon (Eds.), *Encyclopedia of Social Work with Groups.* New York: Routledge.

12
Communicating the values of social work with groups by talking in the idiom of the other
Implications for practice

Dominique Moyse Steinberg and Robert Salmon

Abstract: This paper presents the goals, methods, and implications of a workshop conducted at the XXXI Annual International Symposium of the Association for the Advancement of Social Work with Groups. A conceptual discussion about the need for better communication skills in promoting ethical and effective social work practice with groups sets the stage for a presentation of the workshop's goals and methods, after which implications for practice are offered. It is our hope that sharing the work and *raison d'être* of this symposium session will encourage practitioners to apply the ideas and material to their own agency settings.

Keywords: group work, groupwork, group work practice, social group work, group work method, social work ethics, social work values, effective social work practice, championing, social work with groups, communication, idiom, jargon

Introduction

> The single biggest problem with communication is the illusion that it has taken place. George Bernard Shaw

The purpose of the workshop conducted at the XXXI Annual International Symposium of the Association for the Advancement of Social Work with groups and presented in this paper was to help agency-based group workers to increase their skill at communicating the values of social work with groups to their professional significant others. *Significant others*, in this case, refers to those in a position to advance or impede ethical practice, such as administrators in a position to dictate unrealistic parameters and expectations, colleagues who can withhold referrals or sabotage ongoing practice, individuals from other fields who may not understand the mission or ethics of social work, and those in agency roles who might have goals in some degree of conflict (e.g., reducing costs) with those of social work (e.g., comprehensive psycho-social service).

Effectively communicating the value of group work to potential members and *their* significant others is an essential component of practice, and group workers are generally skilled at engaging people into groups. They are, however, less often skilled at communicating the value of group work to organizational stakeholders with widely differing roles, responsibilities, and vested interests. Thus, the purpose of this workshop was to help group workers to become better *champions* (Doel, 2006) for practice shaped by *social work* theory and ethics. There is no shortage of group-based services in social work today; however, anecdotal evidence from all quarters of the field (students, educational advisors, clinical supervisors, etc.) indicates that there *is* a shortage of ethical group work practice. The workshop presented in this paper is an attempt to respond to this crisis.

We first discuss the conceptual ground that sets the stage for this workshop, highlighting the need for trained group workers to improve their communication skills if they wish to respond effectively to the crisis created by increased use of groups in juxtaposition with decreased attention to the method in social work education. In this discussion we focus on one skill in particular, *talking in the idiom of the other* (Middleman & Wood, 1990), which refers to the ability to communicate to any "other" in a manner that is heard by, and more importantly persuasive to, that "other." We then present the workshop's goals and methods with some illustration of process. Finally, we offer implications for practice. We hope that this paper will both encourage and help interested readers to take, shape, and implement the material in/to their own settings.

Conceptual background

Social work practitioners who are trained in social work with groups must learn how to *talk in the idiom of the other* (Middleman & Wood, 1990a) if they wish to promote ethical and effective group services. *Talking in the idiom of the other* refers to the ability to use the kind of language (verbal and nonverbal) that is heard by, understood by, and ascribed meaning by the receiver (Barnlund, 1974; Doel, 2006; Feil, 1993; Kadushin & Kadushin, 1997; Middleman & Wood, 1990a; Preston-Shoot, 2007).

The tremendous rise in the use of groups across all social work venues today makes very evident, even urgent, the need for skilled communication about the knowledge base and values that drive ethical and effective *social work* practice with groups. Furthermore, communication needs to reach across a myriad types of culture (organizational, social, etc.), multiple and complex relationships (peers, authority figures, other professionals, etc.), and widely-varying realities (ideologies, perspectives, goals, etc.) and needs to be conducted in the many types of "tongues" or idioms that represent these constituencies. This is an enormous challenge! However, if the challenge is not met, group-based services will continue to be implemented according to principles of organizational efficiency rather than professional effectiveness.

Practitioners who know the theoretical foundations of social work and integrate that base into their approach to practice with groups understand the direct correlation between social work values and the characteristics of ethical and effective practice (Bartone, Rosenwald, & Bronstein, 2008; Brower, Arndt, & Ketterhagen, 2006; Doel, 2008; Finn, Jacobson, & Campana, 2006; Galinsky, Turnbull, Meglin, & Wilner, 1993; Gant, 2006; Jacobson & Rugeley, 2007; Macgowan, 2008; Magen, 2006; Pollio, 2002; Preston-Shoot, 2007). Many practitioners who work with groups, however, as well as program directors who design them, administrators who sanction them, and colleagues who refer to them do not (Doel, 2006; Goodman, 2006; Goodman & Munoz, 2004; Preston-Shoot, 2007). Rather, they perceive group services as cost-cutting measures based on organizational c-e-n-t-s rather than vehicles for good professional s-e-n-s-e (Middleman & Wood 1990). In direct violation of the NASW *Code of Ethics* (1999) and the AASWG *Standards for Social Work Practice with Groups* (2005), both of which expect competence, practitioners work according to manuals that offer mechanistic guidelines for covering mission-driven content but without the necessary related skill set to effectively engage clients with that content (Galinsky, Terzian, & Fraser, 2006). The end result is often disastrous to everyone involved (Bernstein, 1993; Freedberg, 1989; Goodman, 2006; Gitterman, 2010; Goodman & Munoz, 2004; Gumpert & Black, 2006; Konopka, 1978; Northen, 2006; Steinberg, 1993). Agency administrators blame practitioners for failures to meet goals in accordance with funding and other organizational mandates. Practitioners blame clients for failures in compliance or in reaching the outcome defined as success by the agency. Clients blame social work in general for being unhelpful and in particular, group work for being not only unhelpful but in some cases, harmful. If, therefore, this "dog kicking" cycle of unrealistic expectations and blame for poor results is to be broken, it is incumbent upon trained group workers to communicate to their professional significant others the value of *social work* practice in helping organizations to meet their goals and the value of method-based training to that end (Breton, 2006; Doel, 2006; Dunst, Trivette, & Deal, 1994; Germain & Gitterman, 1996; Kadushin & Kadushin, 1997; Kurland, 2007; Lietz, 2007; Middleman & Wood, 1990; Northen & Kurland, 2001; Preston-Shoot, 2007; Saleeby, 1994; Steinberg, 2004).

How did this ironic juxtaposition of increasing use and decreasing competence come about? How did the profession arrive at a point at which education does not teach social work students to practice this increasingly widespread method of service delivery? Certainly, it is unreasonable to blame organizations for having discovered the efficiency factor of group-based service, even if they have not discovered its effectiveness! Blame belongs alone to social work education for its complete lack of attention to this discovery. Not only, therefore, is the cold political climate (Goodman, 2006; Goodman & Munoz, 2004) in which social service interventions are shaped by *cents* rather than *sense* here (Middleman & Wood, 1990), the potential for damage in and by this harsh climate is now compounded by a lack of appropriate practice preparation by schools of social work.

In 2007 we presented a keynote address to the XXIX AASWG Annual International Symposium titled *"Joyful Noise." Gateways from Singing the Blues to the Hallelujah Chorus* (*Talking in the Idiom of the Other: A Necessary Skill for Responding to the Current Crisis in Social Work Practice).* In that address we proposed that clarion calls about the survival of group work in our profession are no longer necessary; group work has survived and will continue to do so as witnessed by the continuous articles and books on group work method, practice, and research. Rather, we proposed, the new challenge is to become better communicators about the clinical, organizational, social, and political values of *social work* practice with groups.

Communication is a complex process. Communicating values is particularly complex. It is not simply about choosing the right words, although it does begin with the ability to speak in a manner that carries meaning to the receiver of the intended message. It is about understanding the idioms (such as metaphors) that carry weight for the receiver, or the *other*. It is about skill in selecting the idiom (language, jargon, etc.) that enables an *other* to understand that it is to his or her advantage to adopt or at least seriously consider a given proposition. The goal of this workshop was to help participants to begin to develop such a skill with organizational *others* whose roles and responsibilities have the authority to shape quality of service.

Significant professional others for agency-based social workers are many and represent a wide array of interests: efficient organizational management, financial bottom lines, structural order, social order, efficient service delivery, service-delivery outcomes, behavioral change, psychological insight, individual and social education, physical and mental health, merit and morality, etc. Even within a single organization, representatives from many and more such areas of interest join forces in determining the outcome of every single case that comes through the door. Each such representative adheres to a specific professional ideology; each functions within a conceptual field that has explicit goals, particular definitions of work, and benchmarks for success and failure; each has an action-oriented mindset for carrying out a certain spectrum of tasks. Thus, each works according to particular principles that ultimately lead to a body of actions and related language, or "code" or idiom – a special jargon that represents the full force of its professional package (see diagram below)

At first glance one might think that the idiom of an organization, generally located in its mission statement, policies, rules and regulations, staff mandates, etc., would be enough to create a common conceptual and action ground for the varied professional representatives who function in that setting such that language would also be in common. In other words, one might presume that individuals who belong to a common organization with an overarching mission might use a shared vocabulary to fulfill their roles and responsibilities. This, however, is not at all the case. There may be a common but usually rather vague understanding of an organization's mission, or *raison d'être* (such as child welfare, community service, prevention, education, day treatment, etc.).

A mission statement is purposefully vague – at least vague enough or perhaps said otherwise abstract enough to embrace the plethora of tasks necessary to maintain organizational viability, not only keeping it quite removed from the worlds of work that collide on a daily basis but that may define both the means and end to meeting the mission very differently. Thus, while the various stakeholders may understand and agree on the general intent of an organization, their attempts to translate that mission through their respective conceptual fields (concrete services, for example, or organizational economics or staff management) may well move them farther and farther apart in setting and meeting objectives.

Theoretically, a social welfare organization creates complementary specializations intended to converge on the delivery of holistic service to each client/consumer so that medical service is received from a trained medical provider, vocational rehabilitation received from a trained vocational therapist, psychosocial counseling from a trained social worker, or – given the context of this discussion -- group-based services from a practitioner trained in group work. If there is no point of convergence on requirements for holistic service at the day-to-day level, however, or if there are enough competing interests, the result is misunderstanding, territorial tension, and service fragmentation. Mission statements may be stated in the abstract, but professional ideology is imbued in every "little" action of the daily service world. Thus, the accounting office prioritizes reduced costs, while clinicians prioritize quality of service, and the executive prioritizes quantity of service-delivery goals rather than quality in order to satisfy a funding source. This is the terrain in which much of current agency-based social work practice takes place – one of territorial imperatives and competing interests that result in vastly different idioms that need to be understood and utilized if meaningful communication is to take place. The purpose of the workshop described below was to help participants to increase their skill at speaking in the many idioms of their organizational others in order to become, as Doel (2006) puts it, better at *championing* group work based on social work values, ethics, and skill.

The workshop

Goal

The goal of the workshop was stated as follows:

> To help you to be better at communicating the organizational value of social group work to your organizational significant others – colleagues who can 'make or break' your ability to practice ethical and effective social work with people in groups:
>
> - Administration (go/no go)
> - Colleagues (referral sources or saboteurs)

Method

The following overview of the proposed workshop was then presented:

- Conceptual framework
- Defining 'idiom of the other'
- Effective communication
- Large-group exercise
- Small-group exercise
- Large-group discussion
- Reflections, implications for practice, evaluation

Workshop conceptual framework

With a shared understanding that trained practitioners constantly use the skills of *talking in the idiom of the other* (Middleman & Wood, 1990) in their service to clients, participants were asked to reflect anew on the meaning of and potential for using such a skill in an organizational context while the following passage was read aloud:

> To talk in the idiom of the other is to respond to the other person's disguised, illusory, or veiled messages using the same context and symbols, treating these as if they were real rather than unreal, and as if they were overt rather than covert expressions... the social worker does not force the person to expose herself until she is ready and does not force her to cut off the communication. This behavior is used... as a means of keeping the lines of communication open... The assumption underlying use of this behavior is that the open communication can be threatening, almost devastating to some persons and to all persons under certain circumstances. (Middleman & Wood, 1990a, 66-67)

The primary purpose of reading this excerpt was to note the fact that in the helping context, practitioners need to enter other people's frames of reference in order to help them communicate freely, fully, and honestly about what brings them into contact with the worker. While one might not at first glance think that open communication with professional peers or organizational colleagues might be *threatening* or *almost devastating to some persons,* in effect, to propose that a particular ideology or way of doing things is better (however defined) than another, inheres not just a little threat. Consider the proposal that certain clients would have better outcomes with long-term service in an agency funded for, based solely on, and organized completely toward short-term, cognitive/behavioral service! (The human-service literature has, in fact, for years abounded with debates about the merits of one type of social work practice approach over another in almost every realm imaginable, reflecting the very dynamic that was the topic of this workshop: clear communication, i.e., full agreement and understanding about every single word being bandied about with no room for misunderstanding and every party able to make meaning of the information received. It is, thus, both an intellectual and affective process.)

Participants were then asked to briefly discuss the potential for and possible issues related to transposing this concept from the counseling situation to the myriad requirements for communicating with professional significant others in their respective work settings. A major issue identified was organizational status -- that is, the frequently low status of social workers and the obstacles encountered in attempting to directly access high-level significant others. Another major issue identified was value conflicts -- that is, the often large difference in organizational priorities among staff. Thus, participants felt that even if they were to "scream" the values of group work from a clinical perspective, they would not be heard. Much louder, drowning out their pleas for holistic, strength-centered, long-term service according to ethical mandates of the social work profession would be the hands of the "dollar clock" ticking away, keeping count of the *number* of cases, *number* of referrals, *number* of home visits, *number* of people served in/by groups, *number* of dollars earned, etc.

A passage from *The Validation Breakthrough: Simple Techniques for Communicating with People with "Alzheimer's Type Dementia"* by Naomi Feil (1993) was then read to the group. The title of the passage is *Technique 9: Using a Clear, Low, Loving Tone of Voice*:

> A 90-year-old man, Time Confused and in Repetitive Motion, misses his wife. He cannot see, hear, or distinguish present from past time. Looking for his wife in the middle of the night, he finds a sleeping woman and climbs into her bed. The validating nurse understands that the 90-year-old man is returning to the past to fill his need to be with his wife... the nurse nevertheless uses a nurturing, loving tone to ease both the longing of the 90-year-old man and the terror of the female resident.
>
> 'Mr. Jones, you miss your wife so much, you thought that Mrs. Drew was your wife. Does she look like her?' she asks in a low, nurturing tone full of respect. As the nurse talks, she gently helps Mr. Jones out of Mrs. Drew's bed.
>
> The old man begins to cry as the nurse takes his arm, helping him back to his own room. 'You're a wonderful woman, Molly. You're the tops,' he says.
>
> The validating nurse responds in a loving voice, 'Molly was a wonderful wife. You love her very much. She is your sweetheart.' Together, in a soft voice, they sing, 'Let Me Call You Sweetheart, I'm in Love With You.' His love for his wife expressed, Mr. Jones falls asleep without medication.
>
> This technique should not be used when the disoriented person is

> expressing strong feeling and speaking in an emotional tone of voice. Using a warm, loving voice tone with someone who is angry, for example, will only create withdrawal or increased anger. In this case the Validation worker should match the voice tone...

We then read the last paragraph a second time for emphasis -- to make the point that the advice (noted immediately after) for practice is contrary to what one might ordinarily expect:

> This technique should not be used when the disoriented person is expressing strong feeling and speaking in an emotional tone of voice. Using a warm, loving voice tone with someone who is angry, for example, will only create withdrawal or increased anger. In this case the Validation worker should match the voice tone...

We noted that reflecting on this advice is germane to this workshop on communication, because Feil's advice goes against what we might try if we did not have this guide for tuning in (Shulman, 2006) – that is, if we did not have the required knowledge for appropriate action in this context. Helping professionals are not normally taught to respond to high-level agitation with a like decibel level; rather, they are taught to "de-escalate" the agitation with a calm front, language that appeals to reason, and a soothing voice. Here, however, Feil advises precisely the opposite. She proposes that in this context (i.e., this culture, this idiom) a cool quiet voice will simply push someone away – a kind of de-escalation, yes, but not one that is ultimately productive, because in this case de-escalation leads to withdrawal.

The point is that tuning in (Shulman, 2006) requires both knowledge of and sensitivity to context. Clearly, the concept of tuning in is not new to social work practitioners; in fact, cultural and other types of sensitivity are at the forefront of scholarship today; however, the concept must be adapted to dealing with professional significant others as well if we are to truly communicate in a way that holds meaning and the potential for sway.

In direct service we *talk in the idiom of the other* (Middleman & Wood, 1990a) all the time, but we have neither paid enough attention to the power of this communication skill nor developed our ability to utilize it enough to help our other significant professional *others* understand that it is to their benefit for the organization to practice and to promote *social* work practice with groups. Yet, as Middleman and Wood argue (1990a), it is the use of language -- literal, symbolic, or metaphoric -- *that is understood by and makes sense to* whatever *other* we face at any given moment that has the impact to persuade, convince, change, etc. Thus, to talk *in the idiom of the other* is less about projecting words *at* an *other* than it is about finding the right words – words that are likely to have the desired impact on the receiver or that pack a proverbial punch given that other's world of work. If group workers become more adept at using this skill with their organizational peers, they will go much farther much faster in lifting the field out of the current quagmire of unskilled and unprincipled use of groups that abounds today.

We wrapped up this section of the workshop with an example by Robert Salmon, which illustrates the successful use of this skill many years ago in an exchange with the Commissioner of Mental Health for the City of New York. The result was a unique MSW program track for paraprofessionals already in the public-service arena. The story follows, narrated by Salmon:

> Several decades ago, Dr. Billy Lee Jones, a Psychiatrist, was appointed to be the Commissioner of the New York City Department of Mental Health. He wanted to initiate a new, high quality, innovative program for minority students, who wanted to earn a MSW degree but could not afford the tuition costs. The costs were prohibitive for many of these individuals who were already working as paraprofessionals for the City. He asked his assistant, who was leaving the agency a few weeks later, which school he should approach. The response was immediate: *Hunter!* he replied. *They have a fine MSW program, attract minority students, and have a low tuition.* Accordingly, the Agency contacted the School and invited me to meet with Dr. Jones in his office.
>
> Dr. Jones opened the meeting with a rather aggressive tone: *I am starting my work here... and I want to initiate a high-level social work program for minority social workers. I want 25 students, all minority, to be accepted into your program in two weeks. Are you capable of producing 25 minority candidates in that period of time for your school?*
>
> Rising to the challenge and responding in like tone, I replied, *I can do it in* one *week, but you can't afford it!* to which he replied, *If I produce the money for the tuition, can you produce the students*?
>
> I then said, *We are talking about a quality program, here, and quality is very expensive I can do it, but I don't think you can come up with the money to pay for it.*
>
> The Commissioner replied, *I can come up with the money... No question!*, so I held out my hand and said, *Okay, then, we have a deal... without question*!

Thus was the special program initiated, with funding for full tuition plus two full-time professional development counselors.

This story illustrates the way in which the ability to enter into an *other's* idiom -- in this case a kind of high-level no-nonsense, *mano a mano* "talking turkey" – can enable the parties to communicate in a direct line – ensuring first, attention by the receiver and second, ensuring that the message received is the message sent. The direct and provocative tone (idiom) of the Commissioner was recognized and returned in kind, creating a verbal *pas de deux* with peacock feathers donned by both parties in parallel form, allowing both to immediately cut through to the central drama, *Can you deliver*? Niceties were replaced with directness using tone and language that both understood: professional goals, funding, making education available. Within a very few moments, each one had made a commitment to the other that left nothing to the imagination. One can only wonder what would have resulted had the Commissioner's idiom not been recognized, understood, and met in kind.

From conceptual to practical

The workshop transitioned from conceptual to practical at this point with these initial questions: *What does this mean in the everyday world of work? How can we begin to translate this intellectual appreciation of the power of communication into organizational capital?* To help participants to reflect on these questions they engaged in an activity intended to help them to discover the many languages, jargons, or idioms that organizational colleagues or *others* tend to speak. Here is an outline of the exercise.

Exercise Title: Semantics, Jargon, Metaphors, & Meaning.
A single sheet of newsprint was adhered to the wall, and the purpose of the exercise was explained as follows:

> To identify some of the idioms (components of language, semantics, jargons, metaphors, symbols, etc.) of OTHERS who are significant to our work – idioms or said otherwise, frames of reference in which we must be able to communicate if we are to get what we think needs to happen, to happen.

Initial questions for consideration

Who are some of our *others*, or major players with whom we deal in our agencies? Who do we need to interact with in order to make what we believe to be good group work to happen? Consider planning, forming, defending, designing, and/or otherwise wishing to practice group work. Some might be interested in our s-e-n-s-e of things; some might be interested in the c-e-n-t-s of things. Be specific.

As organizational roles, functions, labels, and interests were identified by participants, they were noted on the newsprint, eventually forming a list of such labels as: *CEO, bookkeeper, doctors, teachers, psychologists, psychiatrists, case managers, intake worker, clergy, psychotherapists, funding sources, managed care representatives, state regulation oversight commissions*, among many others.

As the list drew to an end we noted the many different constituents, idioms, frames of reference, and "cultures" about which we must actually know something if we are to communicate effectively. We also noted that communication is not just about enough knowledge of a jargon or idiom to express an idea but that it must be comprehensive enough to understand responses, using an example of the disastrous consequence of knowing just enough Morse Code to send a distress message but not enough to understand the response. We then engaged the group into a second exercise.

Exercise Title: Getting Your Attention

Participants joined in adhering several sheets of newsprint on the walls, assigning each one a label from the roster of organizational interests identified in the previous exercise, and the purpose of this exercise was explained as follows:

> To identify the idioms of the significant organizational others with whom we interact or who have "make or break" power over the nature and quality of our social work practice.

Initial question for consideration

For each area of interest identified, what key words, terms, phrases, metaphors, symbols, or any other components of language or jargon are likely to get the attention of individuals who represent that area?

Participants walked around the room, noting on each newsprint the words, phrases, or symbols that they believed would be particularly *idiomatic* to each area of interest. After some discussion on commonalities and differences among idioms and the degree to which gaps obviously exist in mindset (as reflected by those idioms) even among individuals who purport to work toward a common mission, participants were asked to try to develop statements on the value of group work as they understand it in the language or idiom of each interest area.

Developing statements that conveyed social work values in idioms that are often very foreign proved to be a daunting task. What makes this task so daunting is not simply the need to use unfamiliar language but the requirement to translate one's own value system into a language that may not have similar words with similar meaning and to do so with integrity. Thus, if one attempts to persuade an *other* of the long-term economic reward of certain interventions, one must be able to substantiate the argument. The challenge, therefore, is developing the ability to convert one's truth into another truth that is convincing to the other without marring the integrity of the original. *Talking in the idiom of the other* (Middleman & Wood, 1990) is not, therefore, simply about using words that are familiar and persuasive. It is the skill of using language to help an other understand the value of what is proposed in and to his or her particular realm of work. For example, talking about the clinical benefits of mutual aid is not likely to convince the finance office that longer or more frequent group sessions or other changes in the characteristics of sessions are necessary. The ability to argue a cost-benefit ratio that places the agency at a financial advantage, on the other hand, might achieve such a goal or at the very least, garner some attention.

Implications for practice

In transitioning to implications for practice, we asked various participants to read the following passages from *The Social Work Interview* (Kadushin & Kadushin, 1997), about "decoding" messages, noting intermittently how well the concept of decoding applies to the task of developing skills that will facilitate communication with others whose *idioms* may be very different:

> The words themselves, the symbols transmitted, are only part of the message communicated. Nonverbal images, smiles, hand gestures, etc.

> accompanying the sounds uttered are communicated simultaneously and modify, cancel, mitigate, or reinforce the meanings being given to the words... Depending on the metacommunication, the message explaining the message, the same words can be a question, a paraphrase, an order, a request, a neutral descriptive statement...
>
> Once the message is encoded and sent, the sender loses control over it. What is done to it, how it is received or ignored or misinterpreted or distorted, is beyond his power to change... Someone once said, *I never know what I said until I hear the response to it.* (1997, p. 25)

We noted that as Kadushin and Kadushin (1997) argue, one cannot assume that even if the ears of the person to whom a message has been sent have physically taken in the words, that he or she has taken in precisely what was intended by communicator *cannot* be assumed. People filter communication in order to guard against messages that make them uncomfortable, that threaten their favorable self-images, or that in some way shake up their psychic "peace and quiet." In short, they may never permit the intended message to *reach their mind*:

> Selective perception permits us to hear only what we allow ourselves to hear, in the way we allow ourselves to hear it... These mental processes protect us from hearing what would be inconvenient, or hurtful, or frightening... Thus we hear what we expect to hear – whether the person said it or not...
>
> Participants in the communicative act are both senders and receivers. Each seeks to influence the other and risks being influenced by the other. This is why communication is a threatening undertaking and why people erect so many defensive barriers to open communication. As Barnlund (1974, p. 163) says, "To communicate fully with another human being since it entails the risk of being changed oneself is to perform what may be the most courageous of all human acts." (1997, p. 26)

Thus, when one discusses the power of group membership, for example, one must be sensitive to the fact that the terms "power" and "membership" may hold very different even negative meanings for some, even though to group workers, it is a positive and desirable construct.

Even further, if someone is psychologically free to receive a message clear and undistorted, Kadushin and Kadushin (1997) argue that communication still has not taken place:

> Spoken language is merely a series of squeaks. The mind has to translate the squeaks so that they make sense. If the message is to be received with the same meaning that was intended when it was encoded, the words received have to be decoded *by shared definitions* (emph. added). The shades of meanings we give to words differ for all of us because our experiences have been different... (p. 26).

In sum, we noted that no two people have identical experiences that cause them to define terms identically, so that even one phrase or a single term evokes different images and meanings. Thus, "It must have been hard for you" may reduce to tears a young girl (but be) received with anger by a 25-year-old male who prides himself on his masculinity ... The message is the same; the reaction is different because the perception of the meaning of the message is different. (1997, p. 27).

Participants were then asked to reflect on the meaning of the issues noted above for their everyday worlds of work. We know that in organizations in which social work takes place we need to communicate to others who have very different frames of reference and perhaps competing values and priorities. What are some of the issues, challenges, possibilities, etc., in your own settings?

Many of the issues noted are common, such as location of the social worker in the organizational power structure including vertical access, low status of social work in the general social environment, widespread misunderstanding about the nature, role, and potential of social work, and the fact that much of what brings people into contact with social welfare agencies that would be best addressed by professional social workers is addressed by preprofessionals, paraprofessionals, nonprofessionals, and/or individuals from other disciplines with different knowledge bases, value systems, skill sets, etc.

Participants were then encouraged to develop statements about the potential of social work practice with groups to help social welfare organizations to meet their missions. As they struggled to communicate their knowledge and beliefs using the various idioms identified on the newsprint (i.e., role-related jargon, metaphors, frames of reference, etc.), they quickly discovered that to "know" or to "understand" is vastly different from communicating the value of that which is known or understood and even further, from doing so in other tongues. During this exercise, a secondary challenge emerged – that of not compromising the integrity of the value being promoted (e.g., clinical power) while focusing on the use of foreign concepts (e.g., financial cost-benefit ratios) in order to gain access to the receiver.

During this exercise three implications of learning to *talk in the idiom of the other* (Middleman & Wood, 1990) within the context of this workshop quickly came to light. First, the gap between some of the frames of reference and thus idioms that co-exist in a single social welfare organization under a common mission is enormous. Second, developing the skills to bridge those gaps is akin to becoming multi-lingual with enough facility in each language to command the use of particular words, phrases, concepts, metaphors, etc. in conveying a message that remains true to the communicator's intent even as it piques the interest of the receiver who may have vastly different goals or priorities. Third, if the values being promoted do not exist in the *other's* frame of reference, effective communication requires the ability to transform or at least translate those values into idioms (concepts, language, etc.) that can, in fact, be understood by the receiver.

A very simple illustration may be useful here. The same word – *aimer* – conveys liking and love in French. Thus, a communicator must:

1. have a basic knowledge of that language in order to know that this one word conveys both sentiments;
2. have a conceptual understanding of the distinction and recognize the potential importance of that distinction [as in, *I like you; let's be friends* vs. *I love you; let's get married*];
3. have enough language facility to express the nature of that difference in another idiom, in this case the French language; and
4. have enough language facility to understand the nature of a response and to continue the communication.

Even if the communicator understands that one word has two meanings, therefore, and further understands their conceptual distinction, he or she must develop enough technical facility to ensure that the meaning assigned in communication is appropriate. This section of the workshop ended with a consensus that such challenges notwithstanding, it is precisely this kind of multi-linguistic undertaking that is necessary for professional social workers to effect and affect practice in social welfare agencies increasingly directed by individuals who have little to no familiarity with the mission, goals, tasks, and benchmarks of successful social work practice.

Application and evaluation

The workshop drew to a close with participant evaluation of the work including the potential for applying the material. Challenges noted above were re-affirmed, but some opportunities were identified as well, as each participant identified at least one organizational other with whom he or she would attempt to communicate using that other's idiom. They also agreed that participating in this workshop re-sensitized them to the fact that the many idioms common to social work are often very unfamiliar to organizational colleagues, that they are therefore neither understood nor valued by those others, and that social workers must, indeed, become better communicators about practice goals and tasks.

Conclusion

As every parent of a teenager knows, one person's music is another person's noise! This is no less true in organizational life: to talk numbers may be off-putting to a clinician but sound like music to the organizational accountant while talking about mutual aid may be music to the ears of practitioners but render the accountant deaf. However, many frames of reference are in fact required to keep a social welfare alive and functioning, and it is not uncommon for tensions to exist between administrative and professional goals. Thus, if social workers wish to have an impact on policy and practice design, they must learn how to communicate the value of their propositions in a way that is heard by those with vastly different frames of reference. *Heard,* in this case, refers to being understood by the receiver as making good organizational s-e-n-s-e-in light of its broad social welfare mission.

References

Association for the Advancement of Social Work with Groups, Inc. (2005). *Standards for social work practice with groups.* (2nd ed.) Alexandria, VA: AASWG, Inc.

Barnlund, D.C. (1974). The public self and the private self in Japan and the United States. In J. C. Condon & S. Mitsoko (Eds.), *Intercultural encounters with Japan: Communication – contact and conflict.* Tokyo: Simul Press, 163-179.

Bartone, A., Rosenwald, M. & Bronstein, L. (2008). Examining the structure and dynamics of kinship care groups. *Social Work with Groups, 31*(3-4), 223-238.

Bernstein, S. (1993). What happened to self-determination? *Social Work with Groups, 16*(1-2), 3-15.

Breton, M. (2006). An empowerment perspective. In C. Garvin, L. Gutierrez & M. Galinsky (Eds.), *Handbook of social work with groups.* NY: Guilford Press, 58-75.

Brower, A., Arndt, R. & Ketterhagen, A. (2006). Very good solutions really do exist for group work research design problems. In C. Garvin, L. Gutierrez, & M. Galinsky (Eds.), *Handbook of social work with groups.* NY: Guilford Press, 435-446.

Doel, M. (2008). Assessing skills in groupwork: A program of continuing professional development. In C. Cohen, M. Phillips & M. Hanson (Eds.), *Strength and diversity in social work with groups: Think group.* NY: Routledge, 69-80.

Doel, M. (2006). *Using groupwork.* NY: Routledge.

Dunst, C., Trivette, C. & Deal, A. (Eds.). (1994). *Supporting and strengthening families: Methods, strategies, and practice, Volume 1.* Cambridge, MA: Brookline Books.

Feil, N. (1993). *The validation breakthrough: Simple techniques for communicating with people with "Alzheimer's type dementia."* Baltimore, MD: Health Professions Press.

Finn, J., Jacobson, M. & Campana, J.D. (2006). Participatory research, popular education, and popular theater: Contributions to group work. In C. Garvin, L. Gutierrez & M. Galinsky (Eds.), *Handbook of social work with groups.* NY: Guilford Press, 326-343.

Freedberg, S. (1989). Self-determination: Historical perspectives and effect on current practice. *Social Work, 34*(1), 33-38.

Galinsky, M., Terzian, M. & Fraser, M. (2006). The art of group work practice with manualized curricula. *Social Work with Groups, 29*(1), 11-26.

Galinsky, M., Turnbull, J., Meglin, D. & Wilner, M. (1993). Confronting the reality of collaborative practice research: Issues of practice, design, measurement, and team development. *Social Work, 38*(4), 440-449.

Gant, L. (2006). Evaluation of group work. In C. Garvin, L. Gutierrez & M. Galinsky (Eds.), *Handbook of social work with groups.* NY: Guilford Press, 461-476.

Germain C. & Gitterman A. (1996). *The life model of social work practice.* (2nd ed.), NY: Columbia University Press.

Gitterman, A. (2010). Mutual aid: Back to basics. In D. M. Steinberg (Ed.), *Orchestrating the power of groups: Beginnings, middles, and endings.* London, England: Whiting & Birch, 1-16.

Goodman, H. (2006). Organizational insight and the education of advanced group work practitioners. *Social Work with Groups, 29*(2-3), 91-104.

Goodman, H. & Munoz, M. (2004). Developing social group work skills for contemporary agency practice. *Social Work with Groups, 27*(1), 17-34.

Gumpert, J. & Black, P. (2006). Ethical issues in group work: What are they? How are they managed? *Social Work with Groups, 29*(4), 61-74.

Jacobson, M. & Rugeley, C. (2007). Community-based participatory research: Group work for social justice and community change. *Social Work with Groups, 30*(4), 21-40.

Kadushin, A. & Kadushin, G. (1997). *The social work interview.* (4th ed.), New York: Columbia University Press

Konopka, G. (2005). The significance of social group work based on ethical values. In R. Kurland & A. Malekoff (Eds.), *A quarter century of classics (1978-2004).* Binghamton, NY: Haworth Press, 17-28.

Kurland, R. (2007). Debunking the "blood theory" of social work with groups: Group workers *are* made and not born. *Social Work with Groups, 30*(1), 11-24.

Kurland, R. & Salmon, R. (2008). Caught in the doorway between education and practice: Group work's battle for survival. In C. Cohen, M. Phillips & M. Hanson (Eds.), *Strength and diversity in social work with groups: Think group.* NY: Routledge, 10-20.

Kurland, R. & Salmon, R. (1996). Making joyful noise: Presenting, promoting and portraying group work to and for the profession. In B. Stempler & M. Glass (Eds.), *Social group work today and tomorrow: Moving from theory to advanced training and practice.* Binghamton, NY: Haworth Press, 19-32.

Lietz, C. (2007). Strengths-based group practice: Three case studies. *Social Work with Groups, 30*(2), 73-88.

Macgowan, M. (2008). *A guide to evidence-based group work.* NY: Oxford University Press.

Magen, R. (2006). Measurement issues. In C. Garvin, L. Gutierrez & M. Galinsky (Eds.), *Handbook of social work with groups.* NY: Guilford Press, 447-460.

Middleman, R. & Wood, G. (1990). From social group work to social work with groups, *Social Work with Groups, 13*(3), 3-20.

Middleman, R. & Wood, G. (1990a). *Skills for direct practice in social work.* NY: Colombia University Press.

Northen, H. (2006). Ethics and values in group work. In C. Garvin, L. Gutierrez, & M. Galinsky (Eds.), *Handbook of social work with groups.* NY: Guilford Press, 76-90.

Northen, H. & Kurland, R. (2001). *Social Work with Groups.* (3rd ed.), NY: Columbia University Press.

Pollio, D. (2002). The evidence-based group worker. *Social Work with Groups, 25*(4), 57-70.

Preston-Shoot, M. (2007). *Effective groupwork.* (2nd ed.), NY: Palgrave MacMillan.

Saleeby, D. (2006). *Strengths perspective in social work practice.* (4th ed.), NY: Pearson Longman Publishers.

Shulman, L. (2006). *The skills of helping individuals, families, groups, and communities.* (5th ed.) Milton, CA: Thomson-Brooks/Cole.

Steinberg, D.M. (1993). Some findings from a study of the impact of group work education on social work practitioners' work with groups. *Social Work with Groups, 16*(3), 23-39.

Steinberg, D.M. (2004). *The Mutual-aid approach to working with groups: Helping people to help one another.* (2nd ed.), NY: Taylor & Francis/ Routledge.

Steinberg, D.M. & Salmon, R. (2007). *Revisiting "Joyful Noise." Gateways from singing the blues to the Hallelujah Chorus (Talking in the idiom of the other: A necessary skill for responding to the current crisis in social work practice).* Keynote, XXIX Annual International Symposium of the Association for the Advancement of Social Work with Groups. Also in G. Tully, S. Palombo, & K. Sweeney, K. (Eds.), (2011). *Groups: Gateways to growth.* London, England: Whiting & Birch, 10-24.

U.S. National Association of Social Workers (1999). *Code of ethics.* Washington, D.C.: NASW Press.

13
The metamorphosis of a university social group work club

Cheryl Lee and Eliette Montiel

Abstract: This paper discusses a longitudinal study (N=222) of a university social group work club affiliated with the Association for the Advancement of Social Work with Groups. The club's purposes were: 1) to nurture social group work; 2) to engage students, practitioners and academics in a collaborative educational group work experience, and; 3) to link members to an international organization that supports all aspects of group work. Members experienced professional growth, satisfaction, and willingness to assume leadership roles to nurture the state chapter. Recommendations include establishing group work clubs in social work schools and departments to support social group work practice.

Keywords: group work club, Association for the Advancement of Social Work with Groups, relational model, social justice

Introduction

This paper describes a follow-up study of a university social group work club that was created to meet the needs of students and practitioners to further group work expertise and foster mutual aid. The university group had a vision to empower students, practitioners and academics with discussions about group work; thus, it was named 'The Group Work Club' after the clubs that developed in settlement houses. Group work has its roots in the settlement house movement in England, the

United States and Canada (Sullivan, Mesbur & Lang, 2009; Toseland & Rivas, 2009). Jane Addams visited Toynbee Hall, a settlement house in London in 1888, before creating Hull House in Chicago to serve new immigrants with adult discussion clubs, children's activity clubs, music, art, and sports clubs among other empowering group activities (Lee, 2009).

Review of the literature

Purpose of the club

The Group Work Club's purposes have roots in the literature. Bergart and Simon (2004) encouraged social group workers to form support groups when they feel isolated in their social work practices. Simon, Webster and Horn (2007) recommended connecting students to professional organizations such as AASWG to provide support, mentoring opportunities, and networking. The decline of social group work in curricula with the advent of generalist social work practice has been documented by Birnbaum and Wayne (2000) and Lee (2005), making it critical to supplement group work education. Sullivan (2006) noted the concurrent loss of members in the international social group work organization, the Association for the Advancement of Social Work and Groups (AASWG). AASWG is a professional organization dedicated to the promotion of group work and the use of ethical multi-cultural group work practice (Sullivan, 2006).
The Group Work Club's purposes address these identified needs. The purposes, which developed over the course of The Club's first year, became: (1) to nurture social group work in agencies; (2) to engage students, practitioners and academics in a collaborative educational group work experience; and (3) to link members to AASWG.

Conceptual framework

The literature is replete with discussion of group development and stages of group (Anderson, 1997; Berman-Rossi, 1993; Garland, Jones

& Kolodny, 1965; Gitterman, 2005; Kurland & Salmon, 2005; Schiller, 1997; 2007; Shulman, 2009; Toseland & Rivas, 2009; Tuckman & Jensen, 1977). The Club's development is best described using Schiller's relational model (Schiller, 1997; 2002; 2007). In this model the stages of development are: pre-affiliation, establishing a relational base, mutuality and interpersonal empathy, challenge and change, and separation/termination. This feminist approach focuses on developing relationships and members connecting with one another. The majority of the members are women and members of different ethnic minority groups that have collectivist cultures in which harmony is valued.

During the first year of The Club, the facilitators and members planned for meetings, attracted members, met often, and developed close relationships with each other while forging a connection with the AASWG state chapter (which was experiencing difficulties) and the international organization. In the second year of The Club, mutuality and interpersonal empathy was evident at meetings. At the first meeting of the second year, a sharing and activity planning meeting, members provided peer consultation about groups they were facilitating. They also planned for upcoming group meetings on topics of interest: groups for victims of sexual assault, people experiencing alcohol and substance addictions, older adults, and social justice. At the social justice group meeting, members shared ideas about what social justice meant to them. They found commonalities and differences but were able to respect members' passions and learn from one another. This is the hallmark of the mutuality and interpersonal empathy stage when members can support others even when there are ideological differences (Schiller, 1997; 2007).

The Group Work Club experienced a challenge during the second year when the State Chapter's President and several board members wanted to resign their positions and dissolve the chapter due to a lack of available leaders. After much discussion among The Club members, consensus was reached to help the chapter by assuming leadership roles. Since it was the second year of The Club, many of the graduate student members of The Club had obtained their masters in social work (MSW degrees) and were practitioners in the community; therefore, they were eligible to serve on the state chapter board and run for office. A meeting was held with the former officers and members of the board who were delighted that The Club was able to keep the chapter alive (although it would be re-located several hours away in a different city). The metamorphosis of The Club into the state chapter is now complete with newly elected officers and board members. The process of transitioning from a university club to a state AASWG chapter fits with the fourth stage of Schiller's Relational Model, 'challenge and change' (Schiller, 1997; 2002; 2007). In this stage of a group's development, members are able to overcome conflict while maintaining connections.

Activities and educational programs

Programs and activities have major value for groups (Comer & Hirayama, 2009; Kurland & Salmon, 2005) and must be related to the group's purposes. The importance of activities was documented by Oborne and Maidment (2007), who wrote about a fathers' group that utilized activities such as indoor and outdoor team sports and an evening barbecue to foster cohesion among the group members as well as to strengthen relationships with their children. The Club had several meetings in which the major theme was activities. One session involved the creation of posters for the Gay and Lesbian Pride Parade. Members brought art supplies and shared their ideas and talents to create posters. A member who has led arts and crafts groups facilitated the activity group. Members not only enjoyed creating posters with a social justice theme but also furthered The Club's goals of providing support and mutual aid.

In addition, there is a need for group work educational programs which The Club provided. Birnbaum and Wayne (2000) documented that group work education has been in a state of decline. Goodman and Munoz (2004) conducted a study demonstrating that many agency supervisors knew little about social group work, and student interns were frustrated when comparing lessons learned in their group work classes. They suggested continuing education for agency personnel so that adequate group work is accomplished. Also, they recommended that educators stay involved with students through professional organizations. Over the course of the two years of meeting, many faculty members have spoken to The Club about different groups with which they have been involved. In addition, Club members have benefited tremendously from educational presentations made by group workers in the community.

Social justice

Social justice is central to empowerment in group work (Breton, 2004; Ephross, 2004; Toseland & Rivas, 2008). According to Breton, every social work group should have a social justice component that is not merely theoretical but results in activities that assist oppressed groups. In his famous book, *The Pedagogy of the Oppressed*, Freire (2007) discusses how teachers can learn much from students and members of other oppressed groups. During the first year of The Club, the members expressed interest in conducting social justice activities together; however, it was not until The Club's second year that they organized a social justice activity, marching in the Gay Pride Parade with signs denoting 'The AASWG Group Work Club', equality for all, and gay/lesbian marriage.

Methodology

Design

To evaluate The Group Work Club, a quantitative/qualitative longitudinal design was employed. The research questions were:

1. What was the satisfaction level of Club members during the second year of The Club as compared to the first year of The Club?
2. What were the strengths of the meetings?
3. What suggestions did members offer to improve The Club?
4. Was there an increase in AASWG's membership as a result of The Club's existence?

Instrument

No group work standardized instruments were found appropriate to evaluate The Group Work Club. Unfortunately, a current social group work instrument created by MacGowan (2003) was not a fit for The Club because it was geared toward treatment groups. Therefore, an instrument from an allied profession was used. The Client Satisfaction Questionnaire (CSQ-8, Attkisson, 1985) is an eight-question scale measuring consumer satisfaction with services rendered. One question was: 'To what extent has the program met your needs?' (4 = almost all of my needs have been met, and 1 = none of my needs have been met). Scores could range from 8 to 32, and higher scores equated with greater satisfaction with the services. The measure's reliability has ranged from .86 to .94 in previous studies (Attkisson, 1985). The reliability of the scale for this sample was excellent (alpha = .92). In addition, the CSQ-8 has good concurrent validity (Attkisson, 1985). A global question was also asked regarding the quality of the meeting: 'How would you rate the quality of tonight's meeting?' (1 = very poor to 5 = outstanding). The last two questions were: 'What were things that you liked about our meeting?' and 'What are your suggestions for future club meetings?'

Data collection and analysis

At the end of each meeting, the participants completed a questionnaire, which included the Client Satisfaction Questionnaire (CSQ-8, Attkisson, 1985) and open-ended questions developed by the researchers. Members were instructed to answer the questionnaire as it related to The Group Work Club. Demographic questions and AASWG records provided additional data.

The quantitative data was analyzed using the Statistical Program for the Social Sciences (SPSS 16). Satisfaction Scores were obtained as an aggregate for the entire sample as well as for individual sessions. Independent means t-tests were used to compare results from Year 1 versus Year 2. Themes were identified and tallied for the two open-ended questions. Two researchers reviewed the open-ended responses to establish inter-rater reliability.

Sample

The sample of those who evaluated the meeting over the eight sessions in the second year of The Club was 107. The general orientation/ sharing group experiences and planning meeting for the second year included 13 members. Session 2 with a speaker on groups for victims of sexual assault included 15 members. For session 3, about alcohol and substance abuse recovery groups, there were 7 members. Session 4, sharing of group work experiences, included 13 participants. Session 5's topic was healthy aging groups for older adults; 18 Club members attended. Session 6 consisted of a group discussion about the meaning of social justice and included 12 members. At session 7, six members created placards to use at the Gay Pride Parade. At the culminating meeting/social justice activity, eight members marched together in the Gay Pride Parade, supporting equality for all and gay/lesbian marriages.

Year 2's Club membership had ethnic/cultural diversity (Table 1). Forty-six percent (n = 49) of The Club members were Caucasians/European Americans, 37% (n = 40) were of Latino descent, 6% (n = 6) were Asian Americans/Pacific Islanders, 6% (n = 6) were bi-ethnic, and 5% (n = 5) were African Americans. The majority of participants were females (n = 83, 78%), social work students (n = 68, 64%), and ages of members ranged from 21 to 61 (M = 33, SD = 13). Most of the members had previously facilitated groups (n = 85, 79%).

Table 1
Sample Characteristics (N = 107)

Variables	n	%
Gender		
Females	83	78
Males	14	22
Ethnicity		
European American	49	46
Latino (El Salvador, Mexico, Nicaragua, Peru)	40	37
Asian Americans/Pacific Islanders (China, Philippines, Vietnam)	6	6
Bi-ethnic/Bi-racial	6	6
African American	5	5

Results

Mean scores for the CSQ-8 were obtained for each of the eight sessions in Year 2 (Table 1). The means ranged from 28.38 (SD = 3.43) to 31.17 (SD = 1.33) out of a possible 32 points. Satisfaction scores were higher in Year 2 as compared to Year 1 (Y2 M = 29.85, SD = 2.86 vs.

Y1 M = 27.95, SD = 3.81, t = -4.05, p = .000). The global question assessing meeting quality resulted in mean scores of 5 out of a possible 5 points for seven of eight meetings. This rating indicates that members found the meetings to be of outstanding quality (Table 2).

Table 2
Member satisfaction with Group Work Club, Year Two (N = 107)

Session Number	CSQ-8			Meeting Quality Question		
	n	*M*	*SD*	*n*	*M*	*SD*
Session 1	13	31.08	1.26	13	5.00	0.00
Session 2	15	29.00	3.72	15	5.00	0.00
Session 3	7	31.14	1.86	7	5.00	0.00
Session 4	13	28.38	3.43	13	5.00	1.00
Session 5	18	29.61	2.87	18	5.00	1.00
Session 6	12	29.25	2.99	12	4.00	1.00
Session 7	6	31.17	1.33	6	5.00	0.00
Session 8	8	31.12	1.81	8	5.00	0.00

One qualitative question asked participants the strengths of the meetings. There were 107 responses to the strengths question (Table 3 overleaf) which were organized into themes. The strengths most frequently noted were: speakers (f = 31, 23%), sharing/mutual aid (f = 27, 20%), skills/knowledge (f = 13, 10%), social environment (f = 12, 9%), and networking (f = 12, 9%).

The 70 suggestions about meetings were grouped into the following themes: *speakers* on a variety of relevant topics who have group work experience; *activities* such as music and art activities and small group experiential exercises; *skills and techniques of group work* such as becoming a more effective facilitator; *social justice activities* such as feeding the homeless; *logistics,* changing day, time, or location; *attracting and maintaining new members; more processing; structure,* starting and ending on time; and *create a strategic plan.*

Table 3
Things you liked about the meeting

Strengths*	*f*	%
Speakers/presentations/topics *(having different speakers in the meetings, writing groups for older adults, groups for sexual assault victims, etc.)*	31	23.13
Sharing/mutual aid *(sharing experiences, helping each other)*	27	20.15
Skills/knowledge *(practice skills learned, Icebreakers, group work knowledge)*	13	9.70
Social environment *(welcoming, friendly, intimate, make friends, relaxing, fun, openness)*	12	8.96
Networking *(meeting new people, reconnecting with old members)*	12	8.96
Food	12	8.96
Participation in social justice activity *(reflections on social justice activity/gay pride parade)*	8	5.97
Cohesiveness *(unity of group)*	7	5.22
Processing	7	5.22
Structure/logistics *(i.e. meeting day and time)*	3	2.24
Link to AASWG *(discussing organization, conferences, etc.)*	2	1.49

*Multiple responses were possible.

In reviewing statistics regarding membership in AASWG, as a result of The Club's formation, AASWG's membership in the state increased by one-third or 17 members during the first year of The Club. Many of these members renewed their memberships. Five additional members joined in the second year.

The following quotes illustrate different members' meeting experiences:

> *My experience at The Group Work Club was a positive one. I did not know what to expect. However, when I arrived, everyone was welcoming. It is nice to know that there is a group on campus that encourages students to get together and share their experiences regarding group work. I also liked the fact that the Club provides guest speakers so that we can gain and enhance skills to be effective group work facilitators.*

> *The discussion of social justice was very interesting because I was able to learn about each individual in the group. It highlighted the reasons we became social workers. We want to make our society just and that is why the group decided to participate in the Gay Pride Parade on May 17. The group has been working towards being a force in the community. Participating in this event will allow the group to bond and to stand up for social justice.*

> *I loved the icebreaker exercise, as I thought it was a good way to acclimate the new people to a group setting. I felt as though people were able to relax and really show their personalities. As I looked around the room during the icebreaker, I felt as if I belonged here because of the great personalities in the room.*

> *I was initially interested in attending The Club to learn more techniques and improve my clinical facilitation skills. I want to become exposed to other types of groups and I am eager to learn from the experiences of other practitioners. Much to my pleasant surprise the individuals who attended The Club meetings were of a diverse academic and professional background. The group appeared cohesive and members interacted well with one another. I decided to join AASWG, and I am looking forward to learning how to improve my skills so that I may better serve my clients. I think it is wonderful to have this recreational club as a way to provide practitioners education on group theory and facilitation.*

Limitations

There were several limitations in this study. The CSQ-8 instrument was not specifically designed to evaluate group work or a group work club. No standardized instrument could be found that was appropriate for evaluating a group work club. Responses on the evaluations might have been influenced by social desirability. A comparison group could not be found. Qualitative data interpretation might be biased (Padgett, 1998); however, the two researchers who analyzed the qualitative data provided a check on each other.

Discussion

The goal of this manuscript was to document the longitudinal evaluation of The Group Work Club whose purposes were: to nurture social group work, to engage students, practitioners and academics in a collaborative educational group work experience, and to link members to an international social work organization AASWG. The first research question examined the satisfaction level of group members during The Club's second year. Members were highly satisfied, exceeding the satisfaction level measured in The Club's first year. This finding converges with the literature which reports that often group workers feel isolated in their practice and benefit from professional consultation, collaboration and support (Bergart & Simon, 2004; Simon et al., 2007). Simon et al. recommend linking students to professional organizations such as AASWG to provide them with support, mentoring opportunities and networking. Group workers benefit when there is ongoing education about group work and group process (Goodman & Munoz, 2004). Club members reported they gained group work knowledge and skills, provided mutual aid, and interacted with members who had similar passions.

The second research question inquired about the strengths of The Club. Members enjoyed the speakers who presented on different types of groups, such as substance abuse, sexual assault and healthy aging for older adults. Another strength was mutual aid and sharing. The group work literature notes the power of mutual aid in groups (Gitterman, 2005). A third strength found that members appreciated learning group work knowledge and skills. Birnbaum and Wayne (2000) and Lee (2005) discuss the decline of social group work in curricula making it imperative to supplement group work education in creative ways.

The third research question explored members' suggestions about The Club as a way to gain insight into hindrances to The Club's success. The number one suggestion was to bring more speakers with knowledge and experience about group work and varied groups. It is sometimes difficult for The Club to obtain volunteer speakers especially because it has a limited budget. The members suggested more activities. One activity that The Group Work Club experienced in the second year involved arts and crafts. Members created posters for the local Gay Pride Parade. This highly rated activity meeting corroborates findings in the literature that activities have value for groups (Comer & Hirayama, 2009; Kurland & Salmon, 2005). The literature also advises that activities should be related to the purpose of the group. The art activity and the marching for equality and gay/lesbian marriage in the gay pride parade aligned with the purposes of The Club and social group work in general. Breton (2004) and Ephross (2004) state that every social work group needs to include a social justice component.

The final research question addressed whether AASWG membership would increase as a result of The Club. Over the course of The Club's two-year existence, membership in the AASWG state chapter has increased due to Club members joining the organization.

Implications for social group work research, education, and practice

Research on group work has increased; yet, there is still a great need for researchers to evaluate the effectiveness of group work interventions (Doel, 2008; Hoyle, Georgesen, & Webster, 2001; McGowan, 2003; Toseland & Horton, 2008). By continuing to collect data and analyze group meetings, group processes will be better understood and evidenced-based practice will develop.

The results of this study suggest that social work departments and schools could greatly benefit by creating social group work clubs. Group work clubs can enhance students' group work education and experience. The Club also provides a place where practitioners can learn about group work from one another.

In addition, AASWG will grow by supporting the formation of group work clubs in schools and departments of social work. The organization needs to think about its future, and students provide new ideas that will insure its growth and sustainability (Freire, 2007). The AASWG state chapter in this community was not only able to survive but thrive due to the energy and leadership of The Group Work Club.

Authors' Note

This article describes a follow-up study to the first year's evaluation of The Group Work Club. For readers interested in learning more about the beginning formulation of The Club, see article by Lee, C.D., Montiel, E., Atchisson, J., Liza, J., Flory, P. & Valenzuela, J. (2009). An innovative approach to support social group work: A university group work club. *Groupwork: An interdisciplinary journal for working with Groups, 19*(3), 11-26.

References

Anderson, J. (1997). *Social work with groups: A process model.* NY: Longman.

Attkisson, C.C. (1985). Client satisfaction questionnaire (CSQ-8). In K. Corcoran & J. Fischer (Eds.), *Measures for clinical practice: A source book.* New York: The Free Press, 120-122.

Bergart, A. & Simon, S.R. (2004). Practicing what we preach: Creating groups for ourselves. *Social Work with Groups, 27*(4), 17-30.

Berman-Rossi, T. (1993). Empowering groups through understanding stages of group development. *Social Work with Groups, 15*(2), 239-255.

Birnbaum, M & Wayne, J. (2000). Group work foundation generalist education: The necessity for curriculum change. *Journal of Social Work Education, 36*(2), 347-356.

Breton, M. (2004). An empowerment perspective. In C.D. Garvin, L.M. Gutierrez & M.J. Galinsky (Eds.), *Handbook of Social Work with Groups.* New York: The Guilford Press, 76-90.

Comer, E. & Hirayama, K. (2009). Activity: Use and selection. In A. Gitterman

& R. Salmon (Eds.), *Encyclopedia of social work with groups* New York: Routledge, 62-63.

Doel, M. (2008). Assessing skills in groupwork: A program of continuing professional development. In C. S. Cohen, M. H. Phillips & M. Hanson (Eds.), *Strength and diversity in social work with groups: Think group.* NY: Taylor & Francis, 69-80.

Ephross, P.H. (2004). Social work with groups: practice principles. In Ephross & Grief (Eds.), *Group work with populations at risk.* (2nd ed.) New York: Oxford University Press, 1-12.

Freire, P. (2007) *The pedagogy of the oppressed.* NY: Continuum.

Garland, J.A., Jones, H.E. & Kolodny, R.L. (1973). A model for stages of development in social work groups. In S. Bernstein (Ed.), *Explorations in group work.* Boston: Milford House, 17-71.

Gitterman, A. (2005). Group formation: Tasks, methods, and skills. In A. Gitterman & L. Shulman, (Eds.), *Mutual aid groups, vulnerable & resilient populations and the life cycle.* (3rd ed.) NY: Columbia University Press, 73-110.

Goodman, H. & Munoz, M. (2004). Developing social group work skills for contemporary agency practice. *Social Work with Groups, 27*(1), 2004.

Hoyle, R.H., Georgesen, J.C. & Webster, J.M. (2001). Analyzing data from individuals in groups: The past, the present, and the future. *Group Dynamics, 5*(1), 41-47.

Kurland, R. & Salmon, R. (2005). *Teaching a methods course in social work with groups.* Alexandria, VA: Council of Social Work Education.

Lee, C.D. (2005). Nuggets of gold from Alex Gitterman. *Reflections: Narratives of Professional Helping, 11*(2), 4-21.

Lee, J.A.B. (2009). Jane Addams. In A. Gitterman & R. Salmon (Eds.), *Encyclopedia of social work with groups.* New York: Routledge, 13-16.

Macgowan, M.J. (2003). Increasing engagement in groups: A measurement based approach. *Social Work with Groups, 26*(1), 5-28.

Padgett, D.K. (1998). *Qualitative methods in social work research: Challenges and rewards.* Thousand Oaks, CA: Sage Publications.

Oborne, M. & Maidment, J. (2007). C'mon guys! A program to facilitate father involvement in the primary school environment. *Groupwork, 17*(3), 8-24.

Schiller, L. (1997). Rethinking stages of development in women's groups: Implications for practice. *Social Work with Groups, 20*(3), 3-19.

Schiller, L. (2002). Process of an idea – how the relational model of group work developed. *Social Work with Groups, 25*(1), 159-166.

Schiller, L. (2007). Not for women only: Applying the relational model of group development with vulnerable populations. *Social Work with Groups, 30*(2), 11-26.

Shulman, L. (2009). Beginning phase. In A. Gitterman & R. Salmon (Eds.), *Encyclopedia of social work with groups*. New York: Routledge, 112-114.

Simon, S., Webster, J. & Horn, K. (2007). A critical call for connecting students with professional organizations. *Social Work with Groups, 30*(4), 5-19.

Sullivan, N.E. (2006). President's pen: Why belong to AASWG?! *Social Work with Groups Newsletter,* 1.

Sullivan, N.E., Mesbur, E.S. & Lang, N.C. (2009). Group work history: Past, present, and future. In A. Gitterman & R. Salmon (Eds.), *Encyclopedia of social work with groups*. New York: Routledge, 3-6.

Toseland, R.W. & Horton, H. (2008). Group work. In T. Mizrahi & H. Horton (Eds.), *The encyclopedia of social work*. Washington DC: National Association of Social Workers.

Toseland, R.W. & Rivas, R.F. (2009). *An introduction to group work practice.* Boston: Pearson.

Tuckman, B. & Jensen, M.A. (1977). Stages of small group development revisited. *Group and Organizacional Studies, 2*(1), 419-417.

14
Generalist social work practice with groups: Sharing the past, present, and future

Stephen J. Yanca and Louise C. Johnson

Abstract: Some believe generalist social work practice developed recently and caused a decline in the study of group work. However, generic curricula and neglect by social work organizations and educators contributed to this decline. Early settlers worked with individuals, families, groups, organizations, and communities. This is generalist practice which cannot exist without group work. Common roots and current relationships between group work and generalist practice are explored. Group interaction, process, and activities are fundamental to traditional group work. Many forms of group therapy use individual methods that evolved from casework. It is proposed that generalists typically use traditional group work originating from settlements. An ecosystem strengths approach to generalist practice with groups is presented using a generalist model as a framework for group work. The potential resurgence of group work is explored. The paper is based on the first text devoted to *Generalist Social Work Practice with Groups* (Yanca & Johnson, 2009).

Keywords: Generalist social work practice, group work, group work history

Introduction

Group work developed early in the history of social work. However, recently it appears that the study of group work as a major method of social work practice in the U.S. has declined (Tropp, 1978; Goldberg & Lamont, 1992; Steinberg, 1993; Birnbaum & Aurebach, 1994; Parry, 1995; Andrews, 2001; Ward, 2003; Kurland et al 2004; Kurland & Salmon, 2005). Most group workers in the U.S. who were specially trained in group work are in their 50s or older. Only a few schools of social work continue to provide a concentration or specialization in group work. This could threaten the education, training, and practice of group work by social workers in the U.S. Those specially trained and educated group workers have knowledge, skills, and experience that may not be available in the future. The education of future social workers is likely to be in the hands of educators who have very limited preparation in group work. This could result in the education of those future generations being limited and unduly influenced by textbooks and publications that may not reflect the importance of group interaction and group process.

Some believe the development of generalist practice has weakened group work as a practice method (Goldberg & Lamont, 1992; Parry, 1995; Ward, 2003). However, we believe social work practice with groups and generalist social work practice share common roots in settlement houses. In addition, we believe that most generalist social workers use traditional social work practice with groups. The fact is that generalist social work practice would not be possible without knowledge and skills in working with groups, because generalists must be prepared to work with individuals, families, groups, organizations, and communities. Families can be seen as a special case of groups. Working within organizations typically involves various task groups. Community work cannot be accomplished without working with task groups. We believe the future of group work may be in the hands of group workers and generalist social workers and, in particular, generalist social work educators. In fact, most MSW social work students have been exposed to group work solely through their first year generalist practice curriculum (Steinberg, 1993; Knight, 1999; Clements, 2008). We believe that social work with groups and generalist practice share a common history, are tied to each other in current practice, and are destined to share a future. We propose this as mainly a position paper to present a different perspective on the relationship between group work and generalist social work practice. The material presented here is based in part on *Generalist Social Work Practice with Groups* (Yanca & Johnson, 2009), the first text devoted to generalist social work practice with groups.

There is a belief that generalist social work practice developed recently. However, we propose that early settlement house workers were the first generalist practitioners. They worked with and developed methods for practicing with individuals, families, groups, organizations, and communities. This is what generalist practitioners are trained to do. Thus, we believe that a major common historical root of group work and generalist practice is the settlement house movement. To demonstrate the relationship between traditional social group work and generalist practice, we discuss historical development of social work in the U.S. from three perspectives. First we look at early social work practice, contrasting the settlement movement (seen as the mother of social group work) and Community Organization Societies (COS). Then we consider social group work as one of the methods of social work. Third we look at generalist practice which also involves some consideration of the historical development of social work generally. We provide a brief description of the Johnson/Yanca model of generalist social work practice with groups and the types of groups that generalist social workers are most apt to facilitate. Finally, we present our vision for the future of group work and generalist social work practice.

What is group work?

Besides considering how group work developed in the U.S., we also provide a contrasting history of the development and functioning of some forms of group therapy or, in some cases, individual therapy in a group. Histories of group work in other countries may have different outcomes. We see some forms of group therapy as emerging out of practice that developed in the COS which focused on working with individuals. Later, when these social workers began to do group work, we believe that many of them gravitated toward approaches that were familiar to them, using individual methods (Kurland & Salmon, 2005). We see much of this as individual therapy or treatment in a group which used methods from psychiatry and psychology.

One of the difficulties in identifying some forms of group therapy as group work lies partly in defining the term group work. It is our contention that we need to identify who is doing the work. We believe that if the group is doing the work, we can logically call it group work. If it is the leader or therapist, then we would label it therapy, not group work. In other words if the therapeutic value or benefit is in group process and the activities and interactions among group members, then we would consider this to be group work. If it is in the interactions between the leader and individuals in the group, then it might be called group therapy if there is sufficient use of group process such as that which Yalom describes in his treatment of group psychotherapy (Yalom & Leszcz, 2005). However, we feel situations in which there is little or no use of group process and interaction and extensive use of individual treatment methods should be called individual therapy in a group if the primary therapeutic value or benefit lies in the interactions of individual members with the leader or therapist. Middleman (1978) pointed out this need for group process and called the focus on individual therapy in groups 'group casework' or 'the hot seat pattern.' Hartford (1978 as cited by Kurland & Salmon, 2005) called it 'aggregational therapy of individuals.' Kurland and Salmon (2005) referred to it as 'casework in a group.' If members are capable of engaging in therapeutic interactions, it is not appropriate for social workers to do the work that members can do for themselves. Doing so creates dependence at the least, or at the worst, it sends the message that the members are not capable of offering anything of value to the group or its members. Failing to use group process wastes an extremely valuable benefit that group work has to offer and sends negative messages to the group and its members.

We should clarify that we are not against group therapy or individual therapy in a group. However, we would not call this group work. There is certainly a need for group therapy and individual therapy in a group to treat people with severe mental impairments that limit or prevent them from successfully participating in group work and group process, especially if their impairment requires complicated or complex interventions that make it difficult if not impossible for other members to use in interactions with each other. However, this is one of the problems with utilizing approaches in groups that have been developed for treating individuals. The skill and complexity that are required for the effective use of these approaches can make it difficult for members to use them in a therapeutic group process with each other. Even higher functioning group members may have difficulty in learning these techniques, let alone those who may need them the most, but may not have the capacity to learn these sufficiently as a member of a group. In group work, the work should not be focused on using particular approaches or techniques. The work should be done by the group through activities and interactions and group process.

History and development of social work with groups and generalist social work practice

Early years: The settlement movement

Traditional social group work evolved largely from the settlement movement. Jane Addams epitomized the settler. Her ethic was to express warm spontaneous affection toward participants, to create cooperation and non resistance, and to build egalitarian or democratic social relationships (Knight, 2005, p.204). The settlement movement emphasized democratic ways of functioning. Addams saw groups as representing the democratic way and allowing group members to experience democracy as part of life (Knight, 2005; Yanca & Johnson, 2009).

According to Wilson (1976), settlers did not set out to use group work to deliver services. Referring to the early settlement houses, she stated:

> ... Few clients came by themselves. Instead they came in twos and threes and larger groups. . . In the beginning, the helpers just responded to what they faced. They did not say to themselves, 'Ah ha, here is the structure of a natural group!' ... (pp.3-4).

Thus, group work developed because people frequently came to the settlements with friends, neighbors, and family members. Settlement social workers worked with people in whatever fashion they presented themselves. As these groups were formed, others joined in and social work with groups and with families began. What is particularly important in how groups developed in settlements was that they were generated by the members. This represented an early version of 'starting where the client is,' a fundamental principle of social work practice, especially for generalist practitioners. In generalist social work practice, the social worker allows the situation to dictate the type of client system, similar to approaches used by settlers.

Another strand of early social work stems from the work of Mary Richmond and the COS that saw the causes of poverty as lying with the individual. This represents the conservative perspective. The COS worked with the poor and new immigrants in ways that sought to enable them to live 'moral lives' and lift themselves up out of poverty or avoid poverty and social problems (Johnson & Yanca, 2007). Services were delivered primarily on an individual basis with some work with families. There was a concern that services be limited to those who were considered 'worthy.' As the name indicates, this was charity work. The COS assumed a cause-effect relationship existed between social problems and their causes. The cause was generally assumed to be either moral inadequacy or lack of appropriate use of social resources. They believed that through the process of careful, thorough, systematic investigation of the evidence surrounding those in need, the worker could gain an accurate picture of the situation (Richmond, 1917; 1971). This was scientific philanthropy, the study of the social situation. It was the forerunner of the use of the scientific method to help people (Johnson & Yanca, 2007).

Settlers developed their own way of working with people and delivering services that was different from the COS. Using Jane Addams as a model, settlement workers were more likely to be warm, accepting, and nonjudgmental (Knight, 2005). They referred to those they served as members. They sought to build egalitarian relationships with individuals and within groups. They saw value in experiencing a sense of belonging and being part of collective action. They felt members were capable of fully participating in the work. This is the root of the importance placed on group interaction, group process, and activities by traditional group workers. Settlers did not assume that poverty and other social ills were caused by individuals. Nor were they interested in establishing eligibility or worthiness for charity. Instead, they saw people as needing access to resources. Often the lack of resources was caused by systems needing to be more responsive. This represents the liberal perspective. Settlers assumed people were capable of meeting their own needs if given the opportunity and made aware of resources and how to access them. This was an early form of a strengths approach to social work practice. Settlers believed that people were capable of taking care of themselves, but sometimes needed help in doing so. New immigrants might not be expected to be very knowledgeable about resources and about life in America under a democratic political system. Knowledge about resources might also be needed by those moving from rural areas where resources were not as plentiful (Simon, 1994).

Settlement houses responded to the same social problems and conditions differently from the COS. Settlers saw the source of problems to be in the environment or society and in a lack of understanding about how to cope with one's surroundings (Johnson & Yanca, 2007). They used educational and enriching group activities and worked to influence political and economic systems. Settlers sought to empower people to act on their own behalf. At times this meant helping them to organize to deal with barriers to accessing resources. Some of this was social action representing the radical perspective which was aimed at changing systems. Settlements often partnered with the emerging labor movement, providing places to meet. In some cases, labor organizers actually lived in the settlement house (Simon, 1994; Fabricant & Fisher, 2002). At this point what was taking place was a movement. Each agency developed its own way of working with the specific groups that existed in their setting. However, they all tended to have at least three focuses: the individual, the group, and the social environment (Yanca & Johnson, 2009; Johnson & Yanca, 2007). The community organization component of social work was developing, particularly social action (Johnson & Yanca, 2010).

The development of group work into a profession

In the 1920s the first course in group work was offered at Western Reserve University. The American Association for the Study of Groups began in the 1930s and published *The Group* (Alissi, 1980). During this time, social work and group work were attempting to be recognized as professions by other professions. This was especially so for group workers who provided recreation or activities. Institutions were offering group work training, mostly in schools of social work. Group work was developing as a method of social work that emphasized assisting people with growth and development and promoting citizen and social responsibility. Group process was an important aspect of social work with groups, as were activities and programming (Yanca & Johnson, 2009). According to Konopka (1972) 'Identification of group work with social work can be dated and credited to a person:

1946, Grace Longwell Coyle.' (p.9). At the National Conference on Social Work at a meeting of the American Association for the Study of Group Work (AASGW), Coyle presented the argument for group work as a method within social work. The AASGW voted to become a professional organization, the American Association of Group Workers (AAGW). Konopka identifies this as the moment when 'group work entered the family of social work' (Konopka, 1963, p.13). Some group workers who identified with recreation, group dynamics, and the like chose not to affiliate with AAGW (Konopka, 1972).

Mary Richmond is the mother of casework and was a leader in the COS. Late in her career she acknowledged that work with groups was an important part of social work (Wilson, 1976, p.5). However, her thinking was not embraced by many caseworkers who began using Freud and psychoanalytic theory which emphasized working with the individual in therapy. They thought that using this as an approach would provide a deeper theory base, along with recognition from other professions. In many respects, they sought to become more like psychiatry and psychology (Yanca & Johnson, 2009). Eventually, psychiatry and psychology began to develop methods for working with groups, as did social caseworkers (Konopka, 1956). We believe that most caseworkers tended to adopt approaches that were similar to psychiatry and psychology as opposed to using the group work that evolved out of the settlements. This may have occurred in part out of their desire to be seen as more professional or more clinical. Konopka (1972) saw this when she expressed concerns about the use of the term 'therapy' in referring to groups:

> Another aspect of the controversy between group work and group therapy should be discussed, namely the question of status. . . For some reason – probably because of the then high status of psychiatry on the North American continent – the term "therapy" seemed to indicate something more precious and more important than the term originally used by social work. This applies to both the individual and group approaches. Group work fought this prestige value from the beginning. This was in accord with the value system of the social group worker who resisted any class system, even in the theoretical or interprofessional realm. To indicate that they were talking about the same method in the framework of their own social work profession and of equal importance and skill, regardless of whether it was practice with healthy or sick people in groups, most social group workers consciously avoided the term group therapy to describe their practice; instead, they called it social

> group work. . . Social workers trained in a period when group work was practiced predominantly in the field of recreation and who had not kept up with its changing focus frequently disregarded the specialization in group method developed within their own profession. They turned to other professions to learn group therapy or practiced it without help in handling a group. . .Such verbal monstrosities as "group casework" were added. . . (pp.36-37).

We see most of these approaches adopted by caseworkers as using what they were familiar with – approaches focused on individuals (Kurland & Salmon, 2005). However, some of this work is, in reality, working with individuals in a group setting with little or no use of group interaction or group process. Most social workers who practice traditional group work view group process as essential to social work with groups (Middleman, 1978). New approaches developed, especially those associated with cognitive behavioral theory, as psychoanalytic thinking became less of an influence in psychiatry, psychology, and social casework. Most of these new approaches have been adopted by social workers who work with treatment groups (Alissi, 1980, p.24).

The National Association of Social Workers (NASW) was formed in 1955 by seven professional organizations including AAGW. Social group work became a method of social work and a field of practice. Several sections were formed including group work. It was assumed that articles on group work would appear in the new publication *Social Work.* So publication of *The Group* ceased. Unfortunately articles on group work did not occur very often. Group workers maintained an identity for a short time through the group work section but in 1962 NASW abandoned sections. Some group workers felt they had lost their identity and group work was losing its importance. Group workers were always much smaller in numbers and caseworkers dominated social work. Many group workers used activities and they felt the emphasis on talk therapy tended to place them in a lesser role. Some social workers saw group workers as primarily recreation workers. Group workers felt there was a loss of emphasis on using group process as an important element in bringing about change. With the increasing use of talk therapy, group workers felt there was less emphasis on social concerns and more on individuals and individual problems. In other words, group workers felt they had become second class citizens in the social work profession (Andrews, 2001). In 1979 some social group workers formed the Association for the Advancement of Social Work with Groups (AASWG) and a journal *Social Work with Groups: A Journal of Community and Clinical Practice* began publication. Today AASWG and a dedicated group of practitioners and educators work to keep traditional social group work alive (Andrews, 2001). The recent NASW agenda has been driven by licensing and vendorship. There is little if any attention paid to issues related to group work, or even generalist practice for that matter.

The emergence of generalist practice

Two other developments in the 1960s significantly affected the practice of social work with groups. First was social systems theory that allowed for a new view of group process. Our understanding of the nature of group process was strongly influenced by this. Social systems theory also provided an understanding about the interactions of various systems with which social workers are engaged – individuals, families, small groups, organizations, and communities. The second development was the beginning conceptualization of integrated social work practice which was the forerunner of today's generalist social work practice. An approach to social work practice was emerging in which a general theory base was used to respond to the initial need and assess person in environment or client in situation. The worker and client used the relationship developed in the process to choose the client system, the unit of attention, and an intervention that was based on one of the more specific approaches from the worker's intervention repertoire. This is the essence of generalist practice that began to emerge (Johnson & Yanca, 2010).

During the 1970s, Baccalaureate Social Work (BSW) Programs began to be accredited. Programs at the baccalaureate level were not new. They had existed for many years, often in sociology departments. They were found in land grant institutions and were particularly strong in southeastern states. They were important providers for line workers in the public social services. When the Council on Social Work Education (CSWE) was formed in 1952, BSW programs were not included. However, they continued to exist and there was pressure from various sources that saw the need for recognition. Manpower shortages in the 1960s placed additional pressure to professionalize baccalaureate graduates. Several formulations of competencies appropriate for BSW graduates were developed (see Southern Regional Conference, Barker/

Briggs Study, and Baer/Federico discussed in McLean, 1979). Generalist practice emerged as the kind of practice that was found to fit the needs of these BSWs. In fact, generalist practice is the required model by the CSWE for the BSW. It has subsequently also been required for the first year of the MSW curriculum. Unfortunately CSWE has not emphasized the need to develop and use group work skills as fundamental to generalist practice. To us, it seems obvious that these skills, especially the ability to understand and facilitate group process, are absolutely essential to generalist practice, but there seems to be a lack of emphasis on this aspect of generalist practice.

At the Association of Baccalaureate Social Work Program Directors (BPD) 2009 annual conference, Dean Pierce, Director of the Office of Social Work Accreditation and Educational Excellence for CSWE, presented a history of CSWE and discussed the origins of the use of the term generalist practice. He identified the Southern Regional Education Board Regional Conference in 1970 as the first recorded use of the term that he was able to find in the records of CSWE. He bemoaned the use of the term generalist practice. Later he was asked what he would have called this practice and he responded 'GOFSWo' or 'good old fashioned social work.'

As authors of this paper, we share Pierce's observation and believe generalist practice evolved out of the early roots of social work, particularly those of the settlement movement. In her practice of social group work in settlements and later in developing a group work program in a large state hospital, one of the authors recognized the need to also work with individuals, families, communities – and, in the later case, with the organization itself. This led to her interest in generalist social work. Her experience exemplifies our position that generalist practice arose out of the settlement houses.

The other author saw a need to work with larger client systems other than individuals in his practice as a caseworker before graduate school. He chose the generalist curriculum for his first year. He chose group work the second year to learn how to work with multiclient systems. He also took courses in community organization and administration to round out his preparation for generalist social work practice. The authors arrived at the same conclusions by different routes. One came from group work to generalist practice. The other from casework to generalist practice to group work. Both concluded that working with only individuals is much too limiting and that generalist practice and group work go hand and hand with each other.

While BSW programs are a majority of the CSWE membership,

issues regarding generalist practice do not seem to be a high priority, especially considering the fact that the generalist model is the fundamental organizing framework for social work practice. BPD was formed to address the needs of BSW programs. However, even BPD does not appear to understand the importance of group work to generalist practice. There seems to be no real sense of urgency regarding the need to preserve and advance the development of group work theory and practice and to understand and use group process as basic to any form of real group work. If there is responsibility for the decline of group work as a method within social work, it would seem to be with the lack of attention from NASW, CSWE, and BPD and not because any of these are preoccupied with developing generalist practice. They do not seem to understand the fundamental role that group work plays in social work practice, particularly generalist practice, and the need to preserve social work with groups as a fundamental method of social work practice. Responsibility also lies heavily with graduate schools of social work, most of which have dismantled their group work sequences and have gone with structures that do not allow for much visibility and attention to group work, like generic approaches or various forms of interpersonal practice, (Tropp, 1978; Goldberg & Lamont, 1992; Steinberg, 1993; Birnbaum & Auerbach, 1994; Parry, 1995; Andrews, 2001; Ward, 2003; Kurland et al 2004; Kurland & Salmon, 2005). We believe that this change to generic curricula is a major cause of the decline in group work education, not generalist practice. Andrews (2001) cited Abels and Abels (1981) who attributed the decline to group workers being overwhelmed by the larger numbers of caseworkers. They referred to the change to generic curricula as the 'generocide of social group work' (Abels & Abels, 1981, p.10, as cited in Andrews, 2001, p.61). It was not necessary to completely dismantle group work education. Several schools have retained group work as a specialization. As a consequence of group work educators being overwhelmed in numbers by caseworker educators, we believe there is much more attention being paid to talk therapy, individual therapy, and individual therapy in a group. This has led to neglecting the importance of group interaction, activities, and group process, and contributes to the decline of real group work and a risk of losing much of our rich group work heritage (Middleman, 1978; Kurland & Salmon, 2005).

The more formal description of generalist practice as an approach to social work practice took place in the 1960s and 70s. Although the formal development of generalist social work practice is more recent, its basic practices have been used since the early beginnings of social work. It evolved from and is a blending of the two major approaches that developed in early social work practice – the settlement houses and the COS. However, as it has evolved, it seems more similar in philosophy to settlement work with its emphasis on client involvement and decision making, empowerment, collective action and group work, building on people's strengths, and working with multiclient systems. This broadened the arena for social work practice considerably. Settlers saw people as struggling to live in an often foreign environment, as needing resources, and as competent to participate in the work to be done. They would work with individuals, families, groups, organizations, or the community to bring about change. This is the basic approach used by the modern generalist social worker. It includes the absolute necessity of understanding and using group work with multiclient systems. Without group work, generalist social work practice is just casework. It is not generalist practice.

Types of groups currently used in generalist social work practice with groups

In 2006 we conducted a qualitative study of generalist practitioners and their work with families, groups, organizations, and communities in preparation for writing companion texts on families and on groups (Yanca & Johnson, 2008; 2009) to go along with our generalist practice text (Johnson & Yanca, 2010). The results were used to focus on the types of groups generalist social workers are facilitating in practice. We categorized these groups into these types: change oriented groups, support and self help groups, growth and development groups, and prevention groups. We identified task groups as being used in organizational and community work.

Change oriented groups facilitate problem solving and decision making or do counseling. We see therapy groups as composed of people who experienced some type of social or emotional damage that creates significant barriers to healthy functioning and requires some reversal. This makes it difficult for members to interact and participate in the work. We view counseling groups as composed of members who are capable of making decisions and carrying them out along with being able to participate in group interaction and process (Yanca & Johnson,

2009). Self help and support groups have seen tremendous growth. The prototype of self help groups is Alcohol Anonymous. Self help groups are included with support groups because we believe that the main benefit is support (Yanca & Johnson, 2009). In support groups, workers facilitate supportive interactions within the group, provide technical information to aid the discussion, and encourage the establishment of support networks outside of the group. These groups can focus on any difficult situation, including illnesses or health problems, cancer, dementia, grief and loss, and the like. One of the strengths of these groups is that other members are usually more available to each other, in some cases the availability is 24/7. Growth and skill development groups are by far the most common type of group found in human services. The purposes include promoting healthy social, physical, emotional, or spiritual growth of their members. These groups tend to make extensive use of activities and educational experiences (Yanca & Johnson, 2009). Groups are offered in various organizations such as YMCAs, YWCAs, community centers, and various modern day descendents of settlement houses. Prevention groups tend to blend activities from growth, support and change oriented groups. Prevention groups generally limit their membership to an identified 'at risk' population. Examples might be those at risk of using drugs or alcohol, becoming delinquent, or engaging in destructive gang behavior (Yanca & Johnson, 2009). Task groups are formed in order to accomplish a task or achieve a goal. Usually they are related to an organization or a community. The purpose for the group lies outside the group and is not focused on meeting individual needs or benefitting individual members. The focus is on a needed change in the ecosystem or the environment (Yanca & Johnson, 2009).

The Johnson/Yanca model of generalist social work practice with groups

We believe that when a group modality is used, group process is of great importance and should receive considerable attention. We believe that activity, group interaction, and group process are powerful tools in facilitating change. We believe the environment has a considerable influence on the functioning of the group and groups are very important in bringing about change in the environment and its agencies and communities. This is the heritage from traditional social group work. We choose to use the term 'social work with groups' rather than 'social group work.' Social work with groups is a more inclusive term and more accurately reflects the thinking used in generalist social work. We do this because we believe it more nearly represents the reality of practice, assessing the situation and deciding that the use of a group is the most appropriate focus rather than automatically applying a method (social group work).

The scientific aspects of the COS approach laid the foundation for the basic method used in generalist social work practice. The current formulation of our model of generalist practice reflects the scientific method. Briefly the model includes assessment, planning, action, and evaluation and termination. Typically before a research study is undertaken, the researcher examines the literature to determine what is known about the subject area. This corresponds to the assessment phase. Next are the hypotheses or research questions. In our model, planning is the second phase and it is similar to creating hypotheses. Essentially goals and objectives are hypotheses regarding what might be done to meet the needs of the client system. The action phase represents implementation of the goals and objectives utilizing any appropriate theory, model, or approach. This parallels implementing the research design in the scientific method. In a sense, the worker and client system are testing whether the theory, model, or approach will work to achieve the goals and meet the needs. Similarly evaluation corresponds to the analysis of the results. In our model, these same phases of the change process are used by group workers whenever they are working with groups throughout each stage of group development.

The Johnson/Yanca (2010) generalist practice model focuses on strengths and resources in the ecosystem during its four phases. We see these as relevant in every group session at every stage of development. Our version of group development includes the following stages:

1. *Orientation stage* – Members come together ... seek similarities in interest, and make an initial commitment ... There is an approach-avoidance ... Patterns of functioning around tasks begin to develop. Task roles ... emerge ... activity and orientation to the situation. Individuals make decisions about ... belonging to the group and whether to become dependent on other group members.
2. *The authority stage* – There is challenge to the influence and control of the group by individual members. Conflict develops;

members rebel and search for individual autonomy; power and control are issues; there may be dropouts. Structure and patterns of functioning are revised. Members share ideas and feelings about what the group should do and how the group should function. Norms and values develop through this sharing.

3. *The negotiation stage* – The group confronts, differs, and engages in conflict resolution. Goals, roles and tasks are designated and accepted. Group traditions are stronger, norms develop, personal involvement intensifies. Group cohesion is stronger, and members are freer in sharing information and opinions.
4. *The functional stage* – A high level of group integration ... little conflict about structure, and ways of functioning have been established. Roles are differentially assigned to members and accepted ... Communication channels are open and functional; goals and norms are known and accepted. The group has the capacity to change and adapt. Conflict and tension are managed ... a problem-solving capacity develops. Members are interdependent. Plans are implemented, tasks are completed, and goals are reached. The group can evaluate itself and its work.
5. *The disintegration stage* – At any of the first four stages, a group may begin to disintegrate. Signs ... include the lessening of the bond ... reduction in the frequency and strength of group interaction, in common norms or values for group members, and in the group's strength of influence on members ... members will ... be strengthening and increasing their interaction with their ecosystem ... (Johnson & Yanca, 2010, pp.344-345; Yanca & Johnson, 2009, pp.93-94)

Before, during, and after each session, the group worker assesses the needs and goals of each member and the group as a whole. For some groups, the group itself engages in assessment as members learn to use the change process for their own benefit or for use on the environment. Similarly, planning occurs before, during, and after each session as the group worker facilitates group development while ensuring that the actions of the group and its members contribute to accomplishing the group's purpose and members benefit from the group experience. Often the group engages in planning as it establishes and works on goals. The worker engages in actions to facilitate group development, to meet group and individual needs, and to ensure successful achievement of group and individual goals. The worker uses theories, models, or approaches that are accepted as good practice. The group acts to carry out its purpose. Evaluation occurs throughout as the group and the worker consider what works and what does not, what is needed and what is not, and what progress has been made and what to do when progress does not occur. Finally, termination occurs at the end of every session and serves to reinforce appropriate termination processes for when the group ends or members leave (Yanca & Johnson, 2009).

The Johnson/Yanca model of social work practice is an ever evolving contemporary generalist model of social work practice. Originally it was a problem solving/social systems model based on need, with intervention in whatever system was most suited for the work that needed to be done. It was an integration of understandings – both theoretical and practice wisdom – from many facets of social work practice. Now instead of social systems we refer to ecological system or ecosystem, which includes client system, environment, and interactions. Problem solving has evolved into a process: assessment, planning, action, and evaluation and termination. We see this as a change process to facilitate growth and change. We still see it as a response to human needs in which the worker partners with the client system to decide where the focus of work should be – whether individual, family, small group, organization, or community will be either the client system or the unit of attention. Vital considerations in this work are diversity and the strengths and resources of individuals and environments. We see this model as very similar in philosophy to the work in settlement houses. We see the work with small groups, their structure, process and development, as a vital component of contemporary generalist practice.

The future of generalist practice with groups

We believe in the potential resurgence of group work. As in the original settlements, this may not be generated so much by workers as by clients. The need for human contact and collective action is as strong as ever. If this resurgence is to take place, then group work research and publication must be expanded and include a strong focus on group process, interaction, and activities, and on other types of groups in addition to treatment and therapy groups. Without this, we are in danger of losing the fundamentals of some of our most important roots – the client driven need for socialization, the benefits of collective activities, mutual aid, and social action, and the importance of group activities, group interaction, and group process.

The increasing expense of individual therapy and the squeeze of managed care are likely to increase the need to provide help through groups. Even individual therapy in a group takes too much time. We believe in the power of the group to bring about change through activities and group process. Participation and belonging, giving and receiving help, support, group interaction, and the desire to receive positive feedback from the group can be highly motivating and rewarding. Increased emphasis on individualism leaves people longing for connections with others. Group work can fill this gap for some. It is likely that both the need and demand for traditional group work are still great. Some of the best evidence for this is the tremendous increase in self help and support groups and in various forms of social networking.

We see a need for more group work with populations who are changing the face of America. An aging population and increasing diversity are projected over the next several decades. The need is there for more traditional settlement work with these populations, but they are much different from those who were served in the past. Instead of coming from Europe and being assimilated into the dominant white culture, there are people of color from all over the world, especially Mexico and Central America, who are not as easily accepted or assimilated. These are not groups typically served by early settlements. There is a need for a diversity competent renaissance or a new version of settlements formed around the needs and aspirations of these diverse populations. Some of these new settlements may exist, but there are too few.

Geriatric social work has tremendous potential. It requires generalist practice skills with case management as the centerpiece. Within this generalist framework, we see group work as fundamental. People who are older are often isolated, especially as they lose spouses, friends, and relatives. Caregivers need respite and support. Socialization and support can best be met through groups. New and different housing and care options may emerge, especially group or congregate care and adult day activity programs, as nursing homes price themselves out of business. Long term care will likely be provided in smaller community based systems based on a social model rather than the medical model that exists in nursing homes. Actually most people in basic skill nursing homes do not need a nurse 24/7. They need assistance with food, clothing, shelter, various forms of self care, and, in some cases, supervision. They also need socialization and stimulation. We can foresee the geriatric social worker of the future serving a string of smaller facilities with 6-20 beds located in the community and operated by social workers or other disciplines trained in serving the basic and social needs of people who are older instead of working in large institutional type settings such as nursing homes. Groups, especially group activities, are vital to providing quality care and experiences in these facilities.

We predict that baby boomers in the U.S. will revisit and reinvent some of the alternative community living arrangements that developed during the 1960s. We think communal living, coops, shared care, and various resident owned systems will emerge. We might call it collective community care. In some of these, people will pool their talents and abilities to provide care for each other. Some will pool resources to pay for and even operate their own caregiving systems. One way to increase efficiency, lower cost, reduce exploitation, and ensure quality care is to own the business that provides one's care instead of relying on distant and detached owners or stockholders. The ultimate in accountability is to have people who are receiving the care also be the people who hire and fire those who deliver the care. Not only will the needs of many people who are older be met within new and recycled versions of collective living, but groups will continue to be vital in reducing social isolation and meeting everyday needs. Collective community care or group living is based on group work and can only be successful if groups are used to oversee the operation, provide services, meet needs, and maintain stability in living together. We see group work with people who are older as expanding and evolving. Senior centers, congregate meal sites, adult day activity programs, support groups, and the like will need to be greatly expanded to meet the needs of increased numbers of people who are older.

We see the development of virtual or electronic settlements. Some might bemoan the loss of personal contact, but young people today are leading the way in developing and using various forms of electronic social networking. We see these emerging into electronic groups. These have been around for awhile now in the form of chat rooms, Facebook, Twitter, etc. For those who would like more face to face interaction, there is video conferencing. We see this expanding beyond interaction between two sites and developing voice activated video conferencing from multiple sites so that one can literally hold a group on line. Some of these forms of electronic group work can serve as support systems and support groups. Some social workers have begun to use electronic media to provide therapy. While we do not see this as totally replacing traditional in person work, we know that some clients may prefer this. We believe that electronic service delivery, networking, and group work is greatly needed in rural areas, especially for people living in remote areas. Currently the lack of infrastructure or the slowness of some systems makes this difficult or impossible, but satellite internet systems hold great promise in potentially making these service delivery systems much more likely even in remote areas of the world.

Conclusion

Social work with groups and generalist social work practice are intertwined with each other. They share a common history, mainly in the settlement houses with the contribution of the scientific method from the COS. The futures of social work with groups and generalist practice continue to be intertwined as generalist practitioners must rely on knowledge and skills in group work in order to work with multiclient systems. This is an essential feature of generalist social work practice. We see the need for group work expanding along with the need to serve new populations in different ways, including electronically. We call on CSWE, BPD, NASW, and graduate schools of social work to join in a partnership along with the AASWG in advancing the study, education, and practice of traditional group work with its emphasis on group process.

We see traditional group work as being practiced by generalist social workers as well as by group workers. To the extent that this occurs now and in the future, it would appear that to some degree the future of group work may very well be in the hands of generalist social workers – and, to a great degree, in the hands of generalist social work educators at the BSW and MSW levels who need to continue to teach the importance of group process to the next generation of social workers. Just as group work made generalist practice possible, generalist social workers cannot abandon the practice of group work without also abandoning generalist social work practice.

References

Abels, S. & Abels, P. (Eds.) (1981). *Social work with groups: Proceedings, 1979 symposium.* Louisville: Committee for the Advancement of Social Work with Groups.

Alissi, A. (1980). *Perspectives on social group practice.* New York: Free Press.

Andrews, J. (2001). Group work's place in social work: A historical analysis. *Journal of Sociology and Social Welfare, 28*(4), 45-65.

Birnbaum, M. & Auerbach, C. (1994). Group work in graduate school education: The price of neglect. *Journal of Social Work Education, 30*(3), 325-335.

Clements, J. (2008). Social work students' perceived knowledge of and preparation for group work practice. *Social Work with Groups, 31*(3/4), 329-346.

Fabricant, M. & Fisher, R. (2002). *Settlement houses under siege: The struggle to sustain community organizations in New York City.* New York: Columbia University Press.

Goldberg, T. & Lamont, A. (1992). The impact of a generic curriculum on the practice of graduates: Does group work persist? In J. Garland (Ed.) *Group Work reaching out: People, places, and power.* New York: Haworth.

Johnson, L. & Yanca, S. (2007). *Social work practice: A generalist approach.* (9th ed.) Boston: Allyn & Bacon.

Johnson, L. & Yanca, S. (2010). *Social Work practice: A generalist approach.* (10th ed.) Boston: Allyn & Bacon.

Knight, C. (1999). BSW and MSW students' perceptions of their academic preparation for group work. *Journal of Teaching in Social Work, 18*(1/2), 133-148.

Knight, L. (2005). *Citizen: Jane Addams and the struggle for democracy.* Chicago: University of Chicago Press.

Konopka, G. (1956). The generic and the specific in group work practice in social work settings. *Social Work, 1*(1), 73-80.

Konopka, G. (1963). *Social group work: A helping process.* (1st ed.) Englewood Cliffs, N.J.: Prentice-Hall.

Konopka, G. (1972) *Social group work: A helping process.* (2nd ed.) Englewood Cliffs, N.J.: Prentice-Hall.

Kurland, R. & Salmon, R. (2005). Group work vs. casework in a group: Principles and implications for teaching and practice. *Social Work with Groups, 28*(3/4), 121-132.

Kurland, R., Salmon, R., Bitel, M., Goodman, H., Ludwig, K., Newman, E. & Sullivan, N. (2004). The survival of group work: A call to action. *Social*

Work with Groups, 27(1), 3-16.

McLean, A. (Ed.) (1979). Competency-based perspectives in Baccalaureate social work education: A report of the Estes Park Workshop, October 3-6,1979. Association of Baccalaureate Social Work Program Directors.

Middleman, R. (1978). Returning group process to group work. *Social Work with Groups, 1*(1), 15-26.

Parry, J. (1995). Social group work, sink or swim: Where is group work in a generalist curriculum?" In M. Feit, J. Ramey, J. Wodarski, & A. Mann (Eds.) *Capturing the power of diversity.* New York: Haworth.

Richmond, M. (1917 & 1971). *Social diagnosis.* New York: Russell Sage Foundation; reprint, Free Press.

Roberts, R. & Northern, H. (Eds.) (1976). *Theories of social work with groups.* New York: Columbia University Press.

Simon, B. (1994). *The empowerment Tradition in American social work: A history.* New York: Columbia University Press.

Steinberg, D. (1993). Some findings from a study on the impact of group work education on social work practitioners' work with groups. *Social Work with Groups, 16*, 23-39.

Tropp, E. (1978). Whatever happened to group work? *Social Work with Groups,* 1, 1, 85-94.

Ward, D. (2003). Where has real group work gone? Reasserting the fundamentals." In J. Lindsay, D. Turcotte & E. Hopmeyer (Eds.) *Crossing boundaries and developing alliances through group work.* New York: Haworth.

Wilson, G. (1976). From practice to theory: A personalized history. In R. Roberts, & H. Northern (Eds.) *Theories of social work with groups.* New York: Columbia Press.

Yalom, I. & Leszcz, M. (2005). *The theory and practice of group psychotherapy.* New York: Basic Books.

Yanca, S. & Johnson, L. (2008). *Generalist social work practice with families.* Boston: Allyn

Yanca, S. & Johnson, L. (2009). *Generalist social work practice with groups.* Boston: Allyn & Bacon.

15
Poster presentations at the 2009 AASWG Symposium

Overview

This section offers abstracts of the posters presented at the 2009 Symposium. As mentioned in our Editors' Overview, the poster session served as a vehicle for engaging students and emerging professionals in both AASWG and the Symposium. Posters provide a less intimidating option for an initial conference presentation. Many who have been able to take this first step in presenting their professional work have gone on to present papers at future symposia and/or to write journal articles. Some have even taken on leadership roles in our group work community. We are proud to feature their work.

Group work as a source of healing in disaster work
Sharima Ruwaida Abbas, Honolulu, Hawaii, USA

This poster explores group work as a source of healing for disaster survivors. Several types of disaster related group work practice are identified. Their commonality, differences, strengths and weaknesses as a source of healing are discussed. Implications for social work education and practice are highlighted.

American Muslims: Demographics, challenges, and possibilities for group-oriented social work
Whitney M. Akhtar, Evanston, Illinois, USA

Recent trends in social work have encouraged inclusion of spirituality as a source of strength for our clients. Becoming more familiar with

Islam and Muslims may help group-oriented social workers to learn how Muslims experience group settings, as well as how social work might be received by this population.

Strategies for school-based education support groups for teen parents

Jill Bajorek and Joni Coleman, Chicago, Illinois, USA

This poster assesses the benefits and challenges inherent in leading school-based educational support groups for teen parents. Issues such as leader qualifications and preparations, contracts, session topics, worker supervision, and the role of mutual aid are discussed. Recommendations for effective implementation of such groups are shared.

Empowering teen girls: A group work initiative

Sarah Buino, Chicago, Illinois, USA

Teen girls universally struggle with self-esteem issues. This poster highlights experiences of a group for teen girls focusing on enhancing self-image and healthy relationships. It reports the impact of instituting this group, which provided opportunities to explore new interests and connect with positive female role models.

Support groups for women who have been trafficked: Benefits and challenges

Smita Ekka Dewan, New York, New York, USA

To what extent can social group work address some of the needs of victims and survivors of human trafficking? This poster highlights the possible benefits of participation in support groups for women who have been trafficked. Unique characteristics of this population that pose challenges for group work are examined.

Support groups for families of neonatal intensive care unit patients (nicu): Benefits and challenges

Eleanor Doar, Chicago, Illinois, USA

Families with children in the neonatal intensive care unit (NICU) need considerable psychosocial support. This poster presents the results of interview-based research conducted with past NICU parents to determine whether support groups were offered and considered helpful. It also describes and assesses one such group conducted by the author.

Group work with at risk adolescent females

Erin Marie Garrity, Chicago, Illinois, USA

Adolescent girls facing significant ecological challenges may be considered "at risk". This poster examines current literature regarding supportive and preventative group work with girls during this vulnerable stage of development. It also assesses the author's experiences facilitating two differing girls groups in urban communities.

Opportunities and challenges in educational support groups for inflammatory bowel disease (IBD) patients

Stephanie Horgan, Chicago, Illinois, USA

This poster describes a patient education support group and the lessons learned from co-leading this group. Emphasis is placed on the need for such groups and the importance of the leaders identifying transference and counter-transference issues.

Multicultural group work in South Africa: Challenging the divide

Reineth Prinsloo, Pretoria, Gauteng, South Africa

This poster illustrates the narrative of successful community engagement projects using group work methodology. Students ran group work programs with members from all ethnic groups and socio-economic levels. The social developmental paradigm is entrenched in all social work intervention methods taught.

Stroke support groups: Topics from the past and ideas for the future

Karolina Lieponis, Lemont, Illinois, USA

This poster discusses stroke support group programs that have been used successfully at hospitals in a Midwestern city, and shares ideas for programs that could be used in the future. Special considerations and suggestions for working with this particular type of group are identified.

Activities for sixth grade girls with attention and behavioral issues

Rebekah Marie Long, Beach Bluff, Tennessee, USA

Middle schoolers that have attention and behavioral difficulties can pose significant challenges for social group workers. This poster describes an approach that facilitates this work without requiring the worker to be an expert on behavior modification or developmental issues.

Integrating film and group work. Putting a face on mental illness: A video narrative

Carrie Beth Parks, Chicago, Illinois, USA

The author created a video that puts a face to mental illness and documents a narrative about the effects of mental illness on the afflicted and the family. This poster aims to demonstrate the value of such a film as a training tool for group work facilitators and as a discussion tool for members of their groups. For more information about the video please contact the author at carriesmurf@yahoo.com.

Human growth, hygiene, and hormones – A "must" group for adolescents with autism spectrum disorders

Kathryn Reibert, Chicago, Illinois, USA,
and Christine O'Toole, Batavia, Illinois, USA

This poster presents a comprehensive human growth and development curriculum for high functioning young adults on the Autism spectrum. Topics include: boundaries, stages of development, self-esteem, friendship, dating, puberty, and hygiene. The presentation also addresses the need for mental health practitioners to be familiar with the issues of this population.

The drop-in group in an acute care hospital: Novel practice rooted in social group work

Joanne Sulman, Toronto, Ontario, Canada

The Daytime IBD Group is a monthly drop-in group for patients and families whose lives are severely affected by inflammatory bowel disease (Crohn's disease; ulcerative colitis). This poster describes the group's genesis, features of collectivity, recruitment strategies, single-session process, worker roles, participant perspectives, and links to a larger IBD group work network.

The Bridge: A group for Chinese immigrant parents interested in transitioning children to an American preschool

Shin Yee Tan, Oak Park, Illinois, USA

Entering the school system is a life-changing experience for immigrant children and families. This poster assesses the role, challenges, and impact of an educational-support group for Chinese immigrant parents who are enrolling their children in an American preschool. The poster delineates essential cultural, worker, and process considerations.

16
When internal processes go astray: Turning points in group

Alex Gitterman

Abstract: This workshop examines interpersonal communication and relationship tensions and obstacles within groups. These internal communication and relationship processes often represent significant turning points in groups. The workshop had two objectives for the participant: 1) to understand what creates these tensions and obstacles; and 2) to learn the methods and skills to effectively deal with them. It focuses on the opportunities and challenges that these internal processes provide and the methods and skills required to achieve turning points which foster mutual support and respect.

Keywords: group work; interpersonal obstacles; group work methods, group work skills

Introduction

Group members often encounter interpersonal obstacles in their group interactions. These obstacles are expressed in dysfunctional communication and relationship patterns. Static is then generated in the group system, hindering mutual aid. Withdrawal, factionalism, alliances, monopolism, and scapegoating are illustrative of these problematic patterns. While dysfunctional for most members, these patterned behaviors also serve a latent need for maintaining group functioning. Scapegoating, for example, "may stave off difficulties in the group while promoting it in the scapegoated member" (Gitterman,

1989, p. 237). After a while these patterns become fixed, and potential changes are resisted. The workshop provides methods and skills to mitigate these dysfunctional patterns.

Summary of content

The interaction between worker, individual members, and the group entity create natural interpersonal tensions and obstacles. These internal communication and relationship processes often represent significant turning points in groups. When they are ignored or ineffectively tackled, internal group processes go astray, mutual aid fails to occur, and the group as a whole is limited in its development.

Internal group obstacles have numerous behavioral manifestations, including scapegoating, monopolizing, factions and cliques, withdrawal, and testing. These manifestations are often identified as an individual's personal problem. However, internal group obstacles are a transactional phenomenon, serving an important latent function for the group. For example, with *factions and cliques,* sub-groups provide members with a greater sense of security and satisfaction than does the group itself. With *scapegoating,* a deviant member serves the function of highlighting group norms and deflecting from similar issues other members have feelings about. Scapegoating reflects the enslavement of other in service of self. For the scapegoatee, negative attention is often preferable to no attention. For the *monopolist,* a self-spotlight keeps the other members from having to deal with intense feelings. In response to a member's *withdrawal,* others protect themselves from dealing with such intense emotions as anxiety related to taboo concerns, anger at worker or peers, sadness, and grief. Finally, there may be *testing* of the worker of of peers. Members test the worker to determine the safety of the group experience, as well as the worker's professional competence. They test peers to determine trust and degree of desired intimacy.

While serving latent functions, internal group obstacles have certain negative consequences. When members' problem-solving is limited, groups are impeded from achieving their potential for mutual aid. Moreover, when group members feel left out and vulnerable to negative behavior, they perceive the group to be unsupportive and dangerous.

Internal group obstacles can be generated by numerous sources. The agency – its structure, culture, processes and representatives – can be one source. Another can be group formation issues such as problematic composition, temporal arrangement, recruitment methods, and organizational contracting. The lack of clarity about purpose creates distrust and testing. Dealing ineffectively with member testing is yet another source. Similarly, members may have different perceptions about how close they want to become to each other and how they want to deal with differences among themselves. The vulnerability and pain associated with taboo material may lead to fight and flight behaviors. Finally, transference and countertransference dynamics also create internal group obstacles.

Since internal group obstacles are powerful deflections from group members' pain and vulnerabilities, the social worker must anticipate *intense resistance* to members' willingness to work on them. As a rule of thumb, the group worker needs to anticipate that the greater the pain and vulnerability, the greater the intensity of resistance. In defining the internal group obstacle, the social worker adopts a transactional definition and perspective, taking into account the members' and worker's contributions to this resistance. Acting on the transactional definition, the social worker describes the observed manifest behavior. For example, "I noticed that when we begin to talk about being a pregnant teenager, Jackie, you begin to clown around – which is followed by everyone joking around. I get frustrated that you are not helping each other with very serious issues and find myself withdrawing." With firmness and consistency, the group worker makes a sensitive demand that the group members examine the pattern of behavior. The group worker provides a great deal of support, integrated with a demand for work. In the face of anticipated resistance, the group worker is persistent in expecting that the members work on the obstacles to mutual aid. The group worker invites and sustains group conflict. When anger is suppressed, participation is thwarted and mutual support is impeded. The group worker reaches for discrepant perceptions and disagreements. In conflict situations, the group worker establishes protective ground rules, and searches for and identifies common definitions and perceptions. The worker also credits the members for sustaining difficult conversations.

Workshop process

The workshop format included presentation, discussion, and role-play. Practice examples were drawn from the practice and teaching experiences of both the participants and the presenter. The workshop focused on *methods and skills* – on what the group worker says and does in dealing with internal group obstacles. The workshop leader presented his ideas and experiences, including obstacles that he had encountered in his practice. For example, the scapegoating of a youngster who had kissed a member's boyfriend; members of different ethnic and racial groups forming cliques; members not talking, etc. The presented illustrations encouraged members to identify their own practice difficulties. Participants were then invited to share examples of actual difficulties in their practice. Using a problem-swapping exercise, a number of difficult situations were selected for presentation. After discussing, role-playing, and reviewing each situation, participants were invited to generalize from the specific situation to their own practice experiences.

From these discussions broader practice principles were formulated. For example, the participants were intrigued by the practice principle of *parallel process*, specifically the distinction between what the group worker *says* members should do and what the worker actually *does* in the group. Group workers model how to listen, explore, and help. As an example of parallel process, when the worker promotes democratic group process, but acts in an authoritarian manner, the members will learn to misuse power. Group members often act out in the group the very experiences they encounter in their lives, and observe how we deal with them. Much, if not more, is *caught by group members* than what we attempt to *teach* them. Paying careful attention to parallel process was an important area of emphasis in this workshop, and examples of this phenomenon were examined as they occurred during the process of the workshop itself.

Conclusion

The behavioral manifestations of internal group obstacles, their latent functions, and their negative consequences were discussed in this workshop. Both the worker's and the participants' professional experiences served as the foundation for these discussions. The opportunities and challenges presented by these obstacles to a group's functioning were addressed. The methods and skills required to utilize these obstacles to foster mutual support and respect were identified.

Recommended Readings:

Antsey, M. (1982). Scapegoating in groups: Some theoretical perspectives and case record of intervention. *Social Work with Groups.* 5(3), 51-63.

Berman-Rossi, T. 1993. The tasks and skills of the social worker across stages of group development. *Social Work with Groups.* 16(1/2):69-92.

Bogdanoff, M. & Elbaum, P. L. (1978). Role lock: Dealing with monopolizers, mistrusters, isolates, helpful Hannahs and other assorted characters in group psychotherapy. *International Journal of Group Psychotherapy.* 28(2), 247-262.

Berman-Rossi, T. 1992. Empowering groups through understanding stages of group development. *Social Work with Groups.* 15(2/3):239-255.

Brown, A. & Mistry, T. 1994. Group work with 'mixed membership' groups: Issues of race and gender. *Social Work with Groups.* 17(3):5-22.

Galinsky, M. J. & Schopler, J. 1994. Negative experiences in support groups. *Social Work in Health Care.* 20(1):77-95.

Gitterman, A. 1989. Building mutual support in groups. *Social Work with Groups.* 12(2):5-22.

Gitterman, A. & Germain, C.B. 2008. *The life model of social work practice: Advances in theory and practice, third edition.* New York: Columbia University Press.

Gitterman and L. Shulman, (Eds.). (2005). *Mutual aid groups, vulnerable and resilient populations, and the life cycle, third edition.* New York: Columbia University Press.

Kurland, R. & Salmon, R. (1998). Purpose: A misunderstood and misused keystone of group work practice. *Social Work with Groups.* 21(3), 5-17.

Malekoff, A. 1999. *Group work with adolescents: Principles and practice.* New York: Guilford Press.

Malekoff, A. (2004). Group work with adolescents: Principles and practice (2nd ed.). New York: Guilford Press.

Schiller, L. Y. 1997. Rethinking stages of development in women's groups. *Social Work with Groups.* 20(3): 3-19.

Schiller, L. Y. 1995. Stages of development in women's groups: A relational model. In R. Kurland and R. Salmon, (Eds.). *Group work practice in a troubled society,* pp. 117-138. New York: Haworth Press.

Shulman, L. (2009). *The skills of helping individuals, families, groups and communities (6th ed.).* Belmont, CA: Thomson/Wadsworth.

Toseland, R. W., & Rivas, R. F. (2005) *An introduction to group work practice (5th ed.).* Boston: Allyn Bacon.

17
More than ice breakers: Teaching social work students how to effectively use activity in the group

Jennifer A. Clements and Samuel R. Benbow

Abstract: Social work educators are continuously challenged with the difficult task of preparing entry level practitioners to apply theories, skills and techniques learned and practiced in class, to that of the real world of work. One way to bridge the gap between classroom knowledge and the demands of social workers conducting group work is the utilization of experiential-based activities. Without question, the classroom setting provides an ideal developmental practice environment for students to serve as group members, facilitators and an informal peer support system in a safe and controlled setting. The experiential-based, five-sectioned manual entitled Effective Activity-Based Group Work was developed for social work students seeking to use activity as a supplement to course requirements and has been well received by students.

Keywords: Group work, activities in group work, use of program in group work, group work education

One of the primary challenges facing entry level as well as experienced social work practitioners is the ability to effectively create working relationships with groups in a very short period of time. Certainly there was a period in social group work where the use of activity in the group setting was discouraged. Ruth Middleman (1980) discussed this loss as 'a flight from activity in favor of talk'. In part due to Middleman and many others writing and teaching during this time period, a resurgence and belief of activity in the group was born. Beginning practitioners and students are often eager to use activity-based group work. The challenge is that activity-based group work has great potential when activities are chosen to deepen relationships as well as provide purpose and meaning for the interaction instead of to fill silence (Doel & Swanson, 1999). The importance of teaching social work students how to use activity in the group and make educated decisions about activity cannot be stressed enough.

Experiential-based group activities in a classroom setting attempt to close the gaps between theory, practice, and the preparations needed to meet the expectations and demands of social group workers and those who seek services (Frumpkin & Lloyd, 1995; Goldstein. 2001). Shulman (2009) refers to this concept as 'a mixed transactional model'. Dennison (2005) describes this as an opportunity for educators and students to learn about experiential-based group activities designed to link classroom learning with real life experiences. Thus the classroom begins to develop the skills needed in the group. Further review of the literature suggests that social service agencies are looking more towards the use of group work. Whether from a cost cutting/dollar maximizing perspective or a greater understanding of the benefits of mutual aid, agencies are recognizing the benefit of groups over individual and family treatment (Daley & Koppenaal, 1989; Garland, 1992; Strom & Gingerich, 1993). The classroom setting serves as a developmental practice environment to methodically identify the when, where, and how to implement group activities as well as assess their effectiveness. Social work students are provided with the opportunity to serve as members, facilitators and most importantly empowering support systems for each other in a safe and controlled environment. The experiential activities must be carefully selected so that they can offer comfort, support and a means of coping at the various stages within the group process (Redmann, 2006). To the contrary, social workers who fail to consider the nuances of the client population being served, fail to understand how to use activity effectively as a therapeutic intervention and/or fail to consider member characteristics, skills and abilities will most likely be a determent to agency and those being served.

The vast majority of the core undergraduate social work courses require small group work and or team-oriented activity as a crucial supplement to the course content. Repeatedly, it has been demonstrated that experiential-based activity serves as an invaluable tool to draw the necessary connections for students in and between textbook knowledge, classroom discussion, and real-life application. The objectives of the classroom-based group sessions are to address the challenges of effectively establishing and maintaining working relationships in a shortened period of time with clients through activity-based group work as a solution to assisting those hard to reach clients. In addition, the course instructors wanted to teach students how to select group activities that are appropriate to the population they intend to served as well as understand how to use activity effectively as a therapeutic intervention.

There was and continues to be the need to develop a manual that provided individual and small group activities for which program students could draw upon at different stages in the group development process to enhance the work within the group session. Curricula-based manuals have been historically developed and utilized to provide 'a means of systematizing practice, so that practice standards may be consistently met across a variety of workers' (Galinsky, Terizan & Fraser, 2006). The manual developed by the course instructors entitled 'Effective activity-based group work' was developed with the objectives of: 1) addressing the challenges of group work and offer activity-based group work as a solution for those hard to reach clients; 2) learning how to select group activities that are appropriate to the population being served ; 3) understanding how to use activity effectively as a therapeutic intervention; and 4) learning numerous group-based activities that participants use in their own group practice. The objectives assist in ensuring that the manual used the most current evidenced-based practices, took into account the realities of implementation by novice/ entry level practitioners, provided information regarding the unique dynamics of group processes, while reinforcing the need for constant mindfulness of group culture (Galinsky, Terizan & Fraser, 2006) .

The manual was designed in five sections which provide specific activities or, as coined by Doel and Sawdon (1999), "action techniques" tailored towards the stages of group development to include beginning, middle and ending phases of therapeutic-based group work, team building exercises for non-therapeutic-based group work, and a planning as well as check sheet of considerations prior to and after selection and implementation of an activity. As activities were shared and practiced, the instructors, using a model discussed by Toseland and Rivas (2005), processed questions to include: 1) at what stage of group development would this activity be useful and why?; 2) how would member characteristics, skills, and abilities influence the way you would modify the activity?; and 3) how would you evaluate the usefulness and impact of this activity on the group and its members? This process has been proven to be an essential component in the student's learning, as it reinforces the need for flexibility in planning to account for the inevitability that an activity may not go as planned (Doel & Sawdon, 1999).

An example of one type of activity in the manual involves members using a basic sentence completion activity about human needs. This activity is placed in the work phase section of the manual since it involves some group member reflection of each other. Each group member completes a 'Need Pie' where slices of the pie are symbolic of types of needs (spiritual, cultural, emotional, physical, etc). Once the individual member completes their pie, they share the sentence completion of 'One need I have that is not getting met is____?' and 'One need I see (insert group member name) has that is not getting met is'. This then begins a process of group discussion, confrontation and processing of observations of each member of the group.

The next step in the student's continued learning was a specific assignment to use activity effectively in a particular stage of group work. Students signed up to facilitate a group at either the beginning, middle or end stage of the group. This was done though a simulated group session in the classroom. As students practiced using activity in their simulated sessions, the classroom professor and the observing classmates would evaluate how effective the student was in their facilitation. Instructors also sought feedback from group participants by requiring them to provide verbal and or written feedback regarding: 1) the effectiveness of the session based on the intended goal and purpose; 2) the appropriateness of the activity for the session; 3) the facilitator's ability to plan, implement and end the activity; and 4) what more could the facilitator have done to enhance the activity.

Students reported that the process for them was extremely helpful. When it came time to develop their group skills in the groups they facilitated in both the field and the classroom simulations, they were better prepared to use activities appropriately. After completion of a consent form defining the confidential nature of the feedback, written and verbal evaluations were completed at the conclusion of the group work course. In order to maintain confidentiality, verbal feedback was given directly to a graduate research assistant. One student shared:

> *... at first I was excited to get some ideas, trying to figure out what to do in an hour group seemed hard. But thinking through even just an ice breaker as a way to really get people talking was awesome.*

Another shared:

I did one activity, just one and then the people in the group started talking and sharing about what came up for them. I was glad I used something from the middle stage since it made people really think about what they wanted out of the group at a time when we were struggling.

As part of the evaluation process, students were highly encouraged to add to the manual content as they further developed their skills and practice experience as entry-level practitioners to address what Galinsky, Terizan and Fraser (2006) identify as the 'cultural characteristics' (p.20) which are ever-changing in group work. The process was developed on-line using web-based software where students could post an activity along with suggestions of how best to implement the activity. They were to indicate the stage of group development the activity was most suited to, as well as any additional information that a group worker would need to implement the activity in a group.

Activity in group work can initially be attractive to a novice group worker. A lack of understanding of the importance and complexity of activity-based group work is a common error in mutual-aid-based groups. By understanding how activity-based group work can enhance mutual aid and deepen intimacy of group members, group facilitators will be better prepared to use these skills in their groups. The classroom becomes the perfect learning lab where students are able to practice activity using the framework from a manual developed out of a group work course. Students walk away from the course more prepared, less likely to want to control the group and, hopefully, more effective mutual-aid-based group workers. This process has been evaluated by the course instructors following video-taped sessions, simulation group sessions in the classroom and feedback given by the students at the end of the course. Due to the way the manual was developed, it is not a published work of any one individual. Similar to great stories that are shared through the years, the manual has become an activity-based story that students carry with them as they leave our program. Interested readers can contact the authors for a digital copy.

References

Daley, B. & Koppenaal, G. (1989). Training mental health clinicians to lead short-term psychotherapy groups in an HMO. *Journal of Independent Social Work, 3*(4), 111-124.

Dennison, S. (2005). Enhancing the integration of group theory with practice: A five-part teaching strategy. *The Journal of Baccalaureate Social Work, 10*(2), 1-17.

Doel, M. & Sawdon, C. (1999). *The essential groupworker: Teaching and learning creative groupwork.* London, Eng: Kingsley Publishers.

Frumpkin, M. & Lloyd, G.A. (1995). Social work education. In *Encyclopedia of social work* (3), 2238-2247. Washington, DC: NASW Press.

Galinsky, M.J., Terzian, M.A. & Fraser, M.W.(2006). The art of group work practice with manualized curricula. *Social Work with Groups, 29*(1), 11-26.

Garland, J. (1992). Developing and sustaining group work services: A systemic and systematic view. *Social Work with Groups, 15*(4), 89-90.

Goldstein, H. (2001). *Experiential learning: A foundation for social work education and practice.* Washington, DC: Council on Social Work Education

Middleman, R. (1983). Activities and Action in Group Work. *Social Work with Groups, 6*(1), 3-7.

Redmann, H. (2006). Warning: There a lot of yelling in knitting: The impact of parallel process on empowerment in a group setting. *Journal of Social Work with Groups, 29*(4).

Shulman, L. (2009). *The skills of helping individuals, families and groups.* (4th ed.) Itasca, IL: Peacock Publishers.

Strom, K. & Gingerich, W. (1993). Educating students for new market realities. *Journal of Social Work Education, 29,* 78-97.

Toseland, R. & Rivas, R. (2005). *An introduction to group work practice.* (4th ed.) Boston, MA: Allyn and Bacon.

Index

www.ingramcontent.com/pod-product-compliance
Lightning Source LLC
Chambersburg PA
CBHW060151280326
41932CB00012B/1715